Eclipse

Other Java™ resources from O'Reilly

Related titles
Java™ in a Nutshell
Head First Java™
Head First EJB™
Programming Jakarta Struts
Tomcat: The Definitive Guide
Learning Java™

Java™ Extreme Programming
Cookbook
Java™ Servlet and JSP™
Cookbook™
Hardcore Java™
JavaServer™ Pages

Java Books Resource Center
java.oreilly.com is a complete catalog of O'Reilly's books on Java and related technologies, including sample chapters and code examples.

OnJava.com is a one-stop resource for enterprise Java developers, featuring news, code recipes, interviews, weblogs, and more.

Conferences
O'Reilly & Associates brings diverse innovators together to nurture the ideas that spark revolutionary industries. We specialize in documenting the latest tools and systems, translating the innovator's knowledge into useful skills for those in the trenches. Visit *conferences.oreilly.com* for our upcoming events.

Safari Bookshelf (*safari.oreilly.com*) is the premier online reference library for programmers and IT professionals. Conduct searches across more than 1,000 books. Subscribers can zero in on answers to time-critical questions in a matter of seconds. Read the books on your Bookshelf from cover to cover or simply flip to the page you need. Try it today with a free trial.

Eclipse

Steve Holzner

O'REILLY®

Beijing • Cambridge • Farnham • Köln • Sebastopol • Taipei • Tokyo

Eclipse
by Steve Holzner

Copyright © 2004 O'Reilly Media, Inc. All rights reserved.
Printed in the United States of America.

Published by O'Reilly Media, Inc., 1005 Gravenstein Highway North, Sebastopol, CA 95472.

O'Reilly Media, Inc. books may be purchased for educational, business, or sales promotional use.
Online editions are also available for most titles (*safari.oreilly.com*). For more information, contact our
corporate/institutional sales department: (800) 998-9938 or *corporate@oreilly.com*.

Editor:	Brett McLaughlin
Production Editor:	Marlowe Shaeffer
Cover Designer:	Ellie Volckhausen
Interior Designer:	David Futato

Printing History:

April 2004:	First Edition.

 This book uses RepKover,™ a durable and flexible lay-flat binding.

ISBN: 978-0-596-00641-9
[C]

Table of Contents

Preface

Welcome to Eclipse, today's premiere Java™ integrated development environment (IDE). Eclipse is an extraordinary tool, and it fills a long-standing need among Java developers—no longer do you have to suffer through pages of errors scrolling off the screen while using command-line Java compilers. Now you've got an IDE that will handle the details for you, letting you get on with writing code. If you've never used Eclipse before, your productivity is about to take a giant jump.

We're going to push the Eclipse envelope in this book, working from the basics up through the advanced. This book has been designed to open up Eclipse and to be more accessible than any other. It's a programmer-to-programmer book, written to bring you up to speed in Eclipse without wasting time.

If you're a programmer, this book is written to give you exactly what you want to see—the good stuff, and only the good stuff. There's as much Eclipse crammed into this book as you need to master the topic, and mastering Eclipse is our goal.

What's Inside

From cover to cover, this book is pure Eclipse, covering hundreds of skills and techniques. We start from the most basic Java development and work up to creating your own plug-in editors for the Eclipse environment. Here are a few of the topics in this book:

- Using Eclipse to develop Java code
- Working with JAR files
- Setting launch configurations
- Selecting Java runtimes
- Creating Javadoc
- Refactoring

- Extracting Interfaces
- Viewing type hierarchies
- Customizing Eclipse
- Testing code with JUnit
- Debugging
- Setting breakpoint hit counts
- Using hot code replacement
- Sharing projects with CVS
- Comparing code with local history
- Using Ant to build Eclipse projects
- GUI programming from applets to Swing
- Using the Standard Widget Toolkit (SWT)
- SWT buttons, text, labels, lists, layouts, and events
- SWT menus, toolbars, sliders, trees, and dialogs
- Developing web applications
- Writing servlet code in place
- Using the Sysdeo Tomcat plug-in
- Debugging and deploying web projects
- Developing Struts applications with Eclipse
- Using the Easy Struts plug-in
- Developing Eclipse plug-ins
- The Plug-in Development Environment (PDE)
- Plug-in manifests
- Extension points
- Using the Run-time Workbench
- Creating a standard plug-in
- Creating an action set
- Creating plug-in menus
- Creating a multipage editor plug-in
- Creating a plug-in wizard
- Creating an Eclipse view supported with a plug-in

We're going to see all these topics and many more in the upcoming pages. Here's an overview of each chapter:

Chapter 1, *Essential Eclipse*

This chapter is all about the basics, including all the details on the Eclipse Workbench and an introduction to the Java Development Tools (JDT).

Chapter 2, *Java Development*

Using the JDT, we're going to create Java projects, create code automatically, implement syntax checking, and start developing significant Java applications.

Chapter 3, *Testing and Debugging*

An IDE wouldn't be much use without a debugger. Eclipse and the JDT give you all the power of a true debugger, including breakpoints, expression evaluators, being able to change values on the fly, and more.

Chapter 4, *Working in Teams*

One of the valuable aspects of Eclipse is that it lets you develop in teams, something that any commercial developer can appreciate, since significant development is usually done in teams. Using Concurrent Versions System (CVS), team members do all of their work in their own workbenches, but they can share and register their work using a CVS repository.

Chapter 5, *Building Eclipse Projects Using Ant*

Ant is a powerful Java build tool, and we'll see in this chapter that you can do things with Ant in Eclipse that Eclipse can't do alone, such as copy and move files.

Chapter 6, *GUI Programming: From Applets to Swing*

This chapter starts our work using Eclipse to handle GUI development with Swing. We'll also take a look at a Swing plug-in for Eclipse here—using this plug-in, for example, you can drag and drop Swing controls.

Chapter 7, *SWT: Buttons, Text, Labels, Lists, Layouts, and Events*

In this chapter and the next, we'll be covering the Standard Widget Toolkit (SWT)—the GUI toolkit for Java developers that provides a portable API and tight integration with the underlying native GUI platform. SWT—a 100% Java alternative to the AWT and Swing—is another reason Eclipse has become so popular, and we're going to spend two chapters on it.

Chapter 8, *SWT: Menus, Toolbars, Sliders, Trees, and Dialogs*

This chapter completes our coverage of the SWT, including dialogs, toolbars, sliders, trees, menus, and more.

Chapter 9, *Web Development*

This chapter gets us started with web development, creating both servlets and JSP using Eclipse and the Tomcat server. We'll also take a look at a Tomcat Eclipse plug-in.

Chapter 10, *Developing Struts Applications with Eclipse*

We continue our web work in this chapter with applications constructed using the Struts framework. We'll also see how to use a Struts plug-in.

Chapter 11, *Developing a Plug-in: The Plug-in Development Environment, Manifests, and Extension Points*

In this chapter, we're going to start creating Eclipse plug-ins to extend Eclipse. We'll use the Plug-in Development Environment (PDE) and other tools in this chapter to create working plug-ins.

Chapter 12, *Developing a Plug-in: Creating Editors and Views*

Here, we're going to get the details on some more advanced aspects of plug-in creation—editors, creating wizards, and how to support Eclipse views.

Chapter 13, *Eclipse 3.0*

In this chapter, we're going to take a look at Eclipse Version 3.0. This will give you a glimpse at the exciting things on the Eclipse horizon.

Conventions Used in This Book

There are some conventions we'll use that you should know about. When we've added a new piece of code and are discussing it, it'll appear in bold face, and when there's more code to come, you'll see three dots. Here's what that looks like:

```
Listener listener = new Listener() {
    public void handleEvent(Event event) {
        ToolItem item = (ToolItem)event.widget;
        String string = item.getText();
            .
            .
            .
    }
};
```

We'll also use the standard convention for selecting menu items in this book; for example, to create a new project in Eclipse, you use the File → New → Project menu item.

The following typographical conventions are used in this book:

Plain text

Indicates menu titles, menu options, menu buttons, and keyboard accelerators.

Italic

Indicates new terms, URLs, email addresses, filenames, file extensions, pathnames, directories, and Unix utilities.

Constant width

Indicates commands, options, switches, variables, types, classes, namespaces, methods, modules, properties, parameters, values, objects, events, event handlers, and XML tags.

Constant width italic

Indicates text that should be replaced with user-supplied values.

This icon signifies a tip, suggestion, or general note.

 This icon indicates a warning or caution.

What You'll Need

All the software you'll need in this book can be downloaded from the Internet for free. You'll need Eclipse—this book was written using Eclipse 2.1.1—and we'll discuss where to get Eclipse in Chapter 1. Other software packages that we'll be downloading throughout the book include the Tomcat web server and various CVS servers (which will allow you to share Eclipse projects with others).

Eclipse is built to be *extendible*, and hundreds of Eclipse *plug-ins* are available for free downloading. Plug-ins let you add functionality to Eclipse—new built-in editors, code generators, software launchers, and more—and we'll take a look at a number of the most popular plug-ins in this book. And in Chapters 11 and 12, we'll develop our own Eclipse plug-ins.

Using Code Examples

All the code in this book is available for download from *http://www.oreilly.com/catalog/eclipse*. See the file *readme.txt* in the download for installation instructions.

This book is here to help you get your job done. In general, you may use the code in this book in your programs and documentation. You do not need to contact us for permission unless you're reproducing a significant portion of the code. For example, writing a program that uses several chunks of code from this book does not require permission. Selling or distributing a CD-ROM of examples from O'Reilly books *does* require permission. Answering a question by citing this book and quoting example code does not require permission. Incorporating a significant amount of example code from this book into your product's documentation *does* require permission.

We appreciate, but do not require, attribution. An attribution usually includes the title, author, publisher, and ISBN. For example: "*Eclipse*, by Steve Holzner. Copyright 2004 O'Reilly Media, Inc., 0-596-00641-1."

If you feel your use of code examples falls outside fair use or the permission given above, feel free to contact us at *permissions@oreilly.com*.

We'd Like to Hear from You

Please address comments and questions concerning this book to the publisher:

O'Reilly & Associates, Inc.
1005 Gravenstein Highway North
Sebastopol, CA 95472
(800) 998-9938 (in the United States or Canada)
(707) 829-0515 (international or local)
(707) 829-0104 (fax)

We have a web page for this book, where we list errata, examples, and any additional information. You can access this page at:

http://www.oreilly.com/catalog/eclipse

To comment or ask technical questions about this book, send email to:

bookquestions@oreilly.com

For more information about our books, conferences, Resource Centers, and the O'Reilly Network, see our web site at:

http://www.oreilly.com

CHAPTER 1

Essential Eclipse

If you're reading this book, you're most likely a Java programmer, and you know how finicky Java can be at times. Missed import statements, forgotten variable declarations, omitted semicolons, garbled syntax, typos—all these problems will cause the Java command-line compiler, javac, to cough in your face and display pages of annoying error messages. The error messages tell you that javac knows what the error is, so why doesn't it just fix the problem and let you get on developing?

Because javac can't fix the problem; it isn't an editor. That makes long streams of errors scrolling off the page an all-too-common experience for Java developers, and leaves them with the feeling that Java is too prickly about what can go wrong. To change all that, you can use an integrated development environment (IDE), which will not only catch errors before you try to compile, but also suggest solutions. Java is badly in need of a good IDE, and a number of candidates are available, but the premiere Java IDE these days is the one this book is all about: Eclipse. You can see Eclipse in action in Figure 1-1.

Eclipse and Java

Although Eclipse can act as an IDE for many different languages—IDEs are available from C/C++ to Cobol—its great popularity is as a Java IDE, and it comes with Java support built-in. Eclipse refers to itself as a *universal tool platform*, capable of handling IDEs for many different languages, but the Java IDE that comes with Eclipse is going to be our main focus, as it is for the great majority of Eclipse users.

The whole Eclipse magic is that it will take the rough edges off Java development in the way you've always imagined. The errors that would cause javac to stumble are usually handled before you even try to compile, and if there is an issue, Eclipse will suggest solutions. All you have to do is point and click—no need for serious head-scratching. If you're like most Java developers, you're going to find yourself thinking, *This is great!*

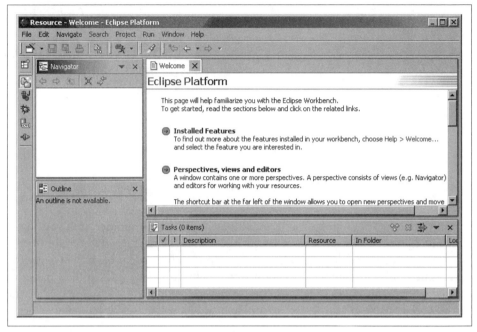

Figure 1-1. Eclipse

Some Background

Eclipse is free for the downloading, like a number of other Java IDEs, but Eclipse has a serious advantage behind it: the power of IBM, which reportedly spent $40 million in the development of the IDE. The first version, Version 1.0, appeared in November 2001 and gradually became popular (although—as with any developer tool— there was a great deal of discussion of its faults).

In time, Eclipse has changed and improved, and the current version, 2.1.1, is getting much praise. In fact, it's become so popular that when Version 2.1 first appeared, the servers at *http://www.eclipse.org* were so busy that it was almost impossible to download a copy for the first few days.

Eclipse was created by IBM in a massive effort that has left Java programmers the winners. It's now an open source project, still largely under IBM's development, but part of a software consortium named eclipse.org. You can see the consortium's page, *http://www.eclipse.org*, in Figure 1-2.

The Eclipse consortium originally consisted of IBM's subsidiary, Object Technologies International (OTI)—who developed Eclipse in the first place—along with Borland, IBM, MERANT, QNX Software Systems, Rational Software3, Red Hat, SuSE, TogetherSoft3, and Webgain2 in November 2001. Since then, the consortium has grown to more than 45 members, including Sybase, Hitachi, Oracle, Hewlett-Packard, Intel, and others.

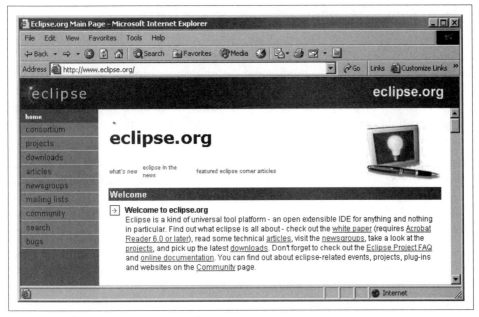

Figure 1-2. The Eclipse consortium's web page

OTI is not a new player either; it's been around for quite some time, and it was responsible for the foundations behind IBM's Visual Age line of products (IBM acquired OTI in 1996). Long ago, OTI created a Java tool written in the Smalltalk language, Visual Age for Java—also called VA4J—that was well received. Eclipse itself is more or less VA4J rewritten in Java and updated—many of VA4J's idiosyncratic features have been removed in favor of more standard ones, and a great deal of development power has been added. In other words, although Eclipse itself is relatively new, it already has considerable history.

The Eclipse project as a whole is divided into three subprojects:

- The Eclipse platform itself, which forms the backbone of the whole application
- The Java Development Toolkit (JDT)
- The plug-in development environment (PDE), which lets you develop your own tools for Eclipse, called plug-ins

These various subprojects are themselves divided into other subprojects—the JDT subproject, for example, is made up of the user interface (UI), core, and debug subprojects. You can learn more about these three subprojects at *http://www.eclipse.org/eclipse/*, and of course you'll learn a lot more about them in this book.

A Word About the Common Public License (CPL)

Eclipse is open source software, which leaves some people uncertain about legal rights when using it. Open source software gives users open access to the software's source code and the right to modify and distribute the software themselves. If you want to modify that software, on the other hand, it's often true that open source licenses don't allow distribution of the modified software unless the end user is also given these rights (as opposed to a copyright, this is sometimes called a *copyleft* in open source projects).

Some open source licenses insist that any software bundled with other open source software also be open source. However, the open source license that Eclipse uses, the Common Public License (CPL), is also designed to allow commercial interests. The CPL allows software bundled with open source software to be distributed under more restrictive licenses for commercial purposes.

If you ever plan to modify and distribute new versions of Eclipse, you can read about the CPL at *http://www.opensource.org* (in particular, at *http://www.opensource.org/licenses/cpl.php*). Among other things, the CPL says, "this license is intended to facilitate the commercial use of the Program."

That's it for the overview—let's get this show on the road.

Getting Eclipse

How do you get and install Eclipse? Eclipse is free for the downloading—all you have to do is navigate to *http://www.eclipse.org/downloads* and select one of the download mirrors available on that page. When you do, you'll be presented with a list of the available downloads, which are of these types:

Release builds

The Eclipse team releases these versions for general use. Usually when you download Eclipse, you'll use one of the release versions. These builds have been thoroughly tested, and the chance of coming across serious bugs is minimal. This is a version of Eclipse comparable to the version that other companies would sell—if Eclipse were for sale.

Stable builds

These are comparable to beta versions. A stable build is a step along the way toward a release version. The Eclipse team considers this build to be relatively stable, but there may be problems. This is where you'll find the new features that are upcoming in Eclipse.

Integration builds

These builds are made up of components that have been fairly well tested, but their operation with other components may still have some issues. If things work out OK and the integration build proves itself, it may be elevated to a stable version.

Nightly builds

These are the most experimental of all publicly available Eclipse builds. They're created nightly by the Eclipse team, and there's really no guarantee that things will work well. Some experience with these builds indicates that they can actually have substantial problems.

Normally, you'll use the most recent release version of Eclipse. To get Eclipse, select the most recent release download for your operating system and click the appropriate link to download it.

Want to learn more about the current and upcoming versions of Eclipse? See *http://www.eclipse.org/eclipse/development/main.html*.

Installing Eclipse is not difficult—all you've got to do is unzip or untar it, depending on your operating system. Since you've downloaded the version of Eclipse targeted to your operating system, you'll find the executable file ready to run as soon as you uncompress Eclipse.

Windows users will be pleased to learn that Eclipse doesn't use the Windows registry, so (re)installation is easy and trouble free.

You start Eclipse by running the Eclipse executable, such as *eclipse.exe*. When you start the program the first time, it may ask you to wait while it completes the installation, which does not take long (Eclipse is creating the workspace directories it'll be using). When you first run Eclipse, you should see something like Figure 1-1, shown earlier in this chapter.

You must have Java installed on your machine when you try to start Eclipse. If you start Eclipse for the first time and see a dialog box with the message that begins "A Java Runtime Environment (JRE) or Java Development Kit (JDK) must be available in order to run Eclipse," you've got to download and install Java first. You can get Java for free at *http://java.sun.com/j2se/*.

In the next chapter, we'll see how to switch the local installation of Java that Eclipse will use if you have multiple installations of Java (for example, you might want to use a newly downloaded JDK instead of the default JRE that comes with many browsers).

To make starting Eclipse easier, you can also connect various shortcuts to the Eclipse executable. In Windows, right-click the executable file in the Windows Explorer and select "Create Shortcut" from the context menu that opens, then drag the new shortcut where you want it. In Linux or Unix, just add the Eclipse directory to your path, or use ln -s to create a symbolic link to the Eclipse executable.

Understanding Eclipse

So what is Eclipse itself? Most people think of Eclipse as a Java IDE, and when you download Eclipse, you get the Java IDE (this is the *Java Development Toolkit*, the JDT) and the Plug-in Development Environment (the PDE) with it. If you only want to develop Java, it's easy to think of Eclipse as a Java IDE because that's the main tool you'll be using.

Eclipse itself, however, is a *universal tool platform*. The JDT is really an addition to Eclipse—it's a plug-in, in fact. Eclipse itself is really the *Eclipse platform*, which provides support for tools beyond just the Java set you get on download. These tools are implemented as plug-ins, so the platform itself only needs to be a relatively small software package.

The platform provides the support the plug-ins need to run; if you want to develop Java, you use the JDT plug-in that comes with Eclipse; if you want to develop in other languages, you'll need to get other plug-ins, such as the CDT, which lets you develop C/C++ code. Installing a plug-in is easy, as we're going to see—all you have to do is drop it into the Eclipse *plugins* directory and restart Eclipse. Eclipse does some checking on each plug-in when it starts, but the plug-ins are not loaded until they're needed in order to save processing time and memory space.

 It's also important to realize that although Eclipse is written in Java, it's intended to be language-neutral. To develop in any programming language, all you need is the corresponding plug-in. In fact, Eclipse is also intended to be spoken-language neutral, too—you can easily change the language that Eclipse uses. To change languages, you can use the same plug-in mechanism that supports plug-ins, except that languages are supported with what are called *plug-in fragments*. OTI has a language pack available that supports a number of languages— Japanese, Korean, German, French, Italian, Portuguese, Spanish, even traditional and simplified Chinese.

The Eclipse Platform

The Eclipse platform is made up of several components: the platform kernel, the workbench, the workspace, the team component, and the help component. You can see an overview of the platform in Figure 1-3.

The Platform Kernel

The kernel's task is to get everything started and to load needed plug-ins. When you start Eclipse, this is the component that runs first, and it loads the other plug-ins that you normally think of as Eclipse itself, such as the workbench.

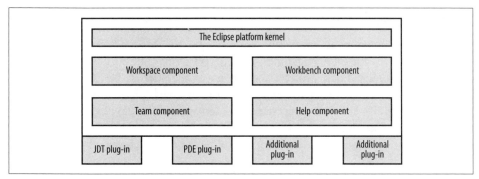

Figure 1-3. The Eclipse architecture

The Eclipse Workbench

The Eclipse workbench is what you saw back in Figure 1-1—it's the basic graphical interface you work with when you use Eclipse. It's got all kinds of toolbars and menus for you to use, and its job is to present those items and the internal windows you saw in Figure 1-1.

Next to the platform kernel, the workbench is Eclipse at its most basic. When you start Eclipse, before working with any specific IDE like the JDT, the workbench displays a Welcome message. When you open another tool like the JDT, that tool takes over.

The workbench looks like a native application, targeted to the operating system you run it on, which is both a feature and a controversial point of Eclipse. The workbench itself—that is to say, Eclipse's graphical user interface—is built using Eclipse's own Standard Widget Toolkit (SWT) and JFace (which is built on top of SWT). The SWT uses the operating system's native graphics support to give the look-and-feel of a native application for the operating system. This is quite different from how most Java applications have worked historically, even those that use Swing.

SWT has to be ported to each operating system that supports Eclipse, and that's been the source of some contention in the Eclipse community, with many people saying that Eclipse, like Java, should be completely operating system–independent. However, that's the way that Eclipse has decided to go, and it's already been ported to most major operating systems, including Windows, Solaris, Mac OS X, Linux/Motif, Linux/GTK2, HP-UX, and a number of others.

In fact, we're going to see how to use SWT and JFace in this book to create Java applications with a totally native look-and-feel. SWT provides some basic graphics and control support, which JFace extends considerably. Eclipse is not only built using SWT and JFace, but it lets you use them as well.

The Eclipse Workspace

The workspace manages all your resources for you—that is, everything you store on disk or connect to on other machines. When you write code in Eclipse, you work with Eclipse *projects*. Each project is given its own folder in Eclipse's workspace directory, which makes it easy to keep track of them. Each project itself can contain many subfolders. Usually, all of a project's folders are subfolders of the main project folder, but they don't have to be—you can include folders anywhere in your machine in a project, and you can include networked folders in a project as well.

When working with code, the workspace component is responsible for managing all the resources connected to a project, which includes all the files in the project. It saves the low-level changes to those resources as well, storing the history of each resource's changes and letting you undo those changes as needed. The workspace informs the plug-ins of those changes.

 The fact that all your Eclipse projects are stored in the same directory has its advantages. For example, if you install a new version of Eclipse, you can often simply copy the workspace directory from the old version directly to the new workspace directory. (Check the new version's release notes to make sure there is no specific problem doing things this way—for example, you can't import Eclipse 1.0 projects into Eclipse 2.0 or later workspaces. If there is a problem, you can always simply delete the new installation and reinstall Eclipse by unzipping or untarring it.)

The Team Component

The team component is the plug-in that supports version control in Eclipse. In version control, program code is checked in to or out of a repository as needed so that the changes to that software can be tracked. This is also done so team members don't overlap or obliterate changes made by other team members as they work on different versions of the code at the same time.

This component acts like a Concurrent Versions System (CVS) client that interacts with a CVS server. If you're not familiar with CVS, don't worry; we'll take a look at using CVS to support version control in Chapter 4. Using the team component, you'll be able to maintain version control over your software, which is a very useful feature when working in teams.

The Help Component

The help component, as you can gather from its name, provides help to the user. It's actually an extensible documentation system for providing Help; plug-ins can provide HTML documentation with XML-formatted data to indicate how that help documentation should be navigated.

That covers the main components of Eclipse in overview. To actually *use* Eclipse, you have to know about a few more concepts: views and perspectives.

Views and Perspectives

When you're working with the workbench, you'll see a number of different internal windows, called *views*, and the idea is that they give you different "views" into your projects. For example, one view may give you an overview of the Java classes in your project, while another may let you navigate between projects. For example, back in Figure 1-1, you can see the Navigator view at the upper left in Eclipse—this is the view that will display all your projects and let you move from one to another.

Because screen space is always at a premium in GUIs, views are often stacked, one on top of another, and you select the one you want to see using tabs that appear on the edge of the stacked views.

 If you ever want to reopen a view you've closed by mistake, select Window → Show View, and select the view you want from the menu that appears.

The editor is one special type of window that usually appears in the center of the workbench. When you open up documents, code, or resources, they'll appear in an editor. Eclipse automatically selects the correct type of editor for the item you're opening: the Java editor for a Java source code file, a GUI you're developing using a plug-in with the editor supplied by the plug-in, and so on. You can even open Microsoft Word documents in the Editor (Eclipse displays an MS Word window in the editor space using Windows Object Linking and Embedding, OLE). In Figure 1-1, the space normally reserved for editors is showing the Eclipse Welcome text.

The editor window is where you do most of the work when developing your code; for example, it's where you enter and edit your code. As we're going to see, the JDT has an editor that is lavish with built-in details, such as syntax checking, code highlighting, and much more. You might have several editors open at once, in which case they'll be stacked with tabs showing at the top of the stack, and you can pick out the one you want by clicking the corresponding tab (or with the Window → Switch to Editor menu item, which displays a list of editors you can switch to). You can close an editor simply by clicking the X in its associated tab (or with the Window → Hide Editors menu item, which toggles to Window → Show Editors after hiding an editor). To sum up: views give you overviews of your projects, and editors let you develop code and resources.

There's one more concept to master here as well: *perspectives*. You don't normally decide what views and editors to display yourself; instead, they're organized into groups called perspectives (although it is easy to customize perspectives yourself).

For example, when you create a Java application, you'll use the Java perspective; when you want to debug a Java program, you'll use the Debug perspective.

Perspectives have a predefined set of views and editors built-in; when you select a perspective, that set of views and editors appears automatically. For example, we'll take a look at the Java perspective here: to select a perspective, you use the Window → Open Perspective menu item, which displays a submenu of the installed perspectives. In this case, we'll choose the Window → Open Perspective → Java menu item to open the Java perspective, shown in Figure 1-4.

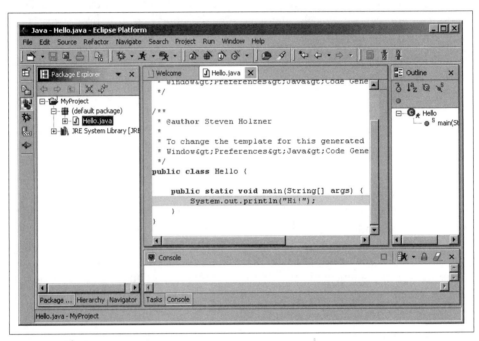

Figure 1-4. The Java perspective

This perspective presents an editor, which appears in the center pane, that lets you write Java code, as well as show several views. For example, the Package Explorer view you see at left gives you an overview of the Java packages and classes in a project, and it lets you move between them. When you debug a Java application, the workbench makes the Debug perspective appear, which you see in Figure 1-5. This perspective displays the code you're debugging, where you are in the program, the values of variables and expressions you want to watch, and so on, in various views.

Much of the time, the idea of views, editors, and perspectives is transparent to the user, and that's certainly the case when you master Eclipse and use it on a daily basis. But they're important concepts for us and ones we'll be referring to by name throughout the book.

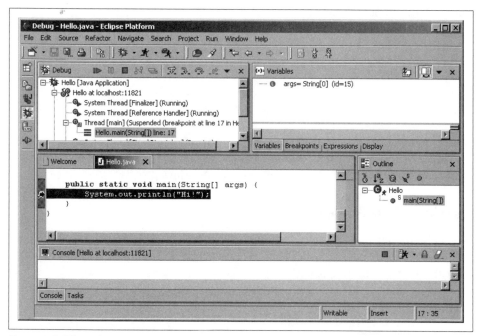

Figure 1-5. The Debug perspective

Now that we're fortified with the concepts and overview that we need, it's time to start actually working with Eclipse. Although Eclipse is a universal tool platform, its great popularity comes from developing Java code, and we're going to put it to work doing that here. When you first start Eclipse, you'll see the Resource perspective, which is the default perspective for developing general resources. But when we put Eclipse to work in this book, we're going to switch to the Java perspective and start developing some code.

Working with Eclipse

You use the Eclipse Java Development Tools (JDT), a series of six seamlessly integrated plug-ins, for Java development in Eclipse. Even if you've written Java for years, you're about to have a whole new experience, one that makes Java development so smooth that when you understand how to use the JDT, you'll wonder what took people so long to make this a reality.

Eclipse is all about code development, and the only way to really understand what's going on is by creating code, so we're going to start by using the JDT to create and run the amazingly useful application you see in Example 1-1. This Java application just displays the message "No worries." on the console.

Example 1-1. The Ch01_01.java example

```
public class Ch01_01
{
    public static void main(String[] args)
    {
        System.out.println("No worries.");
    }
}
```

How can you create this application using Eclipse, and how is Eclipse going to make your job easier? The answers are coming up right now. In Eclipse, all Java code must be inside a Java project, so the first step is to create a Java project.

Creating a Java Project

To invoke the Java perspective, and enter the code for our first example, *Ch01_01. java*, start Eclipse and select the Window → Open Perspective → Java menu item to open the Java perspective using the JDT, as you see in Figure 1-6. This is the perspective you'll use over and over as you start relying on Eclipse for Java development.

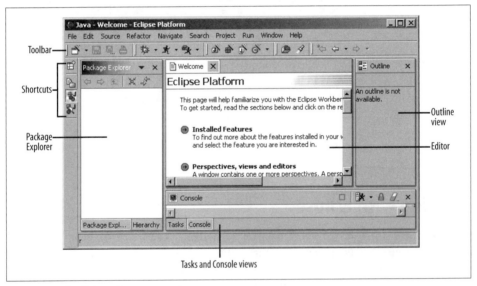

Figure 1-6. The Eclipse Java perspective

It's worth getting to know the Java perspective before we start using it. At the top are the standard menu bars and toolbars, populated with new items for the Java perspective, which we'll become familiar with in the coming pages.

The left pane holds the Package Explorer and Hierarchy views, and you use the tabs at the bottom of this pane to flip between these views. The Package Explorer view gives you an overview of the package you're working on and lets you navigate through Java projects, selecting what files you want to open in the editor. The Hierarchy view lets you examine type hierarchies—you select an item in a code editor, right-click it, and select the Open Type Hierarchy context menu item. When you do, the hierarchy view will display the hierarchy of that item, giving you a clickable inheritance tree for the item, including all members. That can be a big help if you're trying to figure out the syntax of methods you want to override or which methods are available.

The Outline view in the pane at right presents a structured, hierarchical view of the contents of the file open in the main editor pane and lets you jump to elements in it. This is great for developers who are accustomed to using a simple text editor to develop long Java files, because this view organizes the main sections of long code files, letting you move around at will (more on this view in the next chapter).

At the bottom of the Java perspective are the Tasks and Console views, which you can select between using tabs. The Tasks view displays pending tasks, such as errors that the compiler has noticed and which need to be fixed, and the Console view shows you what's going on in the output console—our sample application will write to the Console view, for example.

Editors are stacked in the middle pane and are accessible with the tabs at upper left in that pane. The JDT code editors give you an immense amount of power, far beyond simply entering text. There are all kinds of hidden assets built-in here, most of which are utterly unobtrusive until you decide you want to use them.

That gives us an overview; to create a new Java project in the Java perspective, select the File → New → Project menu item now (alternately, right-click the Package Explorer and select the New → Project context menu item), opening the New Project dialog box, as you see in Figure 1-7.

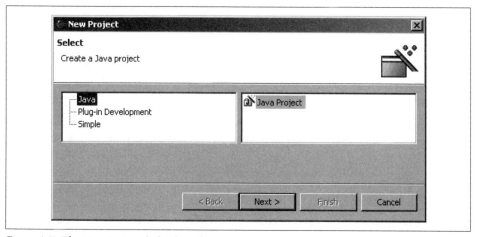

Figure 1-7. The New Project dialog box, first pane

Select the Java and Java Project items and click Next to bring up the next pane of this dialog box. Enter the name of this new project, Ch01_01, in the Project Name box, and click Next, bringing up the next pane of the dialog, which you see in Figure 1-8. As you can see in this pane, we're about to create a new project named Ch01_01 in its own folder. You can use the Projects tab here to include other projects in the build path, something we'll do as our projects become more involved. The Libraries tab lets you browse to libraries and JAR files you want included in the build path; by default, only the JRE System Library is included. The Order and Export tab lets you specify the order of classes in your build path, and gives you the option of whether you want to export the current projects so its code will be available to other projects. In this case, just click Finish to create our new project, Ch01_01.

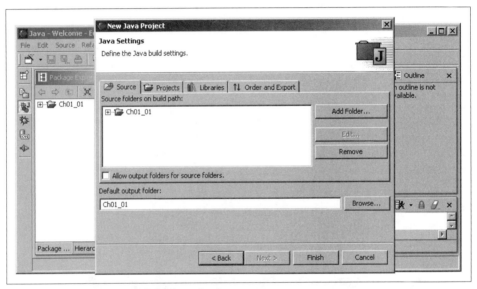

Figure 1-8. The New Project dialog box, third pane

This adds the new Ch01_01 project to the Package Explorer, as you see in Figure 1-9. The project is represented as a folder in your workspace, and, at this point, the folder only contains the libraries we've included on the build path, the JRE System Library.

Projects like this organize your files, classes, libraries, and exports. We don't even have any code in this one yet, so the next step is to add a new public Java class to the project.

Creating a Java Class

In our example, the public class is Ch01_01, and Eclipse stores public classes like this one in their own files. There are several techniques for creating new classes in Eclipse: you can use the toolbar item with the circled C icon, you can use the File → New → Class menu item, or you can right-click a project in the Package Explorer

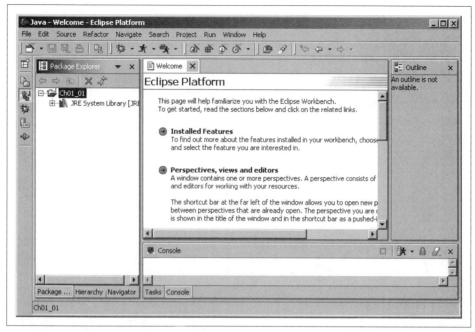

Figure 1-9. A new project in the Package Explorer

and select the New → Class item in the context menu. Any one of these methods opens the New Java Class dialog box you see in Figure 1-10.

Note the options in this dialog. You can set a class's access specifier—public, private, or protected; you can make the class abstract or final; you can specify the new class's superclass (java.lang.Object is the default); and you can specify which, if any, interfaces it implements. We're going to put our examples into Java packages to avoid any conflict with other code; here, we'll use packages named after the example's chapter, like org.eclipsebook.ch01. In this case, just enter the name of this new class, Ch01_01, in the Name box, and enter the name of a new package we'll create for this class, org.eclipsebook.ch01, in the Package box, and click Finish to accept the other defaults. Note, in particular, that under the question "Which method stubs would you like to create?" we're leaving the checkbox marked "public static void main(String[] args)" checked. Doing so means that Eclipse will automatically create an empty main method for us.

Clicking the Finish button creates and opens our new public class, Ch01_01, as you see in Figure 1-11; note the package statement that creates the org.eclipsebook.ch01 package. This new class will be stored in its own file, *Ch01_01.java*, in the Eclipse folder *workspace\Ch01_01*.

So far, so good; you can see the main method that Eclipse has added to our class already. Now let's enter some code of our own.

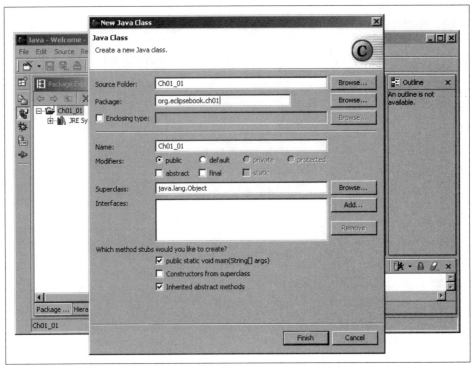

Figure 1-10. Creating a new Java class

Using Code Assist

You can type in code using the JDT's editor as with any editor, as you'd expect, but there's a lot more utility here than in a standard text editor. For example, the JDT also supports a facility named *code assist* that helps you by completing code you've already started to type, and it's a handy tool you'll find yourself using over and over.

For example, say that you want to enter the code System.out.println("No worries."); in the main method. To see code assist do its thing, move the mouse cursor inside the main method's body and type System., and then pause. Code assist will automatically display the various classes in the System namespace, as you see in Figure 1-12.

When you highlight out in the list of possible classes with the mouse, code assist will give you a rundown of what this class does, as you see at left in the figure. Double-click out in the code assist list so that code assist will insert it into your code, and type a period to give you System.out., and pause again. Code assist will display the methods of the out class. Double-click the code assist suggestion println(String arg0), and code assist will insert this code into the main method:

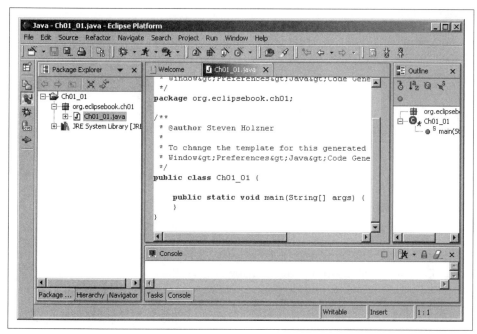

Figure 1-11. A new Java class in Eclipse

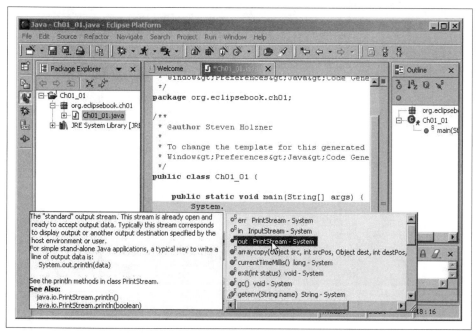

Figure 1-12. Using code assist to create a method call

```
public class Ch01_01
{
    public static void main(String[] args)
    {
        System.out.println( )
    }
}
```

Edit this now to display our "No worries." text (you'll see that code assist adds the closing quotation mark automatically as you type):

```
public class Ch01_01
{
    public static void main(String[] args)
    {
        System.out.println("No worries.")
    }
}
```

However, Eclipse displays this new code with a wavy red line under it, which indicates there's a problem. To see what's going on, rest the mouse cursor over the new code, and a tool tip will appear, as you can see in Figure 1-13, indicating that there's a missing semicolon at the end of the line.

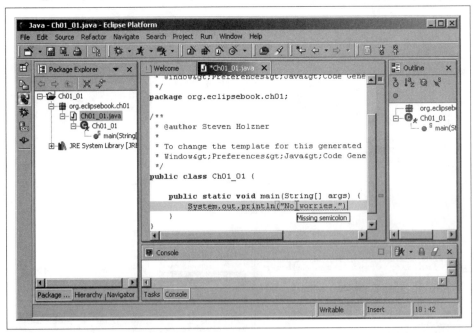

Figure 1-13. Checking an error

Add that semicolon now to give you the complete code and make the wavy red line disappear:

```
public class Ch01_01
{
    public static void main(String[] args)
    {
        System.out.println("No worries.");
    }
}
```

Our code is complete. In Figure 1-13, note that the Package Explorer is giving us an overview of the project, showing the public class Ch01_01 and the main method in that class. In this way, the Package Explorer view gives you access to all the items in a project. To bring an item up in a code editor, just double-click it in the Package Explorer view.

Another handy way to find all the members of a class or object is to highlight an item's name in a code editor, right-click the highlighted name, and select the Open Type Hierarchy item from the context menu. Doing so will open the item's complete type hierarchy in the Hierarchy view, and you'll see all its members, the data types of fields, the arguments you pass to methods, and more. In fact, the code where the selected item is defined will also appear in a code editor (unless that code is inaccessible, as when it's in a JAR file—for example, the System.out class is defined in rt.jar, so no source code is available—although there are now ways to attach source directories to JAR files).

As you can see in this example, the coding was made a little easier because code assist knew all the members of the System.out class and let you select from among them. Code assist will automatically appear when you type a dot (.). You can also make code assist appear at any time while you're typing code—just type Ctrl+Space.

You can also turn code assist off. To configure code assist as you like, select Window → Preferences, then Editor in the left pane of the Preferences dialog, and then the Code Assist tab.

Each time you edit the code in a file, as we're doing here in *Ch01_01.java*, an asterisk appears in front of the filename file in its code editor tab, as you see in Figure 1-13. This asterisk indicates that changes to the file have not yet been saved. There are many ways to save your work: click the diskette icon (for Save) in the toolbar; click the diskette followed by an ellipsis (...) icon (for Save As...) in the toolbar; right-click the code itself and select the Save context menu item; or select the Save, Save As, or Save All menu items in the File menu.

Alright, we've got our first code written and stored to disk. How about running it?

Running Your Code

If you look closely at the Package Explorer view in Figure 1-13, you'll see that the circled C icon for our Ch01_01 class also has a small running figure in it. That is Eclipse's way of indicating this class is *runnable* because it has a main method. To run this code and see the output, select the Run → Run As → Java Application menu item, or open the pull-down menu for the running figure icon in the toolbar and select the Run As → Java Application menu item. This runs our code (Eclipse will ask you to save it first if the code has not been saved yet), and the System.out.println method will write our message to the console. The text of that message, "No worries.", appears in the Console view at the bottom of the Java Perspective, as you see in Figure 1-14.

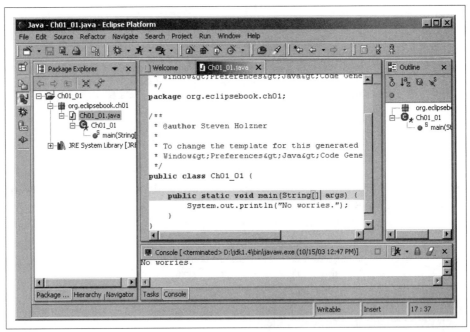

Figure 1-14. Running our Ch01_01 example

Congratulations—now you're an Eclipse developer.

Using the Scrapbook

There's another way to run code in a Java Project, and you don't need a main method to do it: you can use a *scrapbook page* instead. Scrapbook pages give you a way of executing code, even partial code, on the fly—a big help in the development process. This is not an essential skill, but it's a useful one.

To create a scrapbook page, select the File → New → Scrapbook Page menu item to open the New Scrapbook Page dialog box, enter the name Ch01_01Scrapbook in the File name box, and click Finish to create the new scrapbook page, which will be saved as *Ch01_01Scrapbook.jpage*. The new page appears in the Package Explorer and is automatically opened in the editor view, as you see in Figure 1-15. You can enter code or code snippets to run in this page, which helps when your code is getting long and you just want to test part of it. For example, to run our example, enter this code in the scrapbook page (as you see in Figure 1-15)—note that you must include the package name here when referencing the main method in your code:

```
String[] args = {};
org.eclipsebook.ch01.Ch01_01.main(args);
```

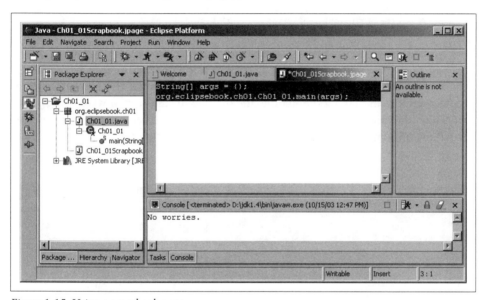

Figure 1-15. Using a scrapbook page

To tell the scrapbook page what code to run, select all the code you've entered, as you see in Figure 1-15, right-click it, and select the Execute context menu item (you can also select the Run → Execute menu item). The results appear in the Console view as before, as you can see in Figure 1-15. In this way, you can execute Java code using a scrapbook page, even snippets of code, and see the results as they'd appear in the console. To close the scrapbook page, click the X button in the tab corresponding to its editor in the workbench's central pane.

If you select the Display item instead of the Execute item, you'll see the net return value of the code you've highlighted in the scrapbook, which is useful for testing methods on the fly. Also, note that you can set imports for the scrapbook page, importing other packages as needed, by right-clicking the scrapbook's code in the editor view and selecting the context menu's Set Imports menu item.

As you can see, the JDT are very helpful. There's also a lot more—for example, what if you've got an error in your code? Eclipse can help here, too.

Using Quick Fix

Quick Fix lets the JDT suggest ways of fixing simple errors, and that's one of the things that Java should have had a long, long time ago. For example, say you change the Ch01_01 code to display the "No worries." message along with today's date:

```
public class Ch01_01 {
    public static void main(String[] args) {
        outString = "No Worries on ";
        Calendar rightNow = Calendar.getInstance();
        System.out.println(outString + rightNow.getTime());
    }
}
```

You can probably spot a few errors here. The variable outString is not declared, which makes the first and last lines of code in main invalid, and the Calendar class has not been imported, making the middle line of code invalid. If you were using javac, you'd have to quit editing and run javac to catch those errors. But the second you enter these lines into Eclipse, they'll be flagged as errors with wavy red underlines, as you see in Figure 1-16.

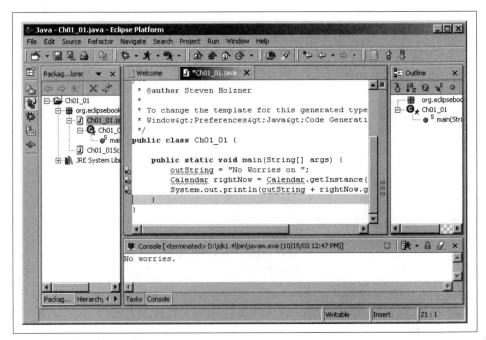

Figure 1-16. Quick Fix indicators

Eclipse doesn't let you down by just showing you the errors—it also suggests solutions. Note the yellow light bulb and red X icons in the bar to the left of the code editor, which is called the *marker bar*. These icons tell you that Quick Fix is available for all the errors. Note also the hollow red rectangles in the bar on the right of the code editor view, called the *overview ruler*. These hollow red rectangles indicate statements that Quick Fix can fix—solid red rectangles flag compiler errors—and you can use these icons to navigate to problems to fix.

If you let the mouse cursor hover over the first light bulb icon in the marker bar, you'll see a tool tip appear with the description of the error ("outString cannot be resolved"), as in Figure 1-17.

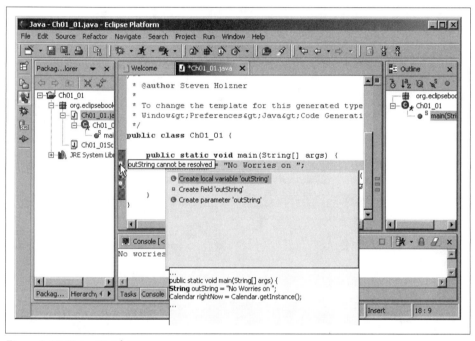

Figure 1-17. Using Quick Fix

To activate Quick Fix and see what the JDT suggests to fix the problem, click the light bulb icon on the affected line. Doing that displays a number of options, the first of which is "Create local variable 'outString'", as you see in Figure 1-17. Quick Fix also indicates what its suggested solution will look like in the context of your code, as you see at the bottom of the figure. To fix the code, select the Create local variable option by double-clicking it, which changes our code to this, declaring outString as a variable of type String:

```
public class Ch01_01 {
    public static void main(String[] args) {
        String outString = "No Worries on ";
```

```
        Calendar rightNow = Calendar.getInstance( );
        System.out.println(outString + rightNow.getTime( ));
    }
}
```

Declaring outString also fixes the last line in the main method, which references that variable, so the light bulb icon disappears from that line as well.

We've still got to fix the problem with the middle line of code in the main method, which uses the Calendar class. You can see what Quick Fix suggests for this problem in Figure 1-18—importing the java.util.Calendar class. (This aspect of Quick Fix alone is worth the price of admission: you no longer have to hunt through entire package hierarchies to find what package to import when you want to use a class whose name—but not package—you remember.)

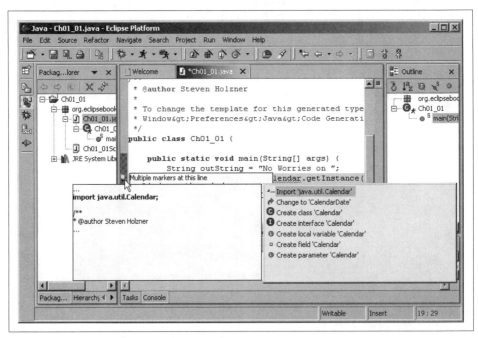

Figure 1-18. Using Quick Fix to import a package

To use this suggested Quick Fix, double-click the "Import 'java.util.Calendar'" line, which imports java.util.Calendar and changes your code to this:

```
import java.util.Calendar;
    .
    .
    .
public class Ch01_01 {
    public static void main(String[] args) {
        String outString = "No Worries on ";
        Calendar rightNow = Calendar.getInstance( );
```

```
        System.out.println(outString + rightNow.getTime( ));
    }
}
```

After resolving these problems with Quick Fix, you can run the code as you see in Figure 1-19. Now you'll see that there are no worries, as the text message in the Console view indicates.

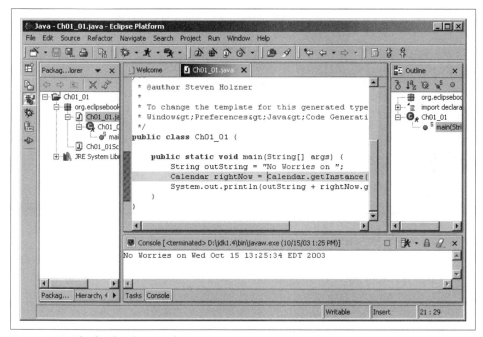

Figure 1-19. The fixed code at work

A Word About Project Management

As you create more projects like Ch01_01, you'll find Eclipse getting more and more crowded, since all your projects are displayed in the Java perspective's Package Explorer view, as well as the Navigator view (recall that the Navigator view is there to let you navigate between projects). If you have 30 projects, there will be 30 entries there. There are various ways to deal with this clutter (such as creating working sets, as we'll see in Chapter 2), but we'll take a look at the simplest one here.

To remove a project from the Package Explorer and Navigator views, you can simply delete it. This does *not* necessarily delete the actual files used for the project, and, whenever you want, you can add the project back to these views. For example, to remove the Ch01_01 project, just right-click its icon and select the Delete item. Eclipse will display the Confirm Project Delete dialog box, as you see in Figure 1-20.

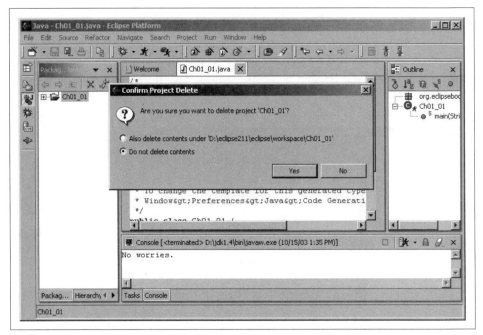

Figure 1-20. Deleting a project

In this case, make sure that the "Do not delete contents" radio button is selected and click Yes to remove the project from Eclipse. The project will disappear from the Package Explorer and Navigator views. Clicking the other radio button will make Eclipse delete all the files and their contents in the project, so don't do that if you want to use the project again later.

When you want to work with the project again, you just import it. To do that, right-click the Package Explorer or Navigator and select the Import context menu item, or select the File → Import menu item. This opens the Import dialog; select the "Existing Project into Workspace" item and click Next. In the next pane, click the Browse button, select the *Ch01_01* folder, and click OK, giving you results like those shown in Figure 1-21.

Click Finish to import the Ch01_01 project again. Now the project is back and ready for use. To run it, select the project in the Package Explorer and select the Run → Run As → Java Application menu item. That's all you need; this is a crude but effective way of doing project management, and we'll see others as we progress.

 You can also close projects if you right-click them and select the Close Project menu item. However, that doesn't remove them from the Package Explorer and Navigator views—it just closes the project folder and changes its icon. The only real benefit of closing projects is that it will allow Eclipse to start up a little faster later because it doesn't have to initialize closed projects.

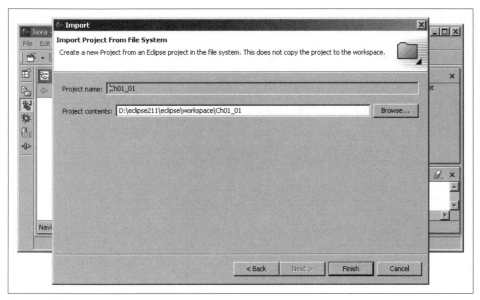

Figure 1-21. Importing a project

That's it for this chapter. We got our start working with Eclipse here, and we're coming up to speed. In the next chapter, we're going to get into more depth on Java development and the JDT.

CHAPTER 2

Java Development

This chapter is where we get down to the business of developing Java using Eclipse. We're going to take a look at using Eclipse for Java development as well as project management, going from the basics to the fairly serious. Nearly everything in this chapter is essential knowledge for the Java developer using Eclipse, so let's jump in.

Developing Java Code

If there's anything that takes more time than it seems to be worth in Java, it's creating code from scratch. While the logic inside a method, interface, or class is unique, the modifiers of a method, the imports for a class, and the syntax involved with new packages is the same over and over again. This often results in a lot of repetitive typing, wasted time, and in many cases, annoying little typo-related bugs. Eclipse can help with all this and more.

Creating New Methods

Eclipse—through code assist—makes it easy to create new methods. As an example, we're going to create and call a new method named printer, which displays the message "No worries.", as you can see in Example 2-1.

Example 2-1. The Ch02_01.java example

```java
public class Ch02_01
{
    public static void main(String[] args)
    {
        printer();
    }

    private static void printer()
    {
        System.out.println("No worries.");
    }
}
```

How do you create new methods? Start Eclipse now and create a new project named Ch02_01. Then create a new Java class named Ch02_01, making it part of the org. eclipsebook.ch02 package. Leave the checkbox for the creation of a stub for the main method checked when you create this new class. This gives you the code:

```
public class Ch02_01 {

    public static void main(String[] args) {
    }
}
```

You could simply type in the printer method, of course, but Eclipse can also be of assistance here. Move the cursor below the body of the main method and type private to make this new method a private method, and then type Ctrl+Space to open code assist, as you see in Figure 2-1.

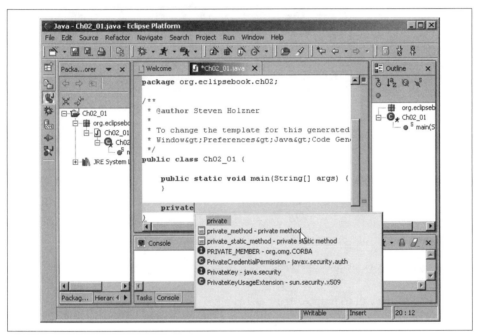

Figure 2-1. Creating a private method

Code assist lets you select the type of private method you want to create—private, private static, and so on. Here, select the private static method, creating the new method template you see in Figure 2-2. The placeholder return_type is highlighted, ready for you to enter in a type; use void. Next, replace the name placeholder with the name printer and delete the arguments placeholder.

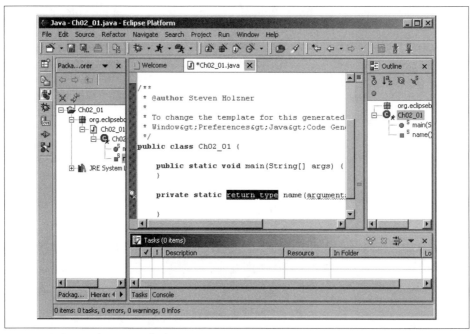

Figure 2-2. Setting the new method's return type

This creates the new method in outline; all that's left is to add the code that will display the message (as before, you can take advantage of code assist to pause after you type each dot for suggestions):

```
public static void main(String[] args) {
}

private static void printer()
{
    System.out.println("No worries.");
}
```

Then just add the call to printer from main:

```
public static void main(String[] args) {
    printer();
}

private static void printer()
{
    System.out.println("No worries.");
}
```

That's all you need; now you can run the example with the Run As → Java Application menu item. You should see "No worries." appear in the Console view—just as before. But this time, we're using a new custom method.

Creating New Classes

We've created a new method and given it a name, but what if you want that new method to be in a different class? For example, say that your main method is in a class named Ch02_02, but the printer method is in a class named Ch02_02Helper:

```
Ch02_02
|
+--------main

Ch02_02Helper
|
+--------printer
```

In this case, you could create a new object of the Ch02_02Helper class in the main method, and then you could call that object's printer method, as you see in Example 2-2.

Example 2-2. The Ch02_02.java example

```java
public class Ch02_02 {
    public static void main(String[] args) {
        Ch02_02Helper helper = new Ch02_02Helper( );
        helper.printer( );
    }
```

The Ch02_02Helper class, with the printer method in it, appears in Example 2-3.

Example 2-3. The Ch02_02Helper.java example

```java
public class Ch02_02Helper {
    public void printer( ) {
        System.out.println("No worries.");
    }
}
```

To implement this example with its two classes in Eclipse, create a new project named Ch02_02 and add the new class Ch02_02Helper to the project. Make this class public and put it into the org.eclipsebook.ch02 package (and make sure that you don't create a main method stub in this class). Next, add the printer method to this class, as in Example 2-1.

Then *save the file*. This is an important step because if you don't save the file, the printer method won't be available to the rest of your project's code. This is essential to know—whenever you want to work with items from file A in file B, you have to save file A first because Eclipse compiles from the files, not what's in its editors.

Having created the new Ch02_02Helper class, the next step is to create the class containing code that will make use of it, the Ch02_02 class. Create that new class in the project and add a stub for the main method to it. Now all you need to do in the main method is add the code to create an object of the Ch02_02Helper class and call that object's printer method:

```
public class Ch02_02 {
    public static void main(String[] args) {
        Ch02_02Helper helper = new Ch02_02Helper( );
        helper.printer( );
    }
}
```

Then save all your work and run the application; Eclipse's compiler handles locating both classes in the same package for you. You should see the "No worries." message as shown in Figure 2-3. As you can see in the Package Explorer, we're using multiple classes in the same project.

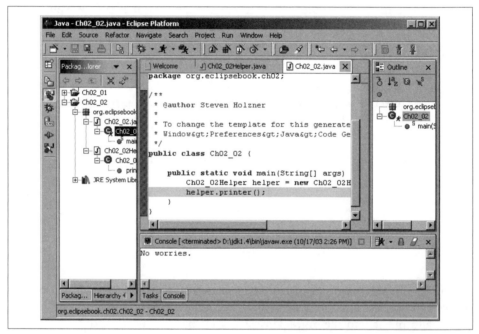

Figure 2-3. Using multiple classes

And there's more you can do with multiple classes here as well. Say you want to override the printer method and change the text it displays. You can do that by deriving a new class based on the Ch02_02Helper class and overriding printer in this new class. To do this, right-click the org.eclipsebook.ch02 package inside the Ch02_02 project and select the New → Class item, opening the New Java Class dialog you see in Figure 2-4.

Name the new class Ch02_02HelperHelper, enter the package name, and deselect the main stub checkbox. To derive this class from Ch02_02Helper, type Ch02_02Helper in the Superclass box (you can also implement interfaces by entering them into the Interfaces box), and click Finish to create the new class. Here's what you get—this new class automatically extends the Ch02_02Helper class:

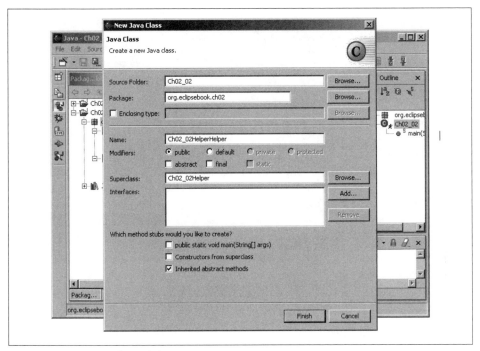

Figure 2-4. Creating a derived class

```
public class Ch02_02HelperHelper extends Ch02_02Helper {

}
```

Notice the "Enclosing type" box in the New Java Class dialog. If you want to enclose one class within another, you can enter the name of the enclosing class here. Note also that if you right-click the enclosing class in the Package Explorer and select New → Class, the enclosing class's name will appear in the Enclosing type text box when this dialog opens, although it won't be used unless you select its checkbox.

We want to override the `printer` method from the base class's version here, so open the new class, `Ch02_02HelperHelper`, and select the Source → Override/Implement Methods menu item, opening the Override/Implement Methods dialog box you see in Figure 2-5 (if you're implementing an interface, you can also find the methods you have to implement here).

This dialog shows a list of possible overrides; all you have to do is pick one. In this case, select the `printer` method and click OK. When you do, you'll see a stub for the new version of the `printer` method in the `Ch02_02HelperHelper` class:

```
public class Ch02_02HelperHelper extends Ch02_02Helper {

    /* (non-Javadoc)
```

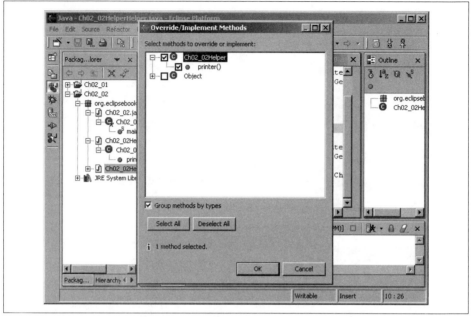

Figure 2-5. Overriding a method

```
    * @see org.eclipsebook.ch02.Ch02_02Helper#printer( )
    */
    public void printer( ) {
        // TODO Auto-generated method stub
        super.printer( );
    }

}
```

In this overriding version, use this code to display a new message, "No problems.":

```
public void printer( ) {
    System.out.println("No problems.");
}
```

And that's it—you've overridden a method in a derived class. As the final step here, change the code in the main method to use your new class:

```
public class Ch02_02 {

    public static void main(String[] args) {
        Ch02_02HelperHelper helper = new Ch02_02HelperHelper( );
        helper.printer( );
    }
}
```

When you run this example, you should see the new message, "No problems.", as in Figure 2-6.

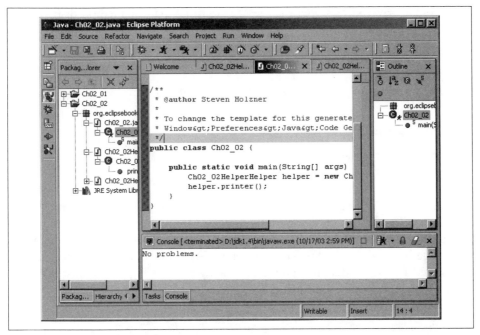

Figure 2-6. Using our derived class

As you can see, automatic code generation can be a timesaver. In this case, you used it to override a method, but there are other options available in the Source menu:

- Source → Comment lets you comment out a section of code. This is great for anyone who's ever had to comment out a long set of lines. All you have to do is select the lines to comment out and choose this menu item. A single-line comment, //, will appear in front of all the lines. Want to uncomment them? Just choose Source → Uncomment.

- Source → Generate Getter and Setter lets you generate standard Java getter and setter methods for a field in a class. For example, if the field is named temperature, the suggested getter and setter methods will be getTemperature and setTemperature.

- Source → Generate Delegate Methods lets you create delegate methods for other methods automatically.

- Source → Add Constructor from Superclass lets you create a constructor that will include code to call the superclass's constructor. (You can also create this constructor automatically when you create a class.)

- Source → Surround with try/catch Block is a great one, and it will surround selected text with a try/catch block for you. This option checks for any uncaught exceptions automatically and adds code to catch them.

For example, say you've stored the message that the `printer` method displays in a class field named `message`:

```
public class Ch02_02HelperHelper extends Ch02_02Helper {

    /* (non-Javadoc)
     * @see org.eclipsebook.ch02.Ch02_02Helper#printer()
     */

    String message = "No problems.";

    public void printer() {
        System.out.println(message);
    }
}
```

Instead of simply storing this data in a class field, you can use getter and setter methods to access it (these methods are of the standard form used in JavaBeans™ to support properties). In this case, you can create getter and setter methods for the value in `message` by selecting the Source → Generate Getter and Setter menu item, which opens the Generate Getter and Setter dialog box you see in Figure 2-7. Just select the checkbox next to `message` and click OK.

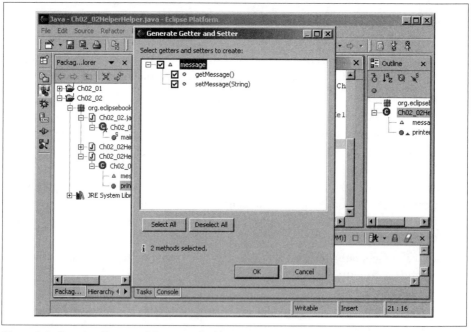

Figure 2-7. Creating Getter and Setter methods

Eclipse will create the new getter and setter methods `getMessage` and `setMessage`; we can use `getMessage` when we want to display the message in the `printer` method this way:

```
public class Ch02_02HelperHelper extends Ch02_02Helper {
```

```
/* (non-Javadoc)
 * @see org.eclipsebook.ch02.Ch02_02Helper#printer()
 */

String message = "No problems.";

public void printer() {
    System.out.println(getMessage());
}

/**
 * @return
 */
public String getMessage() {
    return message;
}

/**
 * @param string
 */
public void setMessage(String string) {
    message = string;
}
```

Another good timesaver is the Source → Surround with try/catch Block menu item. This one checks the code you've selected for uncaught exceptions and writes a try/catch block for any that it finds—another great Eclipse feature worth the price of admission.

Creating New Packages

Besides using multiple classes in the same project, it's also easy to distribute your code over multiple *packages* in the same project. For example, you can break up your code into two packages, org.eclipse.ch02 and org.eclipse.ch02_2, as you can see in the Package Explorer at left in Figure 2-8. Here, we're putting the Ch02_03Helper class, which contains the printer method, into an entirely new package, org.eclipse.ch02_2.

If you want to access a class in another package, just remember to import it—in this case, that means using the fully qualified name of the class you want access to, which is org.eclipsebook.ch02_2.Ch02_03Helper. After you've imported the class, you can create objects using it, like this:

```
import org.eclipsebook.ch02_2.Ch02_03Helper;

/**
 * @author Steven Holzner
 *
 * To change the template for this generated type comment go to
 * Window&gt;Preferences&gt;Java&gt;Code Generation&gt;Code and Comments
 */
```

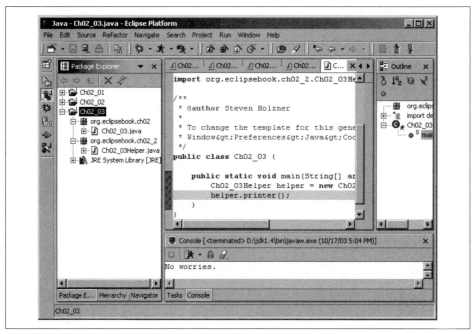

Figure 2-8. Using multiple packages

```
public class Ch02_03 {

    public static void main(String[] args){
        Ch02_03Helper helper = new Ch02_03Helper();
        helper.printer();
    }
}
```

And that's all it takes; as you can see, multiple packages in the same project are no problem at all.

What if the code you want to use is not only in a different package, it's also in another project? When you create a project, you have the option of adding other projects to the build path. For example, if you want to create a new project that works with the code in the org.eclipsebook.ch02_2 package from a new project, Ch02_03, just click the Projects tab in the second pane of the New Java Project dialog and add the Ch02_03 project to the build path, as you see in Figure 2-9.

Now the code in Ch02_03, including the org.eclipsebook.ch02_2 package, is accessible to your new project. You can also add other projects to the build path after a project has been created by selecting the project in the Package Explorer, right-clicking it, and selecting the Properties context menu item. In the Properties dialog that opens, select Java Build Path and click the Projects tab, giving you the same display as in Figure 2-9.

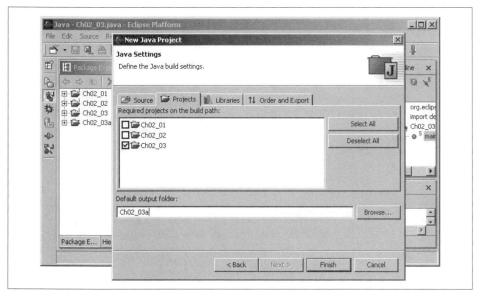

Figure 2-9. Adding a project to the build path

Building and Running Code

How do you create the Java *.class* files that are the end result of developing a project? You use the items in the Project menu. The main menu item here is the Project → Build Project menu item. This item will compile the source code files in your project and leave the resulting *.class* files in the same folder as the source code files by default. For example, if you are working with the Ch02_03 project and select Project → Build Project, the *.class* files for this project will appear in the directory *workspace/ Ch02_03/org/eclipsebook/Ch02* (recall that the classes in this project are in the org. eclipsebook.Ch02 package, which the directory structure reflects). Once created, these *.class* files are ready for use and distribution.

It often makes sense to store all your project's source code in a folder named *src* and the binary output in a folder named *bin*. If you want to set things up this way when you create a new project, open the New Java Project dialog as usual, and, in the second pane, click the Source tab followed by the Add Folder button. Doing so opens the Source Folder Selection dialog; click the Create New Folder button and give the new folder the name *src*. Then click OK twice. Eclipse will recognize that you're creating a source code folder and automatically ask if you want to create a *bin* folder for the binary output, as you see in Figure 2-10.

Configuring a project this way *automatically* stores your source code in the folder named *src* and the binary output in a folder named *bin* (*bin* will not appear in the Package Explorer because it doesn't contain any source code).

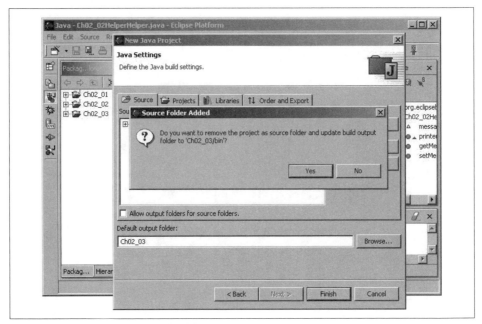

Figure 2-10. Creating source and bin folders

Using JAR and .class Files

Say that you're writing a Java servlet (for more details on servlets, see Chapter 9), shown in Example 2-4.

Example 2-4. The Ch02_04.java example

```
package org.eclipse.ch02;

import java.io.*;
import javax.servlet.*;
import javax.servlet.http.*;

/**
 * @author Steven Holzner
 *
 * To change the template for this generated type comment go to
 * Window&gt;Preferences&gt;Java&gt;Code Generation&gt;Code and Comments
 */

public class Ch02_04 extends HttpServlet {

    public void doGet(HttpServletRequest request,
        HttpServletResponse response)
        throws IOException, ServletException
    {
        response.setContentType("text/html");
        PrintWriter out = response.getWriter( );
```

Example 2-4. The Ch02_04.java example (continued)

```
        out.println("<HTML>");
        out.println("<HEAD>");
        out.println("<TITLE>");
        out.println("A Web Page");
        out.println("</TITLE>");
        out.println("</HEAD>");
        out.println("Hello there!");
        out.println("</BODY>");
        out.println("</HTML>");
    }
}
```

The code in this example relies on classes like HttpServlet that don't come built into the Java core libraries. Since Eclipse can't find some of the required classes, you'll see plenty of wavy red underlines as you enter this code, as in Figure 2-11.

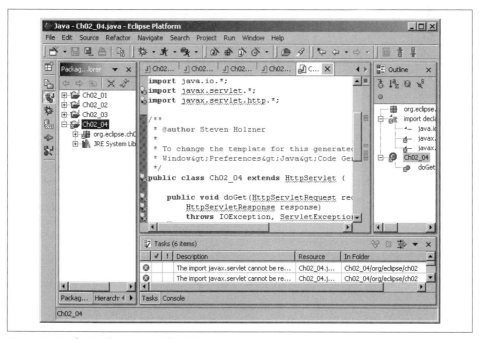

Figure 2-11. Plenty of import not found errors

You can fix this easily by including the correct Java Archive (JAR) file in the classpath, which, in this case, is *servlet.jar*. This JAR file comes with the web server we're going to use later in the book, Apache Tomcat. To add *servlet.jar* to the classpath, right-click the project in the Package Explorer and select the Properties item, opening the dialog you see in Figure 2-12.

In this case, you select the Libraries tab in this dialog, click Add External JARs, navigate to *servlet.jar*, and click OK. Doing so adds *servlet.jar* to the classpath, as you see

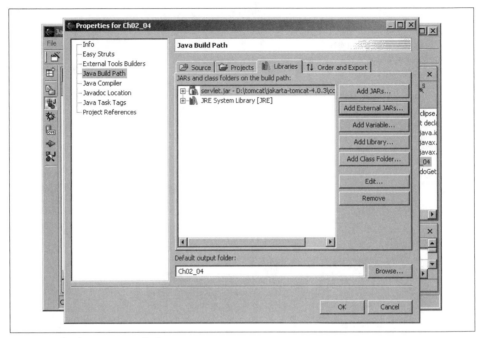

Figure 2-12. The Properties dialog

in Figure 2-12. Click OK to close the Properties dialog and build the project; when you do, things work out fine, as you can see in Figure 2-13, because the needed JAR file is now in the classpath—you can see the reference to *servlet.jar* in this project in the Package Explorer at left.

If you know you're going to be using a JAR file like *servlet.jar* when you first create the project, you can add that JAR file to the project's classpath in the third pane of the New Project dialog. You'll see the same tabs there as you do in Figure 2-12—just click the Libraries tab and add any JAR files you want to the project.

If you add multiple JAR files to the classpath, you can also indicate the order in which you want them searched—just select the Order and Export tab in the Properties dialog, as you see in Figure 2-14, and change the order of imported items with the Up and Down buttons. You can also indicate which items to export by selecting their checkboxes here; when you export an item, it becomes available to any project dependent on the current project.

You can also add *.class* files to the classpath—just use the Add Class Folder button in the Properties dialog to add a folder containing *.class* files.

Say that you're going to be developing more than one servlet; in this case, you might want to make things easier on yourself by creating a *classpath variable* corresponding to *servlet.jar*. You can use that variable to add *servlet.jar* to the classpath. To create a classpath variable, select Window → Preferences, then select the Java item's

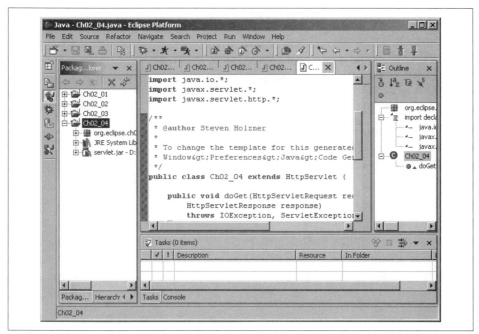

Figure 2-13. A new JAR file in the build path

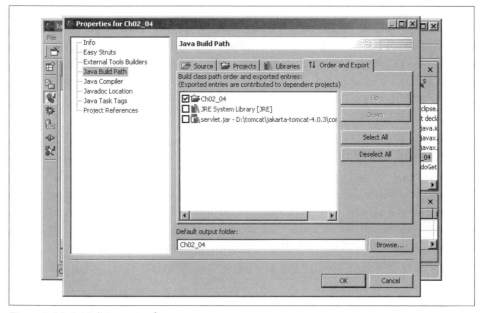

Figure 2-14. Setting import order

Classpath Variables item, as you see in Figure 2-15. To create a new variable, click New, enter the new variable's name—we'll use SERVLET_LIB here—and the path it corresponds to, then click OK. You can see this new variable in Figure 2-15.

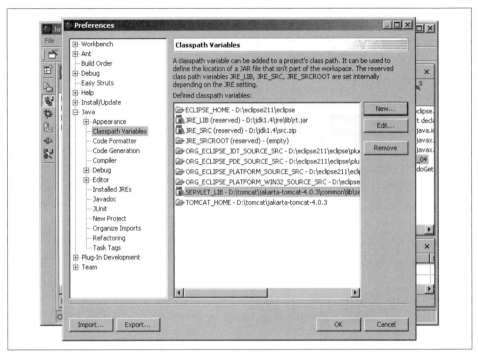

Figure 2-15. Creating a classpath variable

Now, when you want to add this classpath variable to a project's classpath, just open the project's Properties dialog, click the Libraries tab, click the Add Variable button that you see in Figure 2-12, and select the variable you want to add to the classpath. Using classpath variables like this is not only convenient, but it also centralizes your classpath references—for example, if you want to use a new version of *servlet.jar*, all you've got to do is update the classpath variable.

Setting the Launch Configuration

Say that your code needs to read command-line arguments, as you see in Example 2-5, where we're displaying the first word passed on the command line to our code. For example, you could start this program on the command line like this: %java Ch02_05 Hello! (we'll use % for a generic command-line prompt in this book), and you'd expect the program to display the word "Hello!"

Example 2-5. The Ch02_05.java example

```
package org.eclipsebook.ch02;

/**
 * @author Steven Holzner
 *
 * To change the template for this generated type comment go to
 * Window&gt;Preferences&gt;Java&gt;Code Generation&gt;Code and Comments
```

Example 2-5. The Ch02_05.java example (continued)

```
 */
public class Ch02_05 {

    public static void main(String[] args) {
        System.out.println(args[0]);
    }
}
```

Unfortunately, when you run this code as is, you'll get the error java.lang. ArrayIndexOutOfBoundsException at org.eclipsebook.ch02.Ch02_05.main(Ch02_05.java:18) in the console window because we haven't supplied any command-line arguments to be stored in the args array. You can supply command-line arguments in the launch configuration for this project; to set that configuration, select the Run → Run… menu item, opening the Run dialog you see in Figure 2-16.

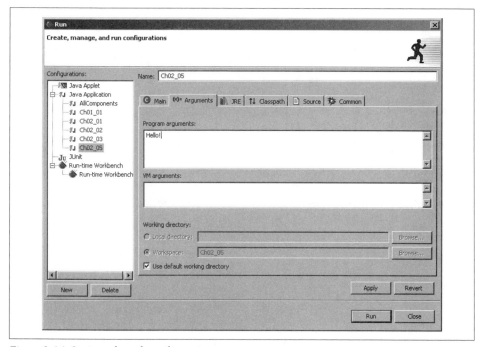

Figure 2-16. Setting a launch configuration

In this dialog, enter "Hello!" in the Program arguments box, as you see in Figure 2-16. If you want to, you can also enter Java Virtual Machine options in the VM arguments box here, as well as select what Java runtime environment you want to work with by clicking the JRE tab. After you enter "Hello!" in the Program arguments box, click Run and the code in your project will read that command-line argument and display it, as you see in Figure 2-17.

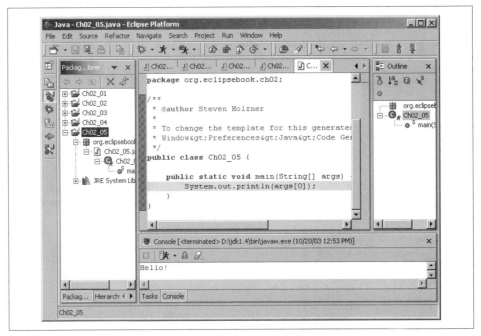

Figure 2-17. Supplying command-line arguments to a program

Selecting the Java Runtime

When you run Eclipse for the first time, it searches for installed Java runtimes, and it may not use the one you want it to use. For example, Eclipse may want to use the outdated JRE that came with your browser instead of the brand new Java SDK you've just downloaded. You can specify what Java runtime you want Eclipse to use by selecting Window → Preferences, selecting Installed JREs, and selecting the one you want, as shown in Figure 2-18 (use the Add button to add JREs and SDKs).

Creating Javadoc

Eclipse also makes it easy to develop Javadoc documentation, the standard Java documentation that accompanies Java programs. You'll notice that in the code it generates, Eclipse inserts some text for Javadoc, as you see in *Ch02_05.java*:

```
package org.eclipsebook.ch02;

/**
 * @author Steven Holzner
 *
 * To change the template for this generated type comment go to
 * Window&gt;Preferences&gt;Java&gt;Code Generation&gt;Code and Comments
 */
```

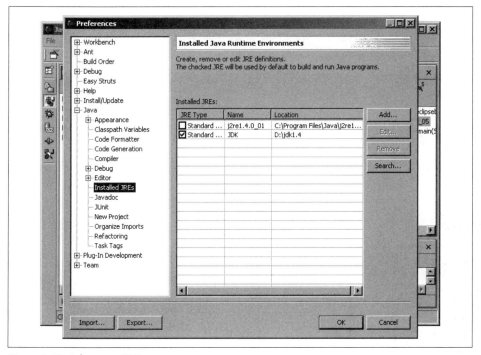

Figure 2-18. Selecting a JRE

If you want to enter your own Javadoc, code assist helps you here, too; for example, if you enter @param and invoke code assist with Ctrl+Space, code assist will list the parameters a method takes. Typing @exception and using code assist will list the exceptions a method throws, and so on. Typing @ in a comment and pausing will make code assist display the Javadoc possibilities, like @author, @deprecated, and so on.

To generate Javadoc from your code, select the Project → Generate Javadoc item, opening the Generate Javadoc dialog, which lets you select the project for which you want to create Javadocs. To browse a project's Javadocs, select the Navigate → Open External Javadoc menu item. For example, you can see the generated Javadoc for the Ch02_05 project in Figure 2-19.

Refactoring

One of the major advantages of using a good Java IDE like Eclipse is that it can let you rename and move Java elements around, and it will update all references to those items throughout your code automatically.

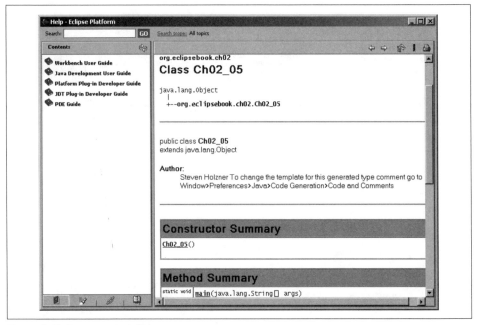

Figure 2-19. Browsing Javadoc

Renaming Elements

For example, take a look at the code in Example 2-6. Here, we've used code assist to create a new method to display a simple message, but we forgot to change the default name for the method that code assist supplied.

Example 2-6. The Ch02_06.java example

```java
package org.eclipse.ch02;

/**
 * @author Steven Holzner
 *
 * To change the template for this generated type comment go to
 * Window&gt;Preferences&gt;Java&gt;Code Generation&gt;Code and Comments
 */
public class Ch0206 {

    public static void main(String[] args) {
        name( );
    }

    public static void name( ) {
        System.out.println("No worries.");
    }
}
```

This default name for the new method, name, is called in the main method, and it could be called from other locations in your code as well. How can you change the name of this method and automatically update all calls to it? Select name in the editor and then select the Refactor → Rename menu item, opening the Rename Method dialog you see in Figure 2-20.

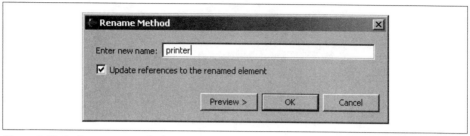

Figure 2-20. Refactoring a method

Enter the new name for the method, printer in this case, and click OK. When you do, the name of this method and all references to it will be updated throughout your code, including all code in the project, as you see here:

```
package org.eclipse.ch02;

/**
 * @author Steven Holzner
 *
 * To change the template for this generated type comment go to
 * Window&gt;Preferences&gt;Java&gt;Code Generation&gt;Code and Comments
 */
public class Ch0206 {

    public static void main(String[] args) {
        printer();
    }

    public static void printer() {
        System.out.println("No worries.");
    }
}
```

We've also misnamed the class in this example—Ch0206, instead of Ch02_06. To rename the class, select Ch0206 in the editor and select the Refactor → Rename menu item, opening the Rename Type dialog you see in Figure 2-21. Enter the new name, Ch02_06, and click OK to rename the class.

Clicking OK not only changes the name of the class in the code, it even changes the name of the class's file from *Ch0206.java* to *Ch02_06.java*, as you can see by checking the Package Explorer. Here's the new code:

```
package org.eclipse.ch02;

/**
```

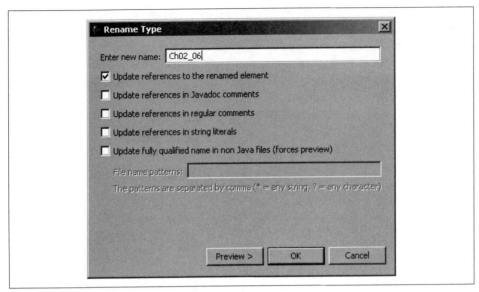

Figure 2-21. Refactoring a class

```
 * @author Steven Holzner
 *
 * To change the template for this generated type comment go to
 * Window&gt;Preferences&gt;Java&gt;Code Generation&gt;Code and Comments
 */
public class Ch02_06 {

    public static void main(String[] args) {
        printer();
    }

    public static void printer() {
        System.out.println("No worries.");
    }
}
```

In fact, we've unaccountably managed to misname the package as well when creating this example—org.eclipse.ch02 instead of org.eclipsebook.ch02. When you refactor it, the name is changed both in the Package Explorer and throughout your code:

```
package org.eclipsebook.ch02;

/**
 * @author Steven Holzner
 *
 * To change the template for this generated type comment go to
 * Window&gt;Preferences&gt;Java&gt;Code Generation&gt;Code and Comments
 */
public class Ch02_06 {

    public static void main(String[] args) {
        printer();
```

```
    }

    public static void printer() {
        System.out.println("No worries.");
    }
}
```

As you can see, it's easy to rename Java elements in your code—Eclipse will handle the details, making the changes throughout your code automatically.

 If you simply type over a Java element in your code, no refactoring happens. You've got to explicitly refactor if you want those changes to echo throughout your code.

Moving Elements

Refactoring works automatically across files as well. Say, for example, that you want to move the printer method to another class, Ch02_06Helper. To see how this works, create that new class now, which Eclipse will put in its own file, *Ch02_06Helper.java*. Then select the method you want to move, printer, by selecting the word "printer" in the declaration of this method. Next, select the Refactor → Move to open the dialog you see in Figure 2-22. To move this method to the Ch02_06Helper class, enter the fully qualified name of that class, org.eclipsebook.ch02.Ch02_06Helper, in the dialog and click OK. This moves the printer method to the Ch02_06Helper class like this:

```
package org.eclipsebook.ch02;

/**
 * @author Steven Holzner
 *
 * To change the template for this generated type comment go to
 * Window&gt;Preferences&gt;Java&gt;Code Generation&gt;Code and Comments
 */
public class Ch02_06Helper {

    public static void printer() {
        System.out.println("No worries.");
    }
}
```

And the call to the printer method is automatically qualified as Ch02_06Helper. printer back in the Ch02_06 class in the main method:

```
package org.eclipsebook.ch02;

/**
 * @author Steven Holzner
 *
 * To change the template for this generated type comment go to
 * Window&gt;Preferences&gt;Java&gt;Code Generation&gt;Code and Comments
 */
```

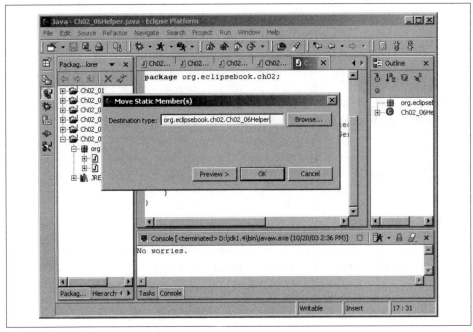

Figure 2-22. Moving a method between classes

```java
public class Ch02_06 {

    public static void main(String[] args) {
        Ch02_06Helper.printer();
    }

}
```

Extracting Interfaces

You can also extract interfaces using refactoring. To see how this works, we'll create an interface for the Ch02_06Helper class (this class has the printer method in it). Convert printer from a static to a standard method by deleting the keyword static in the method declaration. Then select the name of the class, Ch02_06Helper, in the editor and select Refactor → Extract Interface to open the Extract Interface dialog you see in Figure 2-23. Select the printer method to add that method to the interface, and then enter the name of the new interface—Ch02_06HelperInterface—and click OK.

Clicking OK creates a new file, *Ch02_06HelperInterface.java*, where the interface is declared:

```java
package org.eclipsebook.ch02;

/**
 * @author Steven Holzner
 *
```

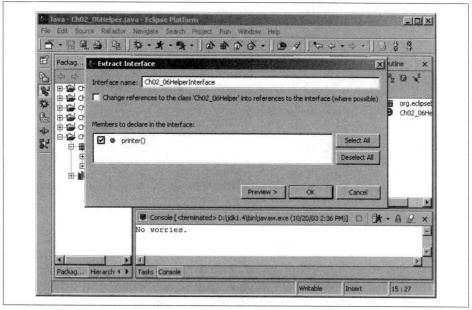

Figure 2-23. Extracting an interface

```
 * To change the template for this generated type comment go to
 * Window&gt;Preferences&gt;Java&gt;Code Generation&gt;Code and Comments
 */
public interface ChO2_06HelperInterface {
    public abstract void printer();
}
```

The original class is now declared to implement this new interface, ChO2_06HelperInterface:

```
package org.eclipsebook.ch02;

/**
 * @author Steven Holzner
 *
 * To change the template for this generated type comment go to
 * Window&gt;Preferences&gt;Java&gt;Code Generation&gt;Code and Comments
 */
public class ChO2_06Helper implements ChO2_06HelperInterface {

    public void printer() {
        System.out.println("No worries.");
    }
}
```

Besides renaming and moving elements and extracting interfaces, there are other operations you can perform with refactoring, such as converting anonymous classes to nested classes, changing a method's signature, and converting a local variable to a class field. For these and other options, take a look at the items available in the Refactor menu.

Some Essential Skills

There are some additional skills that are good to know about. For example, if you highlight an item in the JDT editor, right-click it, and select Open Declaration, the declaration of that item will open. This is great for tracking down where and how methods and fields were created. Several of those are detailed in this section and all are worth adding to your Eclipse toolbox.

Viewing Type Hierarchies

Another menu item in the JDT editor's context menu is the Open Type Hierarchy; when you select an item in the editor and select this menu item, that item's type hierarchy appears in the Java perspective's hierarchy view, as you see at left in Figure 2-24.

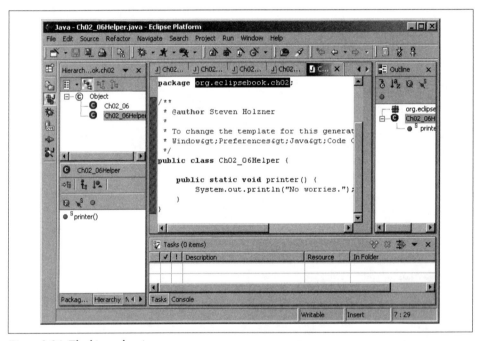

Figure 2-24. The hierarchy view

This view acts like an object browser. It lets you explore a type's Java complete hierarchy, and double-clicking an item in this view opens its definition in the editor. That's useful if, for example, you want to see all the members of the System.out class—just highlight System.out in your code and open its hierarchy. You can also open this view by selecting an item in the editor and selecting the Navigate → Open Type Hierarchy item.

The hierarchy view is not dissimilar from the outline view, which you see at right in Figure 2-24. However, the outline view is designed to show an automatic hierarchy of your code rather than the hierarchy of items you specifically select. As you work in the JDT editor, the outline view is updated automatically to show the hierarchy of the current type you're working with.

Browsing Java Code

There's even another entire perspective dedicated to letting you browse through projects in a Java-oriented way: the Java Browsing perspective. To open this perspective, select Window → Open Perspective → Java Browsing; you can see the results in Figure 2-25.

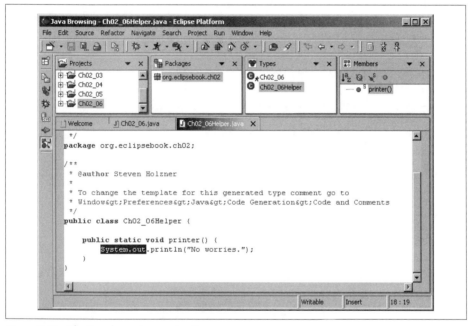

Figure 2-25. The Java browsing perspective

This perspective presents the information you see in the standard Java perspective in a new way, and it breaks type and member information into two new views (the Members view here is much like the Outline view in the standard Java perspective). As you'd expect, the views in this perspective are all coordinated—selecting an element in the Projects views makes its packages appear in the Packages view, for example. And selecting an item in the Members view makes that item appear in the editor, and so on.

Searching Code

Eclipse also has great facilities for searching through code in the Search menu. In fact, the main menu items in the Search menu, Search → Search, Search → File, Search → Help, and Search → Java, all open the Search dialog, although each item corresponds to a different tab in that dialog. Searching is particularly powerful in Eclipse—for example, not only can you search across multiple files, you can also search using wildcards.

The File Search tab in the Search dialog lets you search across multiple files. For example, in Figure 2-26, we're searching for the word main through all *.java* files in the workspace. The scope of the search is set with the radio buttons in the Scope box, and the default is to search all matching files throughout the workspace (that is, all your projects that appear in the Package Explorer). You can also restrict the search to a working set (covered in a few pages) of projects. If you want to search only the current project or just a restricted number of projects, you can select that project or those projects in the Package Explorer, then open the Search dialog and select the Selected Resources radio button in the Scope box.

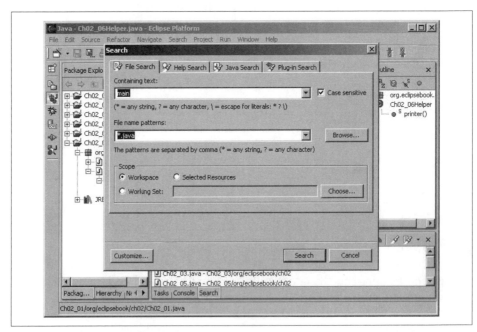

Figure 2-26. Performing a file search

Clicking Search makes Eclipse search for matches to the text you've entered, and you can see the results in the Search Results view, which appears at the bottom in Figure 2-27. Double-clicking a match in the Search Results view opens the match in the JDT editor, as you can see in the figure, and both underlines the match and points to it with an arrow.

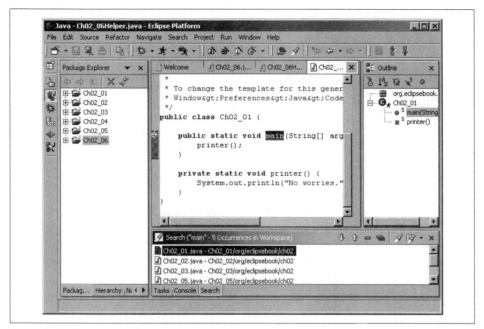

Figure 2-27. Viewing search results

You can also perform Java searches with the Java tab in the Search dialog. This lets you search for Java elements by kind—types, methods, packages, constructors, and fields—as you can see in Figure 2-28. You can also limit the search so that it only matches declarations or references.

Being able to search across files and classes is one of the big advantages of using an IDE—if you've been doing Java development using a text editor and javac, you'll find there's no comparison when you start using the project management capabilities like these in Eclipse.

Customizing the Development Environment

Our last topic in this chapter is all about customizing your development environment. Eclipse is easy to customize, starting from the most basic—you can move any view, editor, or toolbar around simply by dragging it.

 If you don't like to work in an environment where things can move around with mouse movements by mistake, you can lock the toolbars with the Window → Lock the Toolbars menu item. And if a perspective gets all scrambled by inadvertent mouse movements, use Window → Reset Perspective to restore things.

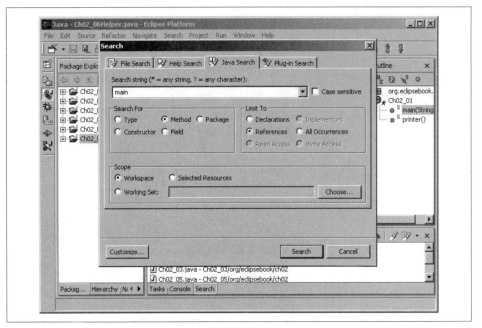

Figure 2-28. Performing a Java search

You can also customize how Eclipse will generate code for you. For example, the default code generation style doesn't place opening curly braces on their own lines:

```java
public void printer() {
    System.out.println("No worries.");
}
```

However, your programming style might be more like this, where each curly brace does get its own line:

```java
public void printer()
{
    System.out.println("No worries.");
}
```

You can customize this with the Windows → Preferences item, opening the Preferences dialog you see in Figure 2-29. Select the Java → Code Formatter item, which lets you specify options for code generation. Here, select the "Insert a new line before an opening brace" item, as you see in the figure; the sample code below will change to match.

Here's another way you can customize how Eclipse generates code. When you create a new file, this kind of comment is inserted automatically:

```java
/*
 * Created on Oct 17, 2003
 *
 * To change the template for this generated file go to
 * Window&gt;Preferences&gt;Java&gt;Code Generation&gt;Code and Comments
 */
```

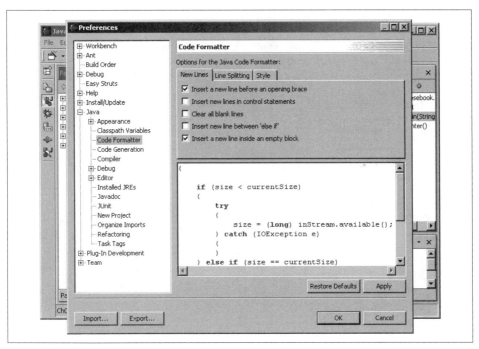

Figure 2-29. Customizing code generation

As this text says, you can change this with the Window → Preferences item, followed by the Java → Code Generation → Code and Comments item (the > you see in the code is the HTML escaped version of >, which is used so the resulting Javadoc can be opened in a browser; the comment actually reads, "To change the template for this generated file go to Window → Preferences → Java → Code Generation → Code and Comments"). When you open the Preferences dialog and select the Java → Code Generation → Code and Comments → Code → New Java files item, as you see in Figure 2-30, you can edit the template Eclipse uses to generate this comment.

You can even create new code assist items in Eclipse. For example, say you want to create a shortcut for the code needed to print out the current date. To do that, select Window → Preferences, followed by the Java → Editor → Templates item. We'll create a new shortcut named ptd to print the date, as you see in the name box in Figure 2-31. In this case, the template System.out.println("${date}"); will be replaced by the code to print out the date. Besides ${date}, you can use other values, such as ${cursor}, to indicate where to place the cursor after the insertion has been performed (when you type ${, code assist will display all the possible values you can use in code assist expressions).

Now when you type ptd in code, followed by Ctrl+Space, code assist will enter the code needed to print out the current date, as you see in Figure 2-32. In fact, if you type p, followed by Ctrl+Space, code assist will list all its options that begin with the letter "p"—including ptd.

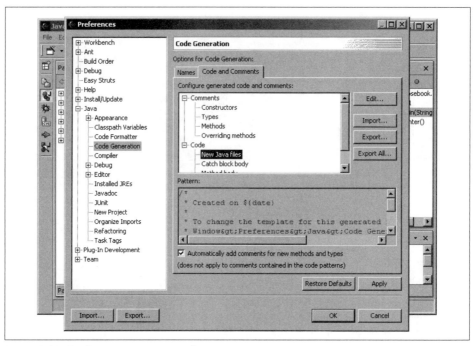

Figure 2-30. Configuring comment templates

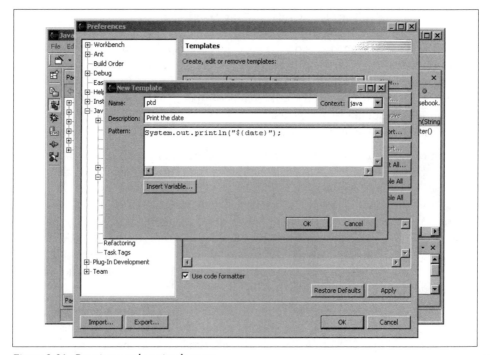

Figure 2-31. Creating a code assist shortcut

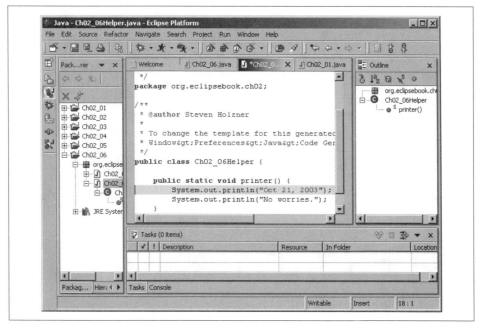

Figure 2-32. Customizing code assist

Another way of customizing your development environment is to create *working sets*. Working sets let you limit what appears in the Package Explorer. For example, to create a working set consisting only of the projects Ch02_01 and Ch02_02, click the Package Explorer's pull-down menu (that's the inverted black triangle at the top of this view) and select the Select Working Set item, opening the Select Working Set dialog. To create a new working set, click the New button and select the Java item in the Working Set Type box in the New Working Set dialog. Then click the Next button. Now you can select the projects for this working set, as you see in Figure 2-33. In this case, we'll create a working set named 1And2Only and select only the Ch02_01 and Ch02_02 projects for this working set.

Clicking Finish creates the new working set and opens the Select Working Set dialog. Select the 1And2Only working set and click OK. When you do, only the Ch02_01 and Ch02_02 projects appear in the Package Explorer, as you see in Figure 2-34.

To restore all projects to the Package Explorer, select the Deselect Working Set item from the Package Explorer's pull-down menu.

In fact, you can customize entire perspectives as well. To do that, select the Window → Customize menu item, opening the Customize Perspective dialog, as you see in Figure 2-35. You can use this dialog to customize menu items available for the current perspective; for example, you can specify what views the user can switch to with the Window → Show View menu item, as you see in the figure.

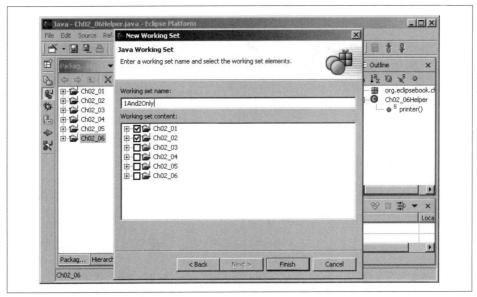

Figure 2-33. Creating a working set

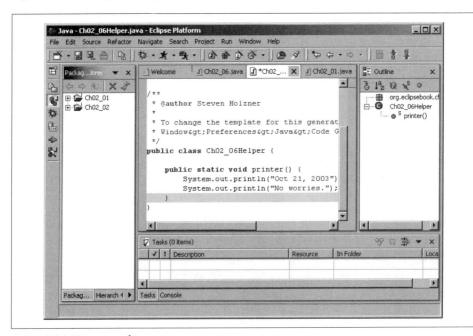

Figure 2-34. Using a working set

After you're done setting Eclipse preferences, you can export those preferences so others can use them as well. To do that, use the Import and Export buttons in the Window → Preferences dialog.

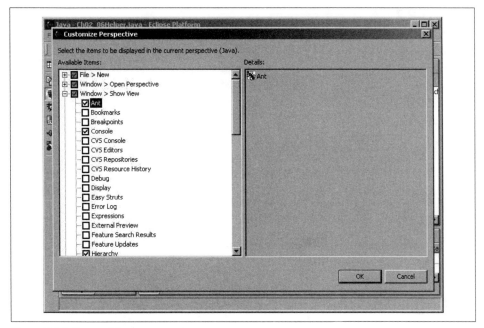

Figure 2-35. Customizing a perspective

And that completes our look at some of the extraordinary power that Eclipse places at your fingertips for Java development. In the next chapter, we're going to discuss testing and debugging your Java code.

CHAPTER 3

Testing and Debugging

Testing and debugging are a way of life in Java development. Eclipse comes with built-in facilities for testing your code using its JUnit framework and some truly exceptional debugging capabilities.

Testing with JUnit

JUnit is an open source testing framework that comes with Eclipse. You can create JUnit-based classes in the same project as other classes, and use this JUnit code to test the other classes in your project. Using JUnit in this way, you can construct a set of standard tests for everyone working on an application, and if they change the application's code, all they'll need is a few clicks to verify that the application still passes the standard set of tests.

JUnit is designed to test your code, and it's made up of assertion methods that can test various conditions. Here they are:

assertEquals(a, b)
> Tests if a is equal to b (a and b are either primitive values or must have an equals method for comparison purposes)

assertFalse(a)
> Tests if a is false, where a is a Boolean value

assertNotNull(a)
> Tests if a is not null, where a is either an object or null

assertNotSame(a, b)
> Tests if a and b both do not refer to the identical object

assertNull(a)
> Tests if a is null, where a is either an object or null

assertSame(a, b)
> Tests if a and b both refer to the identical object

assertTrue(a)
> Tests if a is true, where a is a Boolean value

You construct JUnit tests using these methods; when you run a JUnit application, it opens its own view to give you an immediate indication of which tests have passed and which have failed.

Creating a Test Application

We'll use JUnit in an example here to show how it works by creating an application that we can test, Ch03_01. This application's purpose is simply to fill an array of integers with values and give you access to those values with get and set methods.

In particular, we'll include three methods that return values that may be tested with JUnit:

allocate
:   Allocates an array of integers and fills it with data; returns the newly allocated array.

set
:   Sets a value in the array of integers; returns true if successful, false otherwise.

get
:   Gets a value from the array of integers; returns the requested value.

You can see a first attempt at this code in Example 3-1.

Example 3-1. The Ch03_01.java example

```
package org.eclipsebook.ch03;

public class Ch03_01 {

    private int[] array;

    public int[] allocate() {
        array[0] = 0;
        array[1] = 1;
        array[2] = 2;
        return array;
    }

    public int get(int index) {
        return array[index];
    }

    public boolean set(int index, int value) {
        if (index < array.length && index >= 0) {
            array[index] = value;
            return true;
        } else {
            return false;
        }
    }
}
```

The allocate method allocates an integer array, fills it with data, and returns the array:

```
private int[] array;

public int[] allocate( ) {
    array[0] = 0;
    array[1] = 1;
    array[2] = 2;
    return array;
}
```

The get method retrieves the integer at a given location in the array:

```
public int get(int index) {
    return array[index];
}
```

The set method sets the integer at a given location, returning true or false as appropriate:

```
public boolean set(int index, int value) {
    if (index < array.length && index >= 0) {
        array[index] = value;
        return true;
    } else {
        return false;
    }
}
```

The next step is to test all these methods—allocate, set, and get—with JUnit.

Installing JUnit

To work with JUnit (see *http://www.junit.org* for more details), you have to add *junit.jar* to your project's classpath. In this case, we'll create a new classpath variable, JUNIT. Select the Window → Preferences menu item to open the Preferences dialog, expand the Java node, and select the Classpath Variables item. Then click the New button to open the New Variable Entry dialog, enter the name of the new variable, JUNIT, and the path to *junit.jar*. In Eclipse 2.1.1, you can find *junit.jar* in *eclipse/plugins/org.junit_3.8.1/junit.jar*. Then click OK.

 As is often the case in Eclipse, a task like adding a new classpath variable can be done in more ways than one. Here's another way, with a few more steps: right-click the Ch03_01 project and select the Properties item to open the Properties for Ch03_01 dialog. Select the Java Build Path item and the Libraries tab, then click the Add Variable button to open the New Variable Classpath Entry dialog. Click the Edit button to open the Preferences dialog, and then the New button to open the New Variable Entry dialog. Enter the name of the new variable, JUNIT, the path to *junit.jar*, and click OK. If it can be done in Eclipse, there's usually more than one way to do it.

You may also want to add the JUnit package's source code, for debugging purposes (this is an optional step; we're not going to use the JUnit source in our samples). You'll find the JAR files for many packages' source code in the directory *eclipse/plugins/org.eclipse.jdt.source_2.1.1/src*. To create a new variable for the JUnit source, follow the directions for creating JUNIT, but name this variable JUNIT_SRC (you usually add the suffix _SRC for source code variables) and connect that variable to *eclipse/plugins/org.eclipse.jdt.source_2.1.1/src/org.junit_3.8.1/junitsrc.zip*. After creating this variable, right-click the Ch03_01 project, select Properties to open the Properties for Ch03_01 dialog, click the Java Build Path item and the Libraries tab, and then expand the node for the JUNIT entry as you see in Figure 3-1.

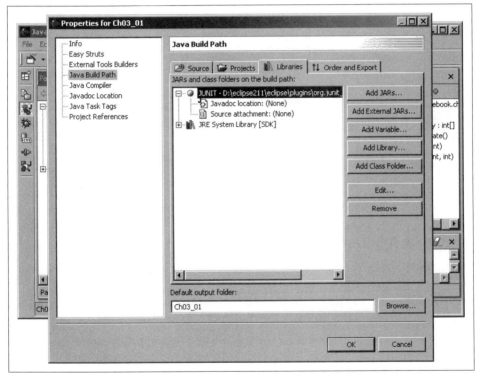

Figure 3-1. Making source code accessible

When you expand a JAR file's node in this way, you can specify where to find both the associated source code and Javadoc. To use JUNIT_SRC for the source code here, select the Source attachment item in the expanded node and click Edit to open the Source Attachment Configuration dialog. Click the Variable button, double-click JUNIT_SRC, and click OK to close this dialog. You can see the results in Figure 3-2, where we've made the source for JUnit accessible to Eclipse. Click OK to close the Properties for Ch03_01 dialog.

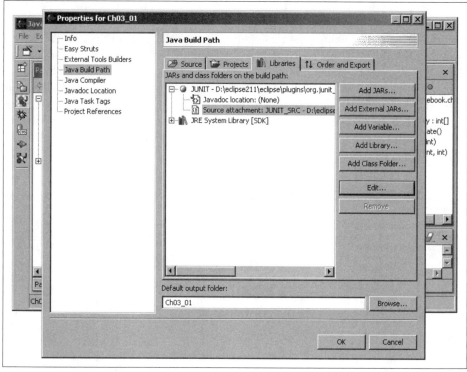

Figure 3-2. Using the JUNIT_SRC variable

Testing an Application with JUnit

We're ready to test the Ch03_01 application. To do so, we'll create a new class that extends the JUnit TestCase class using the JUnit Wizard. To invoke this wizard, you right-click the Ch03_01 class in the Package Explorer and select New → Other to open the New dialog you see in Figure 3-3.

At this point you should be able to expand the Java node in the left pane and select the entry labeled JUnit. In the right pane, select the TestCase entry and click Next, displaying the pane you see in Figure 3-4.

The usual practice is to name JUnit classes using the same name as the classes they test and then adding the word Test at the end, so, in this dialog, enter the name Ch03_01Test in the Test case box. Also, select the setUp and tearDown methods (as you see in Figure 3-4). These methods let you set up and clean up after data and/or objects in the test case (the JUnit term for these items is *fixtures*). Then click Next to open the next pane, shown in Figure 3-5.

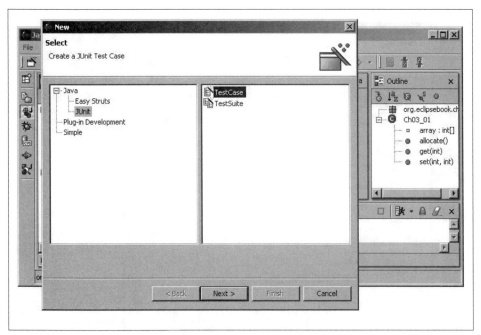

Figure 3-3. Creating a new TestCase-based class

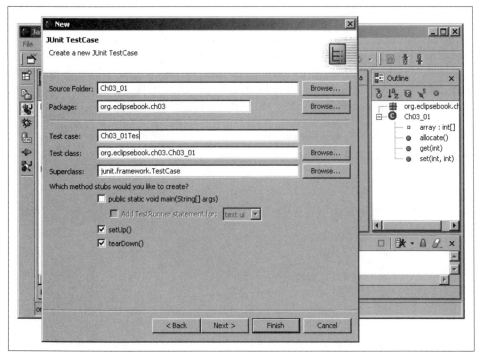

Figure 3-4. Naming a JUnit application

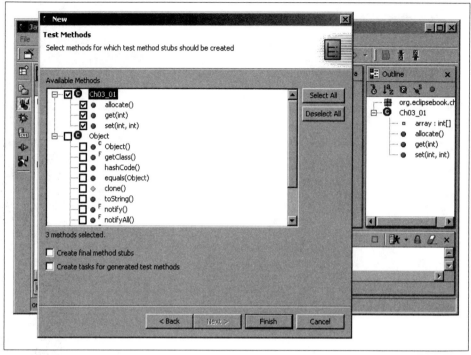

Figure 3-5. Selecting methods to test

In this pane, select the methods you want to test so the JUnit Wizard can create stubs for them. Since we want to test allocate, set, and get, select them as you see in Figure 3-5 and click Finish to create the Ch03_01Test class, which you see in Example 3-2. You can see one method stub in the Ch03_01Test class for each of the allocate, set, and get methods: testAllocate, testSet, and testGet.

Example 3-2. The Ch03_01Test.java example

```
import junit.framework.TestCase;
        .
        .
        .
public class Ch03_01Test extends TestCase {
    /**
     * Constructor for Ch03_01Test.
     * @param arg0
     */
    public Ch03_01Test(String arg0) {
        super(arg0);
    }

    /*
     * @see TestCase#setUp()
     */
```

Example 3-2. The Ch03_01Test.java example (continued)

```
protected void setUp( ) throws Exception {
    super.setUp( );
}

/*
 * @see TestCase#tearDown( )
 */
protected void tearDown( ) throws Exception {
    super.tearDown( );
}

public void testAllocate( ) {
}

public void testGet( ) {
}

public void testSet( ) {
}

}
```

The next step is to add code to these stubs that will call the Ch03_01 class's allocate, set, and get methods so we can use the JUnit assertions on the results. We'll need an object of the Ch03_01 class to call those methods, which we'll name testObject. To create testObject, use the setUp method in the JUnit code. This method is called just before a JUnit test starts, so we'll create testObject from the class we want to test, Ch03_01:

```
Ch03_01 testObject;
    .
    .
    .
protected void setUp( ) throws Exception {
    super.setUp( );
    testObject = new Ch03_01( );
}
```

Now we're free to perform tests with this object. For example, the allocate method is supposed to create an array of integers and return that array, so we can test to make sure that array is not null using assertNotNull in testAllocate:

```
public void testAllocate( ) {
    assertNotNull(testObject.allocate( ));
}
```

The get method is supposed to retrieve a value from the array, so we can test that method using assertEquals with a test value in testGet:

```
public void testGet( ) {
    assertEquals(testObject.get(1), 1);
}
```

And the set method is supposed to return true if it's been successful, so we can test it with assertTrue like this:

```
public void testSet( ) {
    assertTrue(testObject.set(2, 3));
}
```

After you've added this code, select the Ch03_01Test class in the Package Explorer and the Run As → JUnit Test menu item, opening the view you see at left in Figure 3-6.

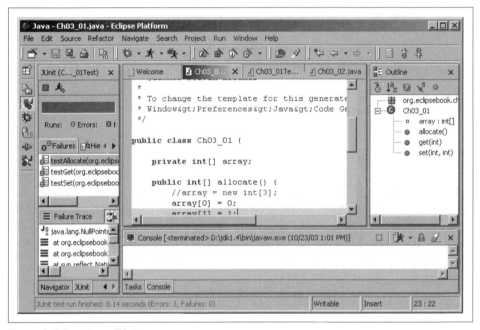

Figure 3-6. Running a JUnit test

A red bar appears at the top of this view (displayed in glorious black and white in Figure 3-6), indicating that there were failures. As you can see in the Failures tab of the JUnit view, all three tests are marked with Xs, which means they've failed. We'll tackle the first test, testAllocate, which asserts that the created array not be null:

```
public void testAllocate( ) {
    assertNotNull(testObject.allocate( ));
}
```

Taking a look at the allocate method reveals the problem—although the code tries to add values to the array, it neglected to actually create the array in the first place. We'll fix that by adding this code to the Ch03_01 class:

```
private int[] array;
        .
        .
        .
```

```
public int[] allocate( ) {
    array = new int[3];
    array[0] = 0;
    array[1] = 1;
    array[2] = 2;
    return array;
}
```

Now when you run Ch03_01Test, you see that only the testGet and testSet methods have failed, as shown in Figure 3-7.

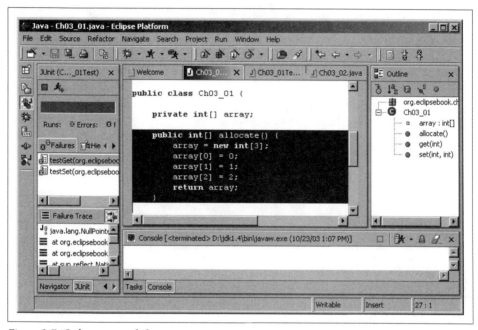

Figure 3-7. Only two tests fail now

What's wrong with the testGet and testSet tests? The problem here is that all JUnit tests are performed *independently*. This means that even though the first test, testAllocate, called the allocate method, that method has not been called as far as the next two tests, testGet and testSet, are concerned. To initialize the array for these two tests, then, we have to call the allocate method in both testGet and testSet. Here's the code we'll add to do that:

```
public void testGet( ) {
    testObject.allocate( );
    assertEquals(testObject.get(1), 1);
}

public void testSet( ) {
    testObject.allocate( );
    assertTrue(testObject.set(2, 3));
}
```

And that's all that was needed. Now when you run the tests they all pass, as you see in Figure 3-8, where there are no failures. And although you can't see it in the black-and-white figure, the bar at the top of the JUnit view is green, which is Eclipse's way of telling you that all systems are go.

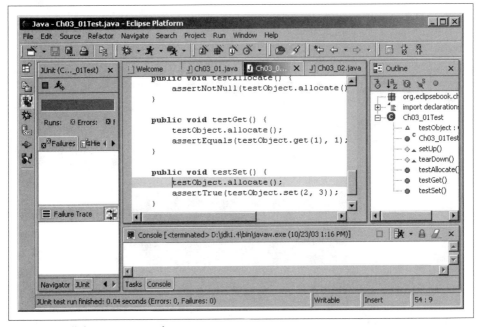

Figure 3-8. All three tests succeed now

As you can see, JUnit provides a relatively simple way to create a standard set of tests that can be applied with a few mouse clicks. Once the tests have been created, you just have to run the JUnit class you've created. That, in itself, can be useful if you want to make sure a number of developers working on your code all apply the same tests.

However, note that JUnit only tests *compliance* with a set of tests—if there's a problem with your code and you don't know what's going on, you need to *debug*.

Debugging

Eclipse's debugging capabilities are impressive, even for a fully featured IDE. To get started, we'll take a look at an example with a logic error that we can then track down. After the example, we'll look at more advanced debugging topics, like setting debug launch configurations, using hot code replacement, suspending a running program that isn't terminating (such as when you have an infinite loop), and more. Being able to interactively debug your code is something you should expect to find in a good IDE—and it's a brilliant improvement over trying to debug your code using only the tools that come with Java—but Eclipse has gone above and beyond the call.

A Buggy Program

Our buggy program appears in Example 3-3. The debugger in Eclipse is especially good at working with *stack frames*, which hold the local variable set for method calls. To get a handle on debugging, we're going to create an example that creates several layers of stack frames: a factorial example (e.g., the factorial of 6, denoted 6!, is equal to 6 * 5 * 4 * 3 * 2 * 1 = 720), which calls itself recursively in order to calculate factorials.

Example 3-3. The Ch03_02.java example

```
package org.eclipsebook.ch03;

public class Ch03_02 {

    public static void main(String[] args) {
        System.out.println(factorial(6));
    }

    public static int factorial(int value) {
        if(value == 0){
            return value;
        }
        else {
            return value * factorial(value - 1);
        }
    }
}
```

You calculate factorials like this: n! = n * (n - 1) * (n - 2) ... * 1. In our example, to calculate factorial(n), the factorial method multiplies n by factorial(n - 1), calling itself to determine the factorial of (n–1). To determine factorial(n - 1), the factorial method multiplies (n–1) by factorial(n - 2), a process that continues all the way down until the factorial has been fully calculated. Here's the code we're using to do that:

```
public static int factorial(int value) {
    if(value == 0){
        return value;
    }
    else {
        return value * factorial(value - 1);
    }
}
```

In this example, we're trying to find the factorial of 6, 6!, which is 720. Here's what the main method looks like:

```
public static void main(String[] args) {
    System.out.println(factorial(6));
}
```

Unfortunately, the first time we run this example, it tells us that 6! = 0, as you can see in the Console view in Figure 3-9.

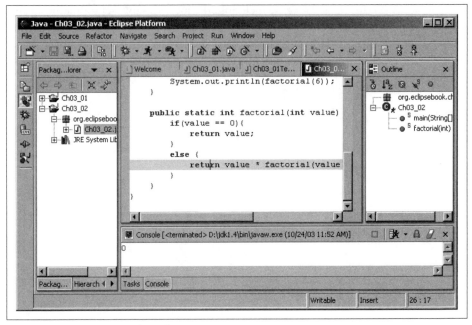

Figure 3-9. First attempt with our buggy program

Setting a Breakpoint

No exception was thrown, so we have a problem in the code's logic, which means it's time to debug. We'll start by examining our code as it's running, halting execution with breakpoints. To set a breakpoint in the JDT editor, just double-click the marker bar next to the line of executable code to which you want to add a breakpoint (alternately, select the line and use the Run → Add/Remove Breakpoint menu item). To remove the breakpoint later, just double-click it again.

In this case, we'll install a new breakpoint next to the code line return value * factorial(value - 1) so we can watch the factorial being created during successive calls to the factorial method. You can see this new breakpoint, which appears as a blue dot in the marker bar, in Figure 3-10.

To debug the code, select the Run → Debug As → Java Application menu item, which makes the debug perspective appear as you see in Figure 3-11.

 Using Run → Run will ignore all breakpoints.

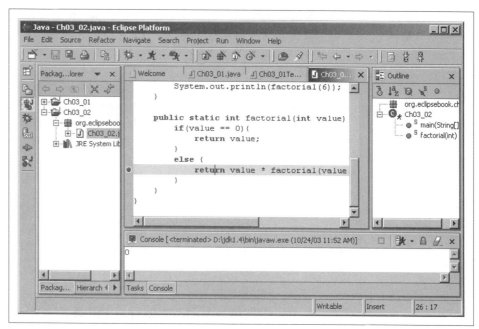

Figure 3-10. Setting a breakpoint

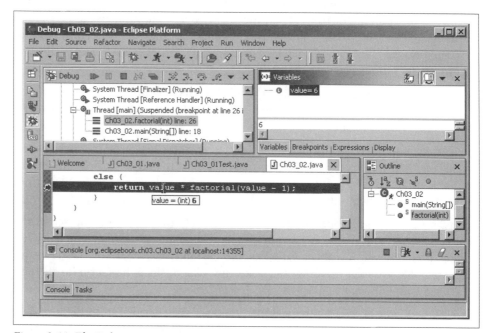

Figure 3-11. The Debug perspective

The code executes up to the breakpoint and stops; the line of code where execution is paused appears in the Debug editor marked with an arrow.

The Debug perspective is worth examining in depth. You can see entries for the programs you're debugging in the Debug view at the upper left. Note, in particular, the stack frames here, marked with three horizontal bars. In this case, we can see we're in the factorial method, which has been called by the main method. The three buttons next to the word Debug in the Debug view are (from left to right) the Resume (start executing code again), Suspend (pause code, as when you've got a runaway infinite loop), and Terminate (stop debugging) buttons.

 Successive debug sessions are added to the Debug view, which can make it pretty crowded over time (these sessions are retained so you can compare what's going on now with what happened before). To get rid of previous debug session's entries in this view, click the Remove All Terminated Launches button in this view's toolbar (the button displaying three overlapping rectangles).

To the right of the Debug view is a set of stacked views—Variables, Breakpoints, Expressions, and Display. The Variables view lets you examine the value of local variables. You can edit these values (as we'll do later in this chapter) to change the value of variables as you debug your code, allowing you to tinker with what's going on in your program interactively. Eclipse will also watch the value in these variables and indicate when they have changed by changing the color of a variable's entry to red. The bottom part of the Variables view is called its *detail pane*, and it displays data in a fuller format.

The Breakpoints view lets you manage the breakpoints in your code by right-clicking a breakpoint in the list and selecting items like Disable, Enable, Remove, or Remove All from the context menu.

The Expressions view lets you evaluate expressions, as we'll see in a few pages. When you select an expression in the editor, right-click it, and select Inspect—it'll be evaluated in the Expressions view. Similarly, when you select the Display item from the context menu, the results will appear in the Display view.

The editor under the Debug perspective is essentially the same one you see in the Java perspective, and it allows you to examine the values of variables simply by letting the mouse hover over those variables. For example, in Figure 3-11, we're examining the value variable, which we see holds the value 6, since the factorial method was called with that value.

Next to the editor is the Outline view at the lower right (also seen in Figure 3-11), which is the same as in the Java perspective. Below the editor is the Console view, which displays program output just as in the Java perspective.

When you end a debug session, the perspective remains in the debug perspective. You can switch back to the Java perspective with the Window → Open Perspective → Java menu item, of course, but during the debugging cycle, it's easier to switch perspectives by clicking the shortcut icons you see at the extreme left in Figure 3-11.

Stepping Through Code

The most fundamental way to move through paused code is by single-stepping. Eclipse offers four options here, corresponding to the four arrow buttons you see in the Debug view toolbar, beginning with the double-headed arrow and moving to the right (these items are also accessible in the Run menu when you're paused in a debugging session):

Step With Filters (also Shift + F5)
> Steps into the selected statement using defined filters. If that statement is a method call, execution continues inside the called method unless you've filtered the method out (see below).

Step Into (also F5)
> Steps into the selected statement. If that statement is a method call, execution continues inside the called method.

Step Over (also F6)
> Steps over the selected statement. Does not step into method calls.

Step Return (also F7)
> Executes until the end of the current method and then returns, pausing after the method returns (or when a breakpoint is encountered).

For example, our debugging session is currently paused at the line `return value * factorial(value - 1)`. Pressing F5 single-steps *into* that line, which means we begin executing the `factorial(value - 1)` call, as you can see in Figure 3-12, where the new value in the `value` variable is 5.

So far, we can see that the `factorial` method is progressing as it should. When it was first invoked, value was 6. In this second call to `factorial`, `value` is 5.

You can also use *step filters* to indicate what code you want to filter out while single-stepping. When you filter out the code in a class or package, that code is not stepped into when you use the Step With Filters option, which is great if you want to avoid stepping through system code. To set step filters, you use Window → Preferences to open the Preferences dialog, then select the Java → Debug → Step Filtering item, as you see in Figure 3-13. To filter out code, use the checkboxes next to the predefined filters you see in the figure, or create a new filter by clicking the Add Filter button.

We could keep single-stepping through our code to try to find the problem with that code. Or we could use the breakpoint we've already set to make things move faster.

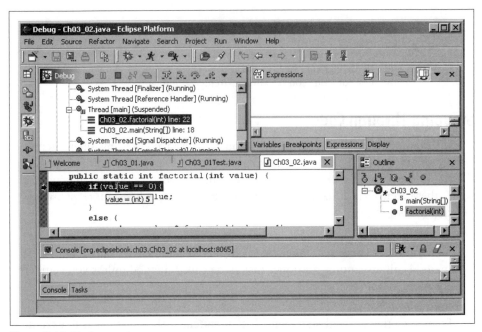

Figure 3-12. Single-stepping

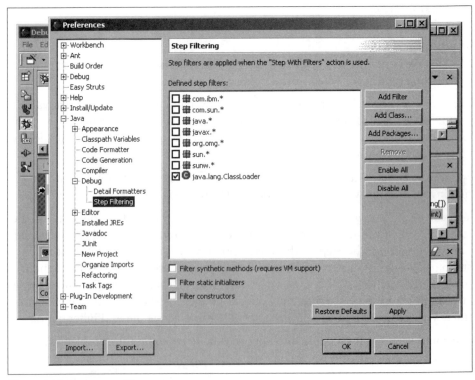

Figure 3-13. Setting step filters

Resuming Execution Until Encountering a Breakpoint

We've been single-stepping through our code, and we can continue doing that, but we'd have to keep going through each line of iteration of the factorial method, which can be a little tedious. Instead, we can simply let our code keep executing until it reaches our breakpoint. To do that, just click the Resume button in the Debug view (the arrow button to the right of the word Debug in the Debug view).

Before doing that, however, we can also set up the Debug perspective to watch the value in our value variable. That way, Eclipse will automatically display the value in that variable, making life a little easier. To watch the value in the value variable, just right-click that variable in the editor and select the Watch item. Doing so will add value to the Expressions view.

Now click the Resume button; when you do, execution resumes until a breakpoint is encountered, as you see in Figure 3-14. You can see that we're still in the same call to factorial by taking a look at the value of the value variable, which is 5. This is apparent because we're watching it in the Expressions view at the upper right.

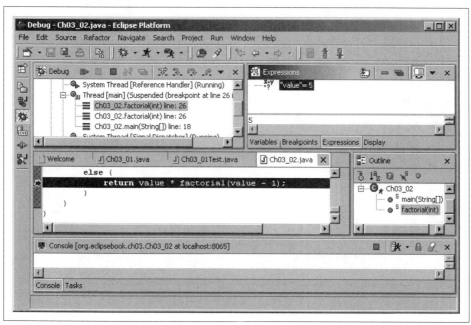

Figure 3-14. Running to a breakpoint

Now all we need to do is keep resuming execution by clicking the Resume button through all the iterations of factorial. But there's an even easier way still!

Setting Breakpoint Hit Counts

There are supposed to be six iterations of the factorial method, so we'd have to hit the Resume button six times. That's not too bad, but you can also configure breakpoints in Eclipse with *hit counts*. When you use a hit count of *n*, the breakpoint won't be triggered until the *n*th time it's encountered, which can save you time.

To set a breakpoint's hit count, right-click the breakpoint in the Breakpoints view and select the Properties item, opening the Java Line Breakpoint Properties dialog you see in Figure 3-15. In this case, select the Enable Hit Count checkbox and enter 6 as the hit count. Then click OK to close this dialog.

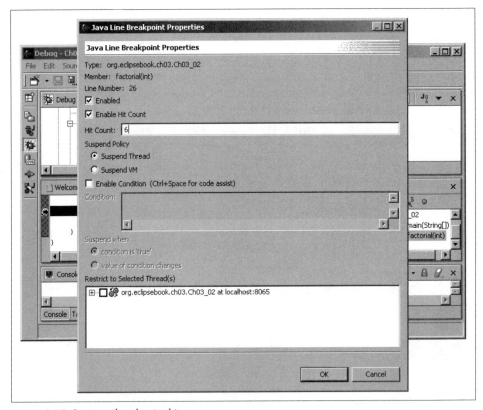

Figure 3-15. Setting a breakpoint hit count

Now restart the debugging session (end the session by clicking the Terminate button or using the Run → Terminate button and start the debugging session again). When you do, execution will be suspended the sixth time our breakpoint is encountered, as you can see in Figure 3-16. Note that value holds 1, as you see in the Expressions view, and that you can see all the stack frames for the successive calls to factorial in the Debug view at left.

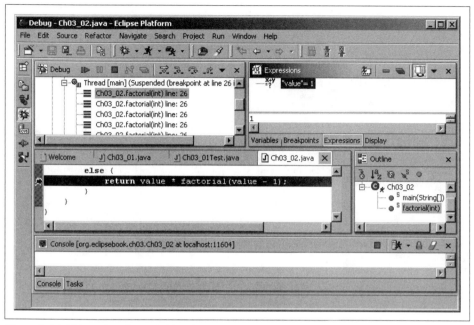

Figure 3-16. Using a breakpoint's hit count

To examine any of the stack frames in the Debug view, and the values of local variables in them, just double-click a frame to make it the active frame. The factorial example generates plenty of stack frames—just double-click one and you'll see that all the local variables like value have been preserved frame-by-frame. In the current stack frame, value = 1, in the next frame under this one, value = 2, and so on.

We've been able to skip to the final iteration of the factorial method just by setting our breakpoint's hit count, and everything still looks fine. We should be able to comfortably single-step to the end of the code at this point. However, when you click the Step Into button, execution unexpectedly enters the factorial method once again, and in the Expressions view you can see that value is set to 0, which is a problem because it should never be set to 0; factorials only work with positive whole numbers (multiplying by 0 always results in 0, of course).

Looking at our code (note the highlighted line in Figure 3-17) reveals the problem—we keep the iterations going until value is set to 0 instead of stopping at 1:

```
public static int factorial(int value) {
    if(value == 0){
        return value;
    }
    else {
        return value * factorial(value - 1);
    }
}
```

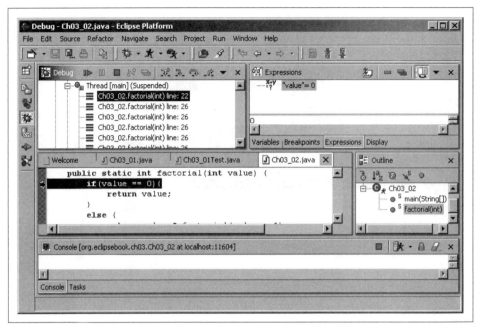

Figure 3-17. Discovering the error

We fix the problem like this:

```
public static int factorial(int value) {
    if(value == 1){
        return value;
    }
    else {
        return value * factorial(value - 1);
    }
}
```

You can see the new, debugged results in Figure 3-18, where we see that 6! is indeed 720.

And that's all it takes—we've debugged the code. This example gave us a start with debugging, but there's much more available in the JDT.

Configuring Breakpoints

We've used a breakpoint hit count to make life easier. Besides using hit counts, you can configure standard breakpoints in several other ways as well; to do that, right-click a breakpoint, bringing up the Breakpoint Properties dialog shown in Figure 3-19. If you select the Enable Condition checkbox, you can enter a condition in the Condition box that will cause the breakpoint to suspend the program. For example, you might be having problems every time a variable named inventory is set to 0; in that case, you might use the condition inventory == 0 and select the "condition is 'true'" checkbox.

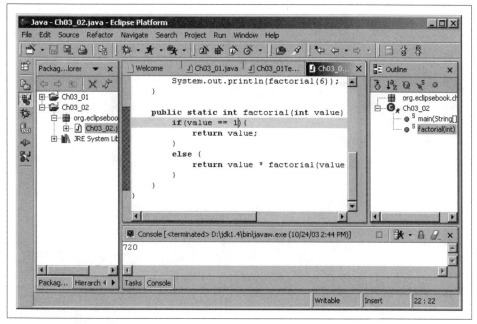

Figure 3-18. The fixed program

Checking a condition

You can also break when the value of a condition changes—for example, if some part of your code is changing the value in a variable named `ipAddress` and it shouldn't, you can type that variable name into the Condition box and click the "value of condition changes" checkbox (you can use any valid expression in the Condition box, of course, not just variable names).

Multithreaded debugging

You can also handle multithreaded debugging here—you can list the threads you want to restrict a breakpoint to with the Restrict to Selected Thread(s) box, and you can also set the suspending policy to either Suspend Thread (the default, which still allows other threads in the application to continue) or Suspend VM (which suspends the entire virtual machine that Eclipse has launched and connected to in order to debug your code).

Watchpoints

The standard breakpoints we've been using are called *line breakpoints*, and besides line breakpoints, the JDT supports other types of breakpoints—field (*watchpoints*), method, and exception.

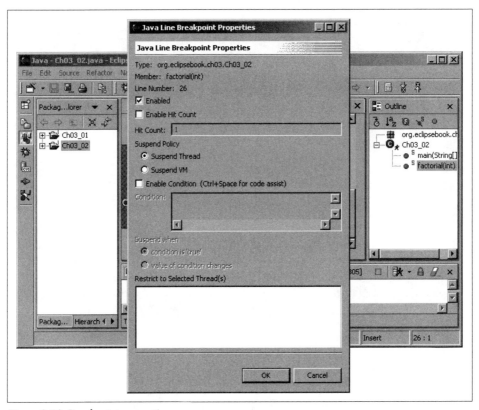

Figure 3-19. Breakpoint properties

Field breakpoints, also called watchpoints, suspend execution when your code is going to access and/or modify the value of a field. Watchpoints may not be set on local variables (such as those you declare inside methods), only on fields (data members of objects). Using a watchpoint is often much easier than trying to catch all the possible points in your code where the field you want to watch may be modified.

To set a watchpoint, select a field in a Java view and select Run → Add/Remove Watchpoint. The new watchpoint will appear in the Breakpoints view, and you can configure it by right-clicking it and selecting Properties, opening the Java Watchpoint Properties dialog you see in Figure 3-20. Note, in particular, that you can select two checkboxes here—Access and Modification—that let you indicate if you want to suspend execution when the field is accessed and/or when it is modified. You can also use a hit count, as with standard breakpoints.

Method breakpoints

Method breakpoints suspend execution when you enter or leave a method, depending on how you configure them, and you usually use these breakpoints on methods you don't have the source code for. To set a method breakpoint, highlight the call to that method in a Java view and select the Run → Add/Remove Method Breakpoint

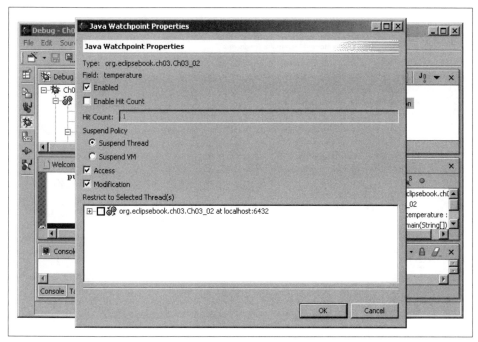

Figure 3-20. Configuring a watchpoint

menu item. You can configure these breakpoints by right-clicking them in the Breakpoints view, opening the Java Method Breakpoint Properties dialog you see in Figure 3-21. You can select whether the breakpoint happens on entry into the method, exit from the method, or both, using the checkboxes in this dialog.

Exception breakpoints

You can also work with exception breakpoints, which let you suspend execution when an exception happens. This is very useful if your code throws an exception, such as a null pointer exception, and you don't know where that exception is happening. You can suspend execution and see what's going on with your code when a thrown exception is caught (or not caught).

To set an exception breakpoint, select Run → Add/Remove Exception Breakpoint, opening the dialog you see in Figure 3-22, which allows you to select which breakpoints you are interested in, as well as whether you want to break when they are caught, not caught, or both.

You can configure the properties for an exception breakpoint as you can for any other breakpoint; just right-click the breakpoint in the Breakpoints view and select the Properties menu item. For example, you can see how we're configuring a breakpoint for uncaught java.lang.NullPointerException exceptions in Figure 3-23. You can restrict the breakpoint to specific locations, and even use hit counts, but you can't specify any conditions for this breakpoint as you can with line breakpoints.

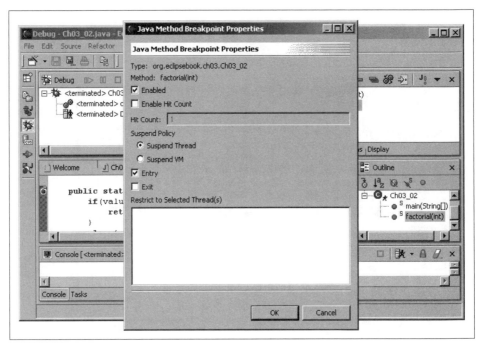

Figure 3-21. Configuring a method breakpoint

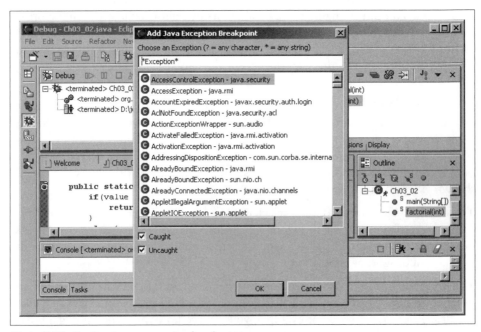

Figure 3-22. Configuring an exception breakpoint

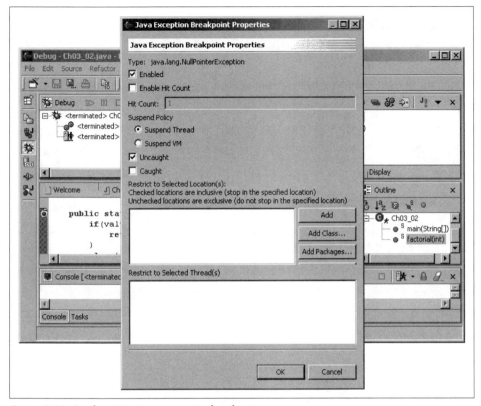

Figure 3-23. Configuring a Java exception breakpoint

Evaluating Java Expressions and Changing Values

While you're debugging, you can enter expressions into the detail pane of the Expressions view (the detail pane is just above the lower horizontal scrollbar in the Expressions view), selecting the expression, right-clicking it, and selecting the Inspect menu item. For example, if the variable value holds 6, you can enter the expression value + 1 in the detail pane, right-click it, and select the Inspect item. Doing that adds value + 1 to the list of expressions in the Expressions view and displays the value of that expression, 7, in the detail pane, as you see in Figure 3-24.

And, as mentioned earlier, you can also edit the values of fields and variables while debugging your code—just double-click a field or variable name in the Variables view, opening the dialog you see in Figure 3-25. In this case, we've double-clicked the variable named value in the Variables view; to change the value in this variable at runtime, just enter a new value and click OK. It's great if you want to check the impact on your code of different test values—for example, to check what happens if you set a variable named denominator to 0—or if you want to avoid known problem values.

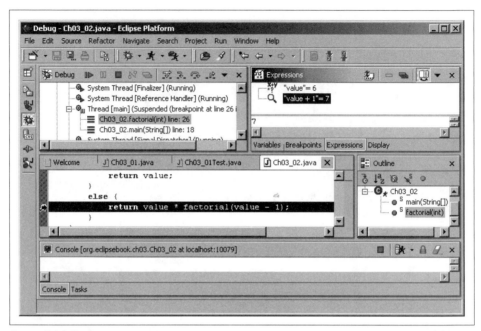

Figure 3-24. Evaluating an expression

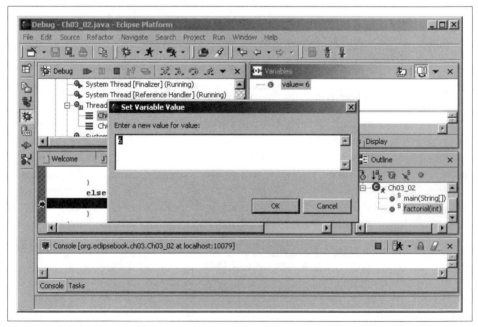

Figure 3-25. Editing a variable's value

Using Hot Code Replacement

You can even edit your code as you're debugging using the JDT debugger, as long as you're working with a JRE that supports it. This is called *hot code replacement*, and it requires a JRE Version 1.4 or later.

The easiest way to use hot code replacement is to enable auto-building of your code each time it's saved (this is not necessary, it just rebuilds your code automatically every time it's been changed and saved). To do that, select the Window → Preferences → Workbench → Perform build automatically on resource modification checkbox and click OK. Then debug your code until execution stops at a breakpoint.

Now you're free to edit your code during a debugging session. After you've changed the code, save it and resume execution (if you haven't enabled auto-build, also select the Project → Rebuild Project or Project → Rebuild All menu item to rebuild the project). That's all it takes.

> You may at times end up with strange results when you edit your code while debugging it; in that case, restart your debugging session.

For example, we can edit our factorial code while debugging (as you see in the highlighted line in Figure 3-26), by changing this line in the factorial method:

```java
public static int factorial(int value) {
    if(value == 1){
        return value;
    }
    else {
        return value * factorial(value - 1);
    }
}
```

The new line is shown here:

```java
public static int factorial(int value) {
    if(value == 1){
        return value;
    }
    else {
        return 2 * value * factorial(value - 1);
    }
}
```

Then just save the code if you have auto-build turned on. That's all it takes—now you've altered the code and you can keep debugging, as you see in Figure 3-26.

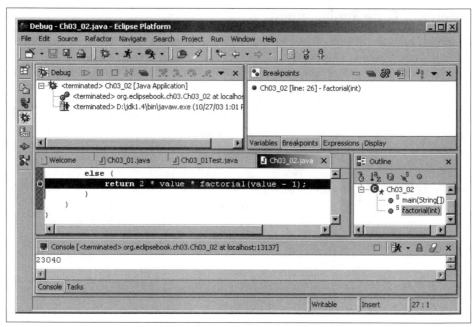

Figure 3-26. Using hot code replacements

Targeting earlier JREs

What if you're creating code that you want to let users with JREs all the way back to Version 1.2 use, but you still want to use hot code replacement, which requires Version 1.4 or later? You can use different JREs for running and debugging your code in Eclipse. To set the debug launch configuration so it uses a different JRE than the default, select Run → Debug, then click the JRE tab and select the JRE you want to use for debugging purposes.

And that's it—that finishes our look at JUnit and JDT debugging. As you can see, both are powerful tools. JUnit is good for creating a standard set of tests that can be applied to code with a few clicks. Debugging in Eclipse offers many options: configurable breakpoints, watchpoints, exception breakpoints, expression evaluation, single-stepping, variable and field modification, hot code replacement, and more. This is a far cry from what you may be used to if you've been using javac for your code development.

CHAPTER 4

Working in Teams

We've been programming solo with Eclipse up to this point, but it's also designed to be used in team environments, and it supports Concurrent Versions System (CVS) to make teamwork go smoothly. Eclipse can be used by any Java developer, and developers often work in teams. This chapter is all about teamwork using Eclipse and CVS.

How Source Control Works

When you work in teams, you have to coordinate. That means discussing and planning, of course, but even with the best of intentions, you can still end up with conflicts. You may have made some brilliant changes to the code—only to find them all wiped out by mistake when another programmer uploads his new version of a file.

Source control stops those kinds of problems by controlling access to code and by maintaining a history of the changes that have been made so things aren't destroyed unintentionally. Storing a history of your code is very powerful—not only can you compare a new (buggy) file against an older one, you can also revert to a previous version in case things have gone awry.

Source control also gives you the ability to coordinate the simultaneous development of several different versions of your software—for example, you might want to work on both a release version and a new beta version. You can do that using *branches*, as we're going to see in this chapter.

Understanding CVS

CVS is an open source project; it started life as a set of Unix shell scripts in 1986 and came into its own with dedicated software in 1989. Support for CVS is available on many operating systems today—Unix, Linux, Windows, and others. For the full CVS story, take a look at *http://www.cvshome.org*.

The idea behind CVS, as with any repository software, is to manage and record changes to source code. In fact, there are many types of repository software available, and some are more powerful than CVS, but CVS is in the most widespread use (perhaps because you can get it for free).

In CVS, a *module* is the basic equivalent of an Eclipse project. Modules are represented by directories in CVS. Standard projects correspond to *physical modules*, while *logical* or *virtual modules* are collections of related resources.

The files you share are stored in the CVS *repository*. When you retrieve a file from the repository, you *check the file out*. After you've modified the file, you *commit* the changes to check it back in and send those changes to the repository. If you want to refresh your own copy of a file, you *update* it from the repository.

In general, there are two models for source code repositories:

Pessimistic locking
> Only one developer can check out a particular file at once—after the file is checked out, the file is locked. It's possible for someone else to check out read-only copies of the file, but not to change it. Access is sequential.

Optimistic locking
> Developers can check out and modify files freely. When you commit changed files, the repository software *merges* your changes automatically. If it can't do that by itself, it'll notify you that you have to resolve the issue yourself. Access is random.

By default, CVS supports optimistic locking—although some CVS software also supports pessimistic locking. We'll be using optimistic locking here, which is what Eclipse supports.

Because each file needs to be kept track of, CVS gives each file a version number automatically. Each time a file is committed, its version number is incremented. When you first commit a file, its version number is 1.1; the next time, it's 1.2, and so on (this can depend on your CVS server; some will start with 1.0). When you commit files to the repository, they'll get a new version number automatically. We'll see these version numbers in the various views you work with when using source control.

When you update a file from the repository, your local version of the file is not overridden. Instead, Eclipse will merge your local file and the one in the CVS repository. If there are conflicts, the conflicting lines will be marked with special CVS markup indicating potential problems. You get the chance to modify your code to handle any conflicts that occurred during the merge operation, after which you can commit your new version of the code. Usually, updating goes smoothly, especially if each developer working on the project has her own set area to work in, but sometimes you've got to spend time resolving the conflicts that CVS points out to you manually.

CVS also supports development *branches*. The main development stream of a project is called the head, and CVS has a special tag name called HEAD that corresponds to that stream. Branches are forks from the head, and, in a branch, you can make changes that are independent of the main development stream, such as when you want to work on a beta version of your project. You tag a branch with a name, and CVS will keep track of the branches using their names. We'll see how all this works later in this chapter.

Finding a CVS Server

To work with CVS, you need access to a CVS server. If you have access to a CVS server already, you're all set. Otherwise, take a look at the overview that follows.

Most Linux and Unix installations already come with a CVS server built-in. To test if you have a working CVS installation, type cvs --help at the prompt; you should see a list of help items. If you can't find a CVS server, you can download what you need from *http://www.cvshome.org*.

In Windows, the story is a little more complex. There are a variety of CVS servers for Windows, such as CVSNT, available for free from *http://www.cvsnt.org*. To install CVSNT, just download the executable file and run it.

Creating a Repository

You'll need to create a repository for your source code using the CVS server. In Linux and Unix, you do that with the command cvs -d *path* init, where *path* gives the location of the directory you want to use as the repository (the permissions and ownership for *path* should be set so all members of your development team can access it).

With CVSNT, you click the Repositories tab in the CVSNT control panel, click the Add button, enter the path of the new repository directory, such as *c:\repository*, and click OK.

Connecting to CVS

In Linux and Unix, you use one of two possible options to reach CVS: SSH (secure shell) or pserver. We'll use pserver here, but you can use either protocol; just make sure that the correct protocol is running on your machine.

In Windows, CVSNT runs as a Windows service, which means it is accessible to Eclipse as soon as you run it. You can start it from the Start menu by selecting the Service control panel item from whatever program group you've added it to, which opens the CVSNT control panel. Click the Start button in both the CVS Service and CVS Lock Service boxes, which will make CVSNT display the message "Running" in both those boxes, as you see in Figure 4-1.

Figure 4-1. Starting CVSNT

With your CVS server running, it's time to start using CVS with Eclipse.

Adding a Project to the CVS Repository

We'll start using CVS by seeing how to add a new project, Ch04_01, to the CVS repository. After this project is in the CVS repository, anyone with access to the repository can check it out and work on it. You can see this sample project in Example 4-1; this sample code does nothing more than display the word "Hello".

Example 4-1. A sample project

```
package org.eclipsebook.ch04;

public class Ch04_01 {

    public static void main(String[] args) {
        System.out.println("Hello");
    }
}
```

Creating a Repository Location

After you've created a project, how do you add it to the CVS repository? You first have to let Eclipse know about the repository, so select Window → Open Perspective → Other, and select the CVS Repository Exploring perspective (after you do this the first time, Eclipse will add this perspective to the Window → Open Perspective, and will add a shortcut for this perspective to the other perspective shortcuts at the extreme left in Eclipse). When this perspective opens, right-click the blank CVS repositories view that appears at left and select New → Repository Location, opening the Add CVS Repository dialog you see in Figure 4-2.

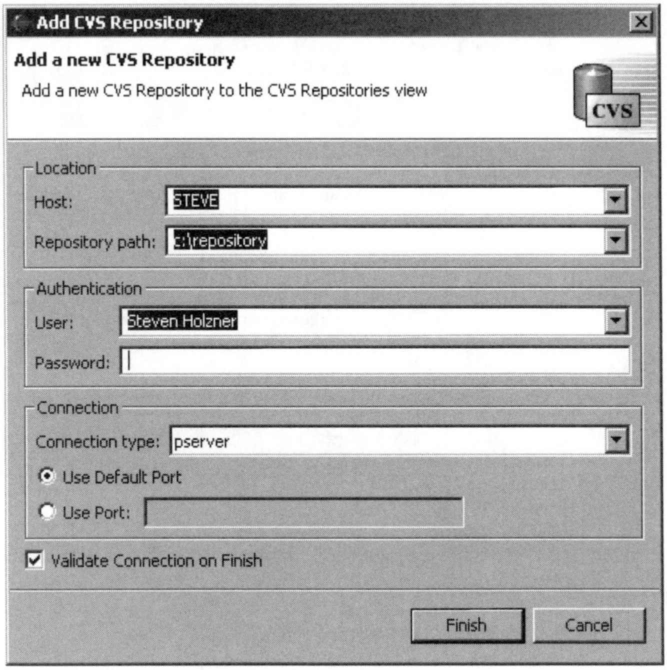

![Add CVS Repository dialog box. Title bar reads "Add CVS Repository". The dialog header reads "Add a new CVS Repository" with subtitle "Add a new CVS Repository to the CVS Repositories view" and a CVS icon. Location section: Host: STEVE, Repository path: c:\repository. Authentication section: User: Steven Holzner, Password: (empty). Connection section: Connection type: pserver, Use Default Port (selected), Use Port (unselected). Validate Connection on Finish (checked). Finish and Cancel buttons.]

Figure 4-2. Connecting a CVS repository to Eclipse

Here, enter the name of the CVS server (usually the name of the computer that hosts the server), the repository path, the username and password, and specify the connection type (here, we'll be using the pserver protocol). Then click Finish to add the new repository to the CVS Repositories view, as you see in Figure 4-3.

Congratulations—now you've connected a CVS repository to Eclipse. The next step is to start sharing your new project.

 There's even a public CVS server for Eclipse and Eclipse code. You can access that server's repository by creating a repository location for `:pserver:anonymous@dev.eclipse.org:/home/eclipse`.

Sharing Projects

To add the Ch04_01 project to the CVS repository, you can use the built-in support for CVS in Eclipse. Open the Java perspective, right-click the project you want to share, and select the Team → Share Project item. This displays the Share Project with CVS Repository dialog, as you see in Figure 4-4.

In this dialog, make sure the "Use existing repository location" radio button is selected, and select the repository you've already created. Click Finish to add the project to the CVS repository.

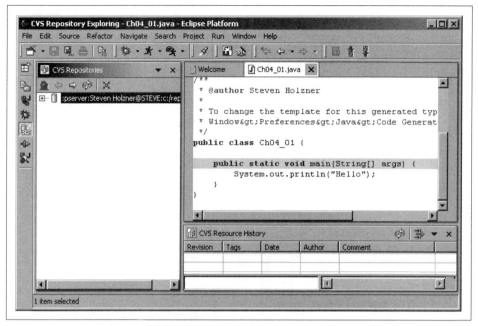

Figure 4-3. A new repository in the CVS Repositories view

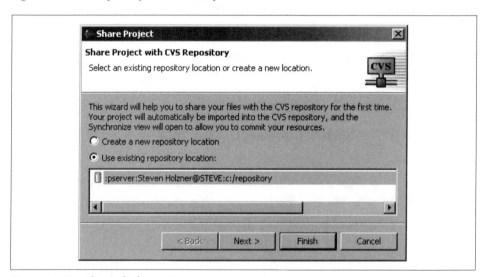

Figure 4-4. Specifying which repository to use

 This gives the CVS module the same name as the project. If you want to give the created CVS module a different name, click Next instead of Finish, enter the name of the CVS module you want to create, enter a new module name, and click Finish.

The Share Project operation adds the project to the CVS repository and also opens a Synchronize view that overlaps with the Console view. The Synchronize view lets you synchronize files, but it's not of much use to us at this point; we'll see how to work with it later in this chapter when we synchronize our local code with code in the repository that's been changed by someone else.

 If you want to see what commands Eclipse is sending to the CVS server, you can open the CVS console by selecting Window → Show View → Other → CVS → CVS Console. The CVS console will appear overlapping the standard Console view.

Committing Files

So far, we've just added the Ch04_01 project to the CVS repository; now we've got to start checking in some files. There are two steps here: first, you *add* the file to CVS (which just notifies CVS of the file but doesn't actually upload the file), then you *commit* it (which makes the file appear in the CVS repository so it can be shared).

You can add individual files by right-clicking them and selecting the Team → Add to Version Control item. Then you can select the Team → Commit menu item to commit them.

However, there's an easier way. Eclipse gives you a shortcut here—just right-click the project in the Package Explorer, and select Team → Commit. When you do, Eclipse will display the Add to CVS Version Control dialog, listing the files that have not yet been added to the CVS repository. Make sure all filenames are checked in this dialog by clicking the Select All button and then clicking the Yes button. Eclipse will prompt you for a comment for the set of files you're committing, giving you the chance to label that set of files and indicate what makes them different from other files in the repository. In this case, just enter some text, such as Build 1.0, and click OK.

 If you want to check in and check out projects as Eclipse projects, be sure to commit the *.project* file itself.

To verify that the project is connected to the CVS repository, select Windows → Preferences → Workbench → Label Decorations, select the CVS checkbox, and click OK. This displays a gold cylinder next to files in the CVS repository, as you see in the Package Explorer in Figure 4-5. Files in the repository will also have a CVS version number showing; that version is 1.1 here.

Switch to the CVS Repository Exploring perspective now, as you see in Figure 4-6. You can see your entire project, now the Ch04_01 CVS module, in the repository's HEAD section, which is the main development stream. Also note the *CVSROOT* directory, which holds CVS administrative data, and the Branches node, which will hold any files in other branches of development.

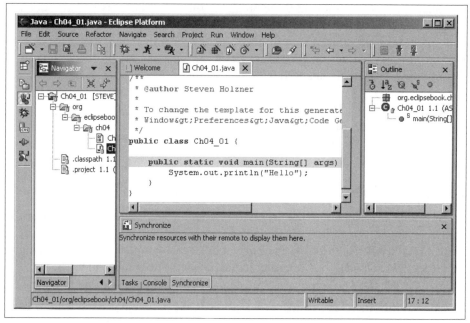

Figure 4-5. Verifying CVS connections

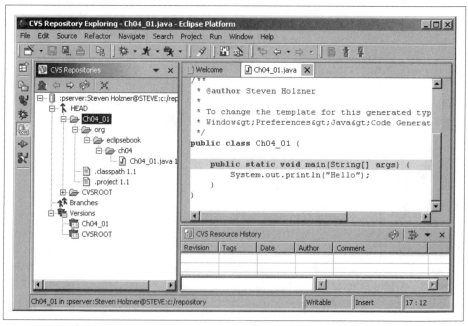

Figure 4-6. Examining files in the CVS repository

Checking Projects Out

How does someone else check out your new CVS module? To check out a module, he'd first create a connection to the repository in the same way as we have—by right-clicking the CVS Repository view, selecting New → Repository Location, and entering the name of the CVS server, the location of the repository, username, password, and the type of the connection.

He can then open the Repository view to explore the files in the repository. To check out the Ch04_01 module, right-click the module in the Repository view and select the Check Out As item from the context menu, opening the Check Out dialog you see in Figure 4-7.

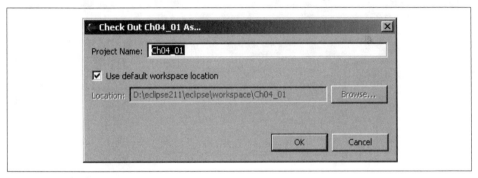

Figure 4-7. Checking out a project

In this case, clicking OK checks out the Ch04_01 project and tries to build it. If you're sharing an Eclipse project and each CVS module has its own Eclipse *.project* file, you can simply select the Check Out As Project item from the Repository view's context menu, which will check out an Eclipse project and build it locally. If your code isn't in a project of a kind that Eclipse can recognize, it will ask you what type of project to create; select the Java entry, followed by the Java Project entry.

Updating Code

So what if you and other members make changes to the files in the Ch04_01 project and save them? For example, say you change the code from this, where we're displaying "Hello":

```
public class Ch04_01 {

    public static void main(String[] args) {
        System.out.println("Hello");
    }
}
```

to this, where we're displaying the message "Hello there":

```
public class Ch04_01 {

    public static void main(String[] args) {
        System.out.println("Hello there");
    }
}
```

When you make these changes and save the file *Ch04_01.java*, you'll see a ">" appear in front of various files in the Package Explorer, as you see in Figure 4-8, indicating there are outgoing changes that have yet to be committed.

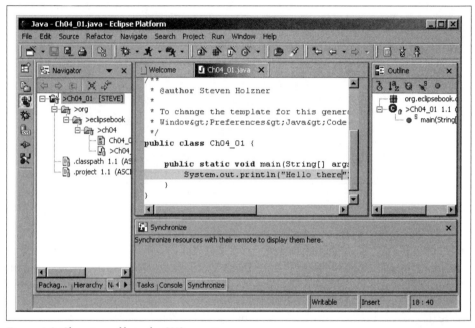

Figure 4-8. Changing a file in the CVS repository

You could commit your changes to the CVS repository, but, as a general rule, it's a good idea to first check and see how your changes will be received. Say, for example, that someone else has already checked out the same code and modified it to display the message "No worries.":

```
public class Ch04_01 {

    public static void main(String[] args) {
        System.out.println("No worries.");
    }
}
```

He's committed the changes by right-clicking the file in his version of Eclipse and selecting the Commit item, so his version of the file is now version 1.2. With changes like this being made to the code, you can see why it's a good idea to check what other changes have been made before committing a file. To check on changes that have already been made to the file you've checked out, right-click it and select the Team → Update menu item. Doing so imports *Ch04_01.java* version 1.2 into your Eclipse, as you can see in the Package Explorer at left in Figure 4-9. And in this case, it also indicates that there's a conflict between your code and the code in the repository, as you see in the editor.

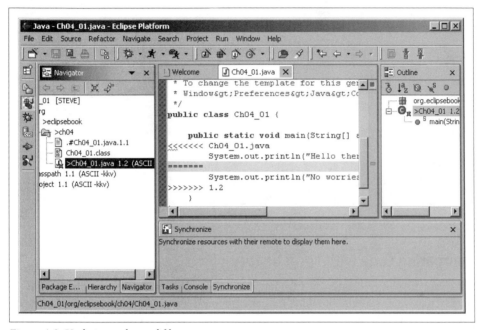

Figure 4-9. Updating a changed file

If there was no conflict, any changes would simply have been merged into your version of the file. But since both you and the other developer have changed the same line, there is a conflict. The CVS support in Eclipse indicates that there's a conflict by listing both versions in your code with some added CVS markup:

```
public class Ch04_01 {

    public static void main(String[] args) {
<<<<<<< Ch04_01.java
        System.out.println("Hello there");
=======
        System.out.println("No worries.");
>>>>>>> 1.2
    }
}
```

To get more information, right-click the changed file, *Ch04_01.java*, and select the Team → Show in Resource History item. You'll see the CVS Resource History view appear, as you see in Figure 4-10, and you can see the comments for each version of the code in that view.

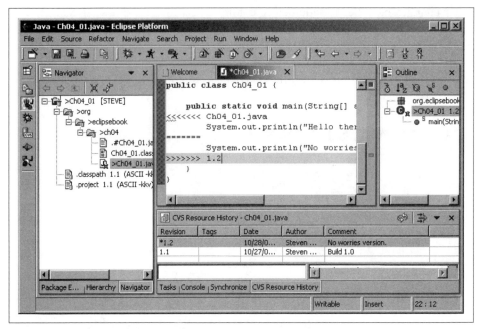

Figure 4-10. Looking at the resource history

Comparing Code with Local History

To make it a little clearer as to what CVS-generated changes have been made in longer files, you can check *Ch04_01.java* against its local history, which is a useful thing to know. To compare a file against its history, right-click that file and select Compare With → Local History, opening the Compare with Local History dialog you see in Figure 4-11. This dialog points out in a graphic way the changes that the CVS support in Eclipse added to the code.

Committing Code

Before you commit a file, it's up to you to resolve the conflict that the update has revealed. In this case, we're going to accept the other developer's version of the code, but with modifications—instead of "No worries.", we'll display "No worries at all.":

```
public class Ch04_01 {

    public static void main(String[] args) {
        System.out.println("No worries at all.");
    }
}
```

Now right-click *Ch04_01.java* and select Team → Commit, which opens the Commit dialog you see in Figure 4-12. This dialog asks for a new comment for the file you're about to commit; in this case, we'll use the comment "No worries at all version."

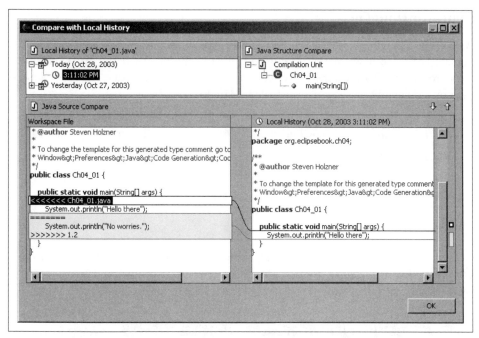

Figure 4-11. Checking a file's local history

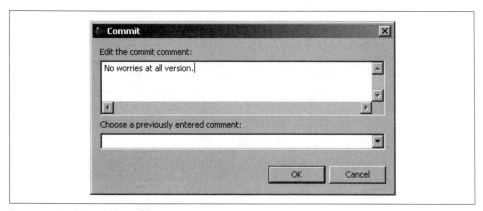

Figure 4-12. Committing a file

Click OK to commit your changes to the CVS repository. Doing so creates version 1.3 of the file. And that's all you need—now you've committed a new version of your code to the CVS repository. We've gone through the whole cycle now—checking code in, checking it out, updating code to check on changes made by other developers, and committing it. There's also another way to update your code if the differences between your version and the repository are fairly extensive: you can *synchronize* your code.

Synchronizing Code

When the differences between your code and repository code are relatively minor, an update is fine. But when the differences are substantial, it's better to synchronize. Synchronizing with the repository lets you compare changes that have been made side-by-side in an easier format than the update merge format.

For example, say that someone else works on the same file that you're working on, *Ch04_01.java*, and adds a new line of code and then commits her file as version 1.4:

```
public class Ch04_01 {

    public static void main(String[] args) {
        System.out.println("No worries at all.");
        System.out.println("Got any problems with that?");
    }
}
```

To synchronize your code (version 1.3) with the new version of *Ch04_01.java* (now at version 1.4 in the repository), right-click the Ch04_01 project and select Team → Synchronize with Repository. You can see the results in Figure 4-13.

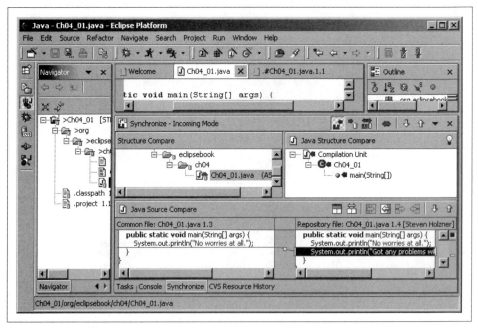

Figure 4-13. Synchronizing a project

When you first synchronize with the repository, you'll see the name of the files where there are differences marked with a stubby red double arrow (which looks almost like a diamond in Figure 4-13) in the Synchronize view. Double-clicking a file so marked opens the full display you see in Figure 4-13, where you can compare the

---

repository version of the file (version 1.4) to your version (version 1.3) directly in the Java Source Compare view at the bottom of the window.

Note, in particular, the line connecting the two code boxes in the Java Source Compare view and the small white box in the middle of that line. If you let the mouse hover over that box, it'll change into a button with a left-pointing arrow. Clicking that arrow will import the change into your version of the file, making the synchronization process a little easier. After you've synchronized your version of the code with that in the repository, commit your changes back to the repository.

In this case, the repository file has been changed since the last time we synchronized/updated with the repository, and the Synchronize view opened in *incoming mode* (as you can see in this view's title bar in Figure 4-13), which displays the changes in repository code. There are three such modes in the Synchronize view:

Incoming
   Displays those files that have changed in the repository since the last time you synchronized, updated, or committed your code with the repository.

Outgoing
   Displays those local files that you have changed since the last time you synchronized, updated, or committed your code with the repository.

Incoming/outgoing
   Displays the local or repository files that have changed since the last time you synchronized, updated, or committed your code with the repository.

You can select the Synchronize mode with the buttons you see at right in the Synchronize view's title bar. In Figure 4-13, Eclipse saw some incoming changes and automatically selected incoming mode, which means the incoming mode button is down. To the right of that button is the outgoing mode button and to the right of that button is the incoming/outgoing mode button.

For example, say that you've changed the local version of *Ch04_01.java* so that instead of displaying the message "No worries at all.", it displays "No worries at all today!":

```java
public class Ch04_01 {

    public static void main(String[] args) {
        System.out.println("No worries at all today!");
    }
}
```

Now when you save these changes locally and synchronize, selecting outgoing mode, you'll see your local changes compared to the repository version, as in Figure 4-14.

These modes are designed to let you filter the changes that have happened to make synchronizing/updating more tractable. If there are a lot of changes going on, make sure you synchronize/update frequently—although it can feel like an unpleasant task, it's necessary when you're working in teams, and, if you wait too long, merging with the repository code can become just about impossible.

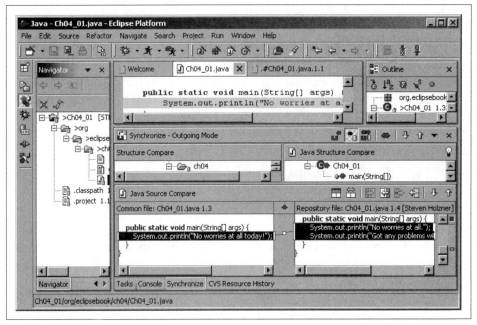

Figure 4-14. Outgoing mode

Here's something else to be careful about: although you can undo changes in a file with Eclipse's Edit → Undo menu item, those changes are local and not necessarily reflected in the code in the CVS repository. So if you update and find that there are too many changes that appear in the merged code, you can select Undo. But Eclipse will treat that Undo operation as a local edit to the file, so when you then synchronize with the repository version of the file, you may be presented with different options than the ones we've discussed here. In general, it's not a big problem, and updating and merging your code is still the best general policy before committing your code. However, if you suspect there may be big changes, either synchronize instead of updating, or back up the file you're going to update first.

Creating a Patch

Not everyone you deal with is going to have access to your CVS repository. To update those users without changing the version number of the software, you can create a *patch*. For example, say that you added this line to your example code locally but didn't change the code in the repository:

```
public class Ch04_01 {

    public static void main(String[] args) {
        System.out.println("No worries at all.");
        System.out.println("Got any problems with that?");
```

```
        System.out.println("Didn't think so.");
    }
}
```

You can create a patch that will convert the standard code for this version to the new form of the code. When you create a patch, Eclipse will compare your local code to what's in the repository and create a patch file holding the differences.

To create a patch to let users of your code come up to speed without needing access to the CVS repository, save the modified file locally, right-click it, and select Team → Create Patch, opening the dialog you see in Figure 4-15.

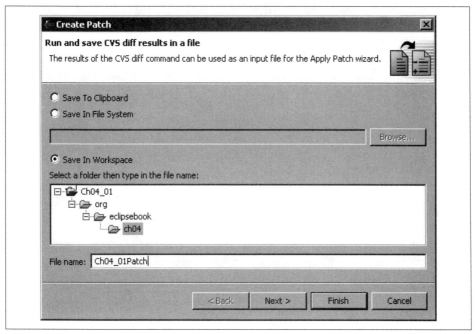

Figure 4-15. Creating a patch

You can save the patch file where you want; in this case, we'll save it as a file named *Ch04_01Patch* in the workspace. That's all you need; click the Finish button to save the patch. This creates the file *Ch04_01Patch* with these contents—as you can see, this is simple text, suitable even for emailing (note that the new line of code is marked with a +, which means Eclipse will add it to the code you're patching):

```
Index: Ch04_01.java
===================================================================
RCS file: c:/repository/Ch04_01/org/eclipsebook/ch04/Ch04_01.java,v
retrieving revision 1.4
diff -u -r1.4 Ch04_01.java
--- Ch04_01.java28 Oct 2003 21:13:46 -00001.4
+++ Ch04_01.java29 Oct 2003 17:34:54 -0000
@@ -17,5 +17,6 @@
```

```
    public static void main(String[] args) {
        System.out.println("No worries at all.");
        System.out.println("Got any problems with that?");
+       System.out.println("Didn't think so.");
    }
}
```

To apply the new patch to code that has not yet been patched, right-click the file to be updated in Eclipse and select the Team → Apply Patch item, opening the dialog you see in Figure 4-16.

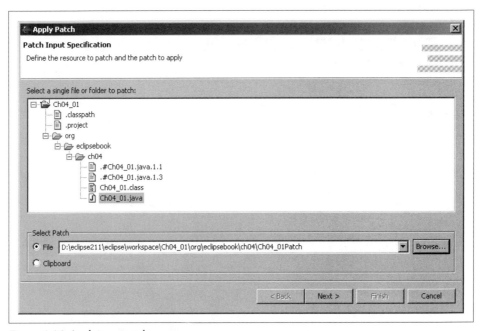

Figure 4-16. Applying a patch

Browse to the patch file and click Next, opening the dialog you see in Figure 4-17. Here, you can review the changes the patch will create in your local version of the file. As you can see, Eclipse is proposing to add the line System.out.println("Didn't think so."); to your code. Click Finish to apply the patch.

Applying the patch adds the new line of code to the local version of the file, as you see in Figure 4-18. The version number of the file wasn't changed, but your code was. Using Eclipse in this way automates the entire patching mechanism.

Tagging Versions

When you create a milestone version of your code, you can tag it with a version label, which will make CVS store that version so that you can access it at will later. To tag a project with a version label, right-click the project and select Team → Tag As Version, opening the dialog you see in Figure 4-19.

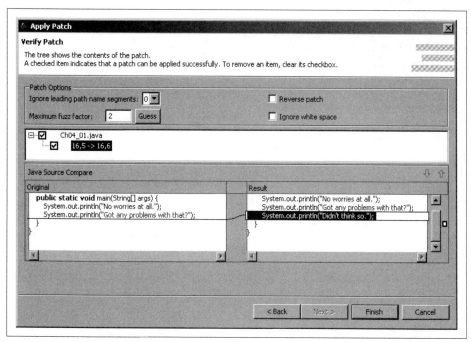

Figure 4-17. Configuring a patch

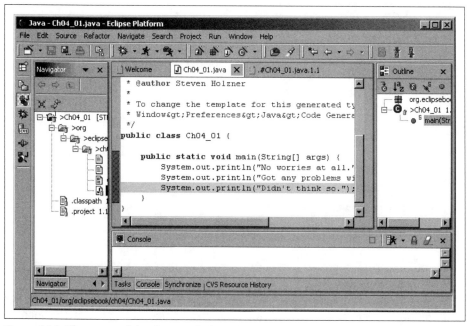

Figure 4-18. The new patch has been applied

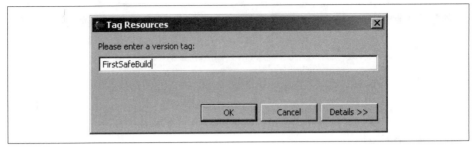

Figure 4-19. Tagging a version

In this case, we're going to tag the current version of the project as FirstSafeBuild, so enter that name and click OK. Version labels must start with a letter, and they may not include spaces or these characters: `` `$,.:;@|' ``. After tagging the current version with this name, you can find it in the Versions node in the CVS Repositories view, as you see in Figure 4-20.

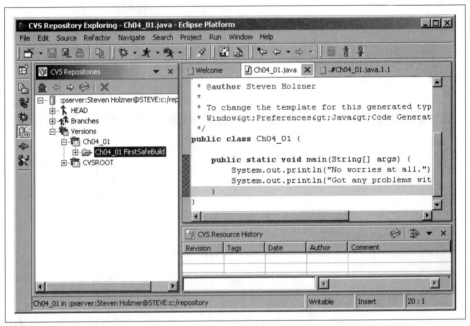

Figure 4-20. Examining a tagged version

You can check out a tagged version of a module by right-clicking it in the CVS Repositories view and selecting context menu items such as Check Out as Project, as with any other CVS module. Alternately, you can right-click a project in the Package Explorer and select the Replace With → Another Branch or Version item, opening the dialog you see in Figure 4-21. Select the version you want to replace the current project with and click OK.

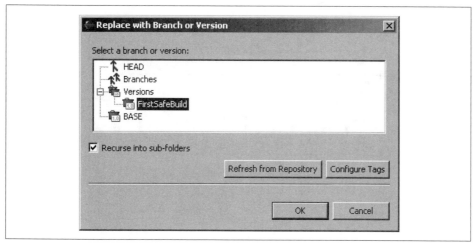

Figure 4-21. Replacing the current project with another version

Tagging a project with a version label like this is very useful because it lets you store a snapshot of the project that can be retrieved by name later.

Creating Branches

Besides storing versions, you can also create new branches, which act as alternate streams of development. For example, you might want to create an Internet-enabled branch of your software for testing, so you'd split a new branch off from the main development tree to do that.

To create a branch, right-click a project and select Team → Branch, opening the Create a new CVS Branch dialog you see in Figure 4-22. Give the new branch a name—we'll use InternetEnabledBranch here (note that branch names have the same restrictions as version labels). You can also create a new version name that will act as the start of the branch, giving Eclipse a starting point for merging the branch back into the main development stream.

If you leave the "Start working in the branch" checkbox checked, you'll start working with the branch's code immediately. Alternately, you can check out a branch from the CVS Repository view, as you see in Figure 4-23.

If you want to merge a branch back into the main development stream, right-click it in the Package Explorer and select the Team → Merge item, opening the Merge dialog. Select the merge starting point (this is the version name you gave when you created the branch) and click Next. In the next pane, select the branch you want to merge from, and click Finish.

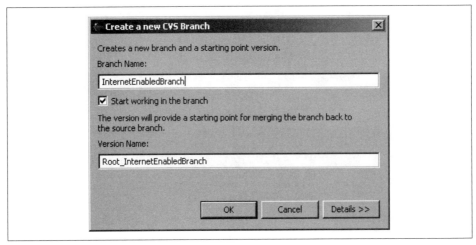

Figure 4-22. Creating a new branch

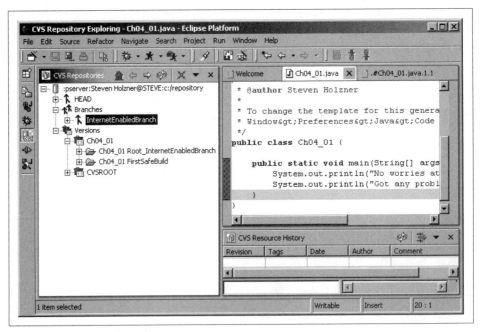

Figure 4-23. Exploring branches

This finishes our chapter on teamwork using CVS. A natural part of developing code with Eclipse is to share that development with others in teams, and, as you can see, Eclipse is up to the task.

CHAPTER 5

Building Eclipse Projects Using Ant

Eclipse is great for building your code. But for more advanced project development, there's still something missing. For example, what if you want not only to compile several files at once, but also to copy files over to other build directories, create JAR files and Javadoc, create new directories, delete previous builds, and create deployment packages all at once?

You can do that with a build tool like Apache's Ant (*http://ant.apache.org/*). Ant is a Java-based build tool that can perform all these tasks and much more. You can download Ant and run it on the command line, automating your build tasks to not only compile code, but to create JAR files, move and create classes, delete and make directories, and a great deal more.

The good news here is that Ant comes built into Eclipse, ready to use. Ant is the premier build tool for Java development, and we'll get an idea why in this chapter. As your projects become more and more elaborate, Ant can automate dozens of tasks that you'd otherwise need to perform manually. When you have things set up to run with Ant, all you've got to do is point and click to perform a complete build without having to take dozens of separate steps, which can save many steps omitted in error over the development process.

The fact that Ant comes built into Eclipse means that it's easier to use for us than for all those developers who use it on the command line. To see how this works, we'll start with a quick example.

Working with Ant

To use Ant from Eclipse, create a new project, Ch05_01, and add a new class to it, Ch05_01. In this class's main method, we'll just display the message "No worries.", as you see in Example 5-1.

Example 5-1. A sample project

```java
package org.eclipsebook.ch05;

public class Ch05_01 {

    public static void main(String[] args) {
        System.out.println("No worries.");
    }
}
```

To work with Ant, we'll need an Ant build file, which is named *build.xml* by default. To create that file in this project, right-click the project and select New → File. Enter the name of the new file, *build.xml*, in the File name box and click Finish. You use the XML in this file to tell Ant how to build your project. Although Eclipse can automate the connection to Ant, Ant needs this XML build file to understand what you want it to do, which means that we will have to master the syntax in this file.

Eclipse recognizes that *build.xml* is an Ant build file and marks it with an ant icon, as you see at left in Figure 5-1.

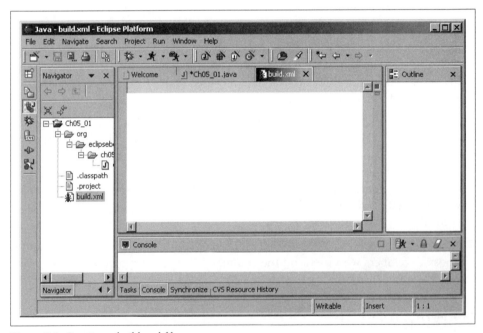

Figure 5-1. Creating a build.xml file

Enter this simple XML into *build.xml*—all we're going to do here is have Ant echo a message, "Ant at work!", to the console:

```xml
<?xml version = "1.0" encoding="UTF-8" ?>
<project name = "Ch05_01" default = "Main Build">
    <target name = "Main Build">
```

```
            <echo message = "Ant at work!" />
        </target>
</project>
```

This XML makes the *target*, which we've named "Main Build," into the *default target*.
An Ant target specifies a set of tasks you want to have run, similar to a method in
Java. The default target is that which is executed when no specific target is supplied
to Ant. In this case, we're just going to have this default target echo a message to the
console; nothing's going to be compiled.

You can see this new XML in the Ant editor in Figure 5-2. The Ant editor uses syntax
highlighting, just as the JDT editor does, and you can see an outline of the *build.xml*
document in the Outline view at right.

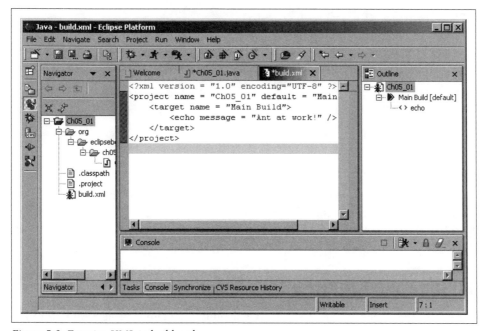

Figure 5-2. Entering XML in build.xml

Save *build.xml* and right-click it, selecting the Run Ant item. This opens the Ch05_01
build.xml dialog you see in Figure 5-3. You can see that the default target, Main Build,
is already selected.

Click the Run button in this dialog to run Ant. When you do, you'll see something
like this in the Console view (note that your message was echoed here):

```
Buildfile: D:\eclipse211\eclipse\workspace\Ch05_01\build.xml

Main Build:
        [echo] Ant at work!
BUILD SUCCESSFUL
Total time: 430 milliseconds
```

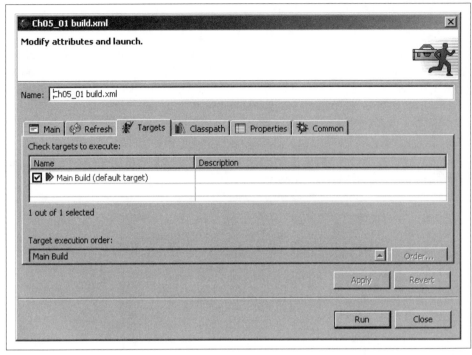

Figure 5-3. Running Ant

That's exactly what we wanted this example to do. That's a quick example to show how to interact with Ant from Eclipse, but all it does is display the message "Ant at work!" It doesn't compile anything, it doesn't create any JAR files, but it does give us a start on using Ant in Eclipse. We'll get more advanced in our next example.

JARing Your Output

Here's another example; in this case, we'll build an Eclipse project and store the resulting class in a JAR file. You won't need to be an Ant professional to follow along because we're interested in looking at Ant from an Eclipse point of view, not in the details of Ant *per se*. This example is designed to give you the basics of creating a working Ant build file in Eclipse; if you want more details on Ant itself, take a look at the manual at *http://ant.apache.org/manual/index.html*.

Our goal here is to create a new Java project in Eclipse, use Ant to compile it, and store the resulting *.class* file in a JAR file. To follow along, create a new Java project, Ch05_02. To emulate a somewhat real-world project, we're going to store the example's source code in a directory named *src* and its output in a directory named *bin*. You can set those directories up when you create the project in the third pane of the New Java Project dialog by clicking the Source tab, then clicking the Add Folder button, then the Create New Folder button to open the New Folder dialog. Enter the name src in the Folder name box and click OK twice. Eclipse will ask if you want to remove the project as source folder and update the build output folder to *Ch05_02/bin*. Click Yes, then click Finish to create the new project, which will be complete with *src* and *bin* folders.

Next, add a new class, Ch05_02, in a package named org.eclipsebook.ch05, to the project. Add code to the main method in this example to display the message "This code was built using Ant.", as you can see in Example 5-2.

Example 5-2. A sample project

```
package org.eclipsebook.ch05;

public class Ch05_02 {

    public static void main(String[] args) {
        System.out.println("This code was built using Ant.");
    }
}
```

Finally, add *build.xml* to the project by right-clicking the project in the Package Explorer and selecting New → File. Type *build.xml* in the File name box and click Finish, which creates the file and opens it in the Ant editor. We'll start writing *build.xml* with the standard XML declaration and a <project> element that identifies the Main Build task as the default:

```
<?xml version="1.0" encoding = "UTF-8"?>
<project name="Ch05_02" default="Main Build" basedir=".">
        .
        .
        .
</project>
```

Next we'll create the properties corresponding to the directories we'll use—src, bin, a directory for the JAR file, jardir (we'll create a *lib* directory under the *bin* directory to store JAR files), and the JAR file itself, jarfile (we'll call this file *Ch05_02.jar*). Setting up properties this way lets you access these directory names later in the build file. We'll also set the build.compiler property to the adapter for the JDT compiler, org.eclipse.jdt.core.JDTCompilerAdapter, which Ant will use:

```
<?xml version="1.0" encoding = "UTF-8"?>
<project name="Ch05_02" default="Main Build" basedir=".">

    <property name="bin" location="bin"/>
    <property name="src" location="src"/>
    <property name="jardir" location="${bin}/lib"/>
    <property name="jarfile" location="${jardir}/Ch05_02.jar"/>
    <property name="build.compiler"
        value="org.eclipse.jdt.core.JDTCompilerAdapter"/>
        .
        .
        .
</project>
```

Now we'll create the main task, Main Build. We'll use three stages in this Ant file—an initialization stage, a compile stage, and a JAR-creation stage—each with its own task: Initialize, Compile, and Jar. To make sure that all those tasks are performed, we'll make the main, default task dependent on them using the depends attribute. Then the main task only has to echo a message to the console indicating that Ant is at work—Ant will take care of the details of running each needed task:

```
<?xml version="1.0" encoding = "UTF-8"?>
<project name="Ch05_02" default="Main Build" basedir=".">

    <property name="bin" location="bin"/>
    <property name="src" location="src"/>
    <property name="jardir" location="${bin}/lib"/>
    <property name="jarfile" location="${jardir}/Ch05_02.jar"/>
     <property name="build.compiler"
        value="org.eclipse.jdt.core.JDTCompilerAdapter"/>

    <target name="Main Build" depends="Initialize, Compile, Jar">
        <echo message="Ant at work!"/>
    </target>
         .
         .
         .
</project>
```

The Initialize task will delete everything in the output ${bin} and ${jardir} directories and then recreate them:

```
<target name="Initialize">
    <delete dir="${bin}"/>
    <delete dir="${jardir}"/>
    <mkdir dir="${bin}"/>
    <mkdir dir="${jardir}"/>
</target>
```

The Compile task will compile the source files in ${src} (which is just *Ch05_02.java*) and put the resulting *.class* file into ${bin}:

```
<target name="Compile" depends="Initialize">
    <javac srcdir="${src}"
        destdir="${bin}">
    </javac>
</target>
```

Finally, the Jar task will compress *Ch05_02.class* into a JAR file and store that file as ${jarfile}—note that this task depends on the Initialize and Compile tasks:

```
<target name="Jar" depends="Initialize, Compile">
    <jar destfile="${jarfile}" basedir="${bin}"/>
</target>
```

That completes *build.xml*; you can see the whole file in Example 5-3.

Example 5-3. A sample Ant build file

```xml
<?xml version="1.0" encoding = "UTF-8"?>
<project name="Ch05_01" default="Main Build" basedir=".">

    <property name="bin" location="bin"/>
    <property name="src" location="src"/>
    <property name="jardir" location="${bin}/lib"/>
    <property name="jarfile" location="${jardir}/ch05_01.jar"/>
     <property name="build.compiler"
        value="org.eclipse.jdt.core.JDTCompilerAdapter"/>

    <target name="Main Build" depends="Initialize, Compile, Jar">
        <echo message="Ant at work!"/>
    </target>

    <target name="Initialize">
        <delete dir="${bin}"/>
        <delete dir="${jardir}"/>
        <mkdir dir="${bin}"/>
        <mkdir dir="${jardir}"/>
    </target>

    <target name="Compile" depends="Initialize">
        <javac srcdir="${src}"
            destdir="${bin}">
        </javac>
    </target>

    <target name="Jar" depends="Initialize, Compile">
        <jar destfile="${jarfile}" basedir="${bin}"/>
    </target>

</project>
```

Eclipse can generate Ant scripts for you under certain circumstances. If your project already has an XML-based manifest file, as the plug-in projects we're going to create in Chapters 11 and 12 will have (the plug-in manifest file is named *plugin.xml*), all you have to do is right-click the manifest file and select the Create Ant Build File item.

When you enter this XML into *build.xml*, you can see its properties and tasks in the Outline view, as in Figure 5-4.

To build the project, right-click *build.xml* in the Package Explorer and select Run Ant. This opens the Ch05_02 *build.xml* dialog you see in Figure 5-5. You can see the various Ant targets we've set up here, which you can build independently. The default target, Main Build, is already selected, so just click Run now to build the project.

You can see the results in Figure 5-6—the build was successful, as you see in the Console view.

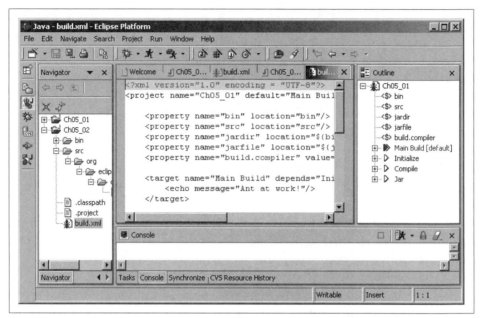

Figure 5-4. Our new build.xml

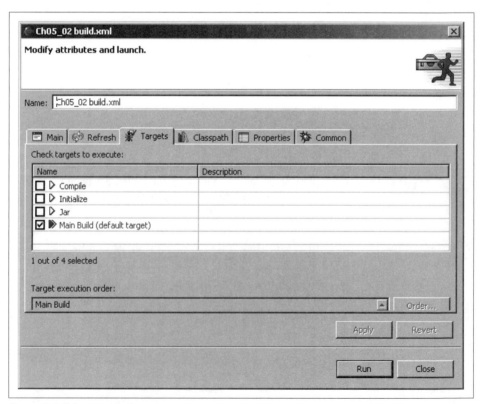

Figure 5-5. Selecting which target to run

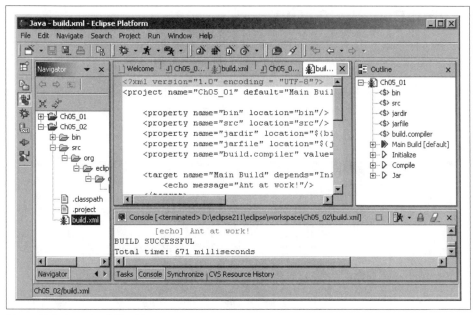

Figure 5-6. A successful build

Here's the complete text that appears in the Console view—you can see the results of each task as it runs:

```
Buildfile: D:\eclipse211\eclipse\workspace\Ch05_02\build.xml

Initialize:
    [delete] Deleting directory D:\eclipse211\eclipse\workspace\Ch05_02\bin
    [mkdir] Created dir: D:\eclipse211\eclipse\workspace\Ch05_02\bin
    [mkdir] Created dir: D:\eclipse211\eclipse\workspace\Ch05_02\bin\lib

Compile:
    [javac] Compiling 1 source file to D:\eclipse211\eclipse\workspace\Ch05_02\bin
    [javac] D:\eclipse211\eclipse\workspace\Ch05_02\src\org\eclipsebook\ch05\Ch05_
02.java
    [javac] Compiled 20 lines in 210 ms (95.2 lines/s)
    [javac] 1 .class file generated

Jar:
      [jar] Building jar: D:\eclipse211\eclipse\workspace\Ch05_02\bin\lib\ch05_01.
jar

Main Build:
      [echo] Ant at work!
BUILD SUCCESSFUL
Total time: 1 second
```

And that's it—the project was built and *Ch05_02.jar* was created in the *bin/lib* directory. As you can see, Ant lets you go far beyond the normal Eclipse build process to copy files, create directories, create JAR files, and so on.

Configuring Ant in Eclipse

Eclipse also lets you configure its internal version of Ant. To configure how Ant will run, select Window → Preferences, followed by the Ant item, as shown in Figure 5-7. In Eclipse, you don't need to name your build file *build.xml*; Ant will try to guess which file is the build file (the build file does need to be an XML file, with a name that has the extension *.xml*). You can help Eclipse out by giving an alternate name, or a list of names, in this dialog.

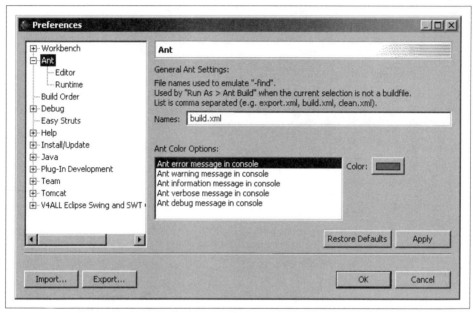

Figure 5-7. Configuring the build file

You can also set Ant runtime options by selecting the Runtime node, as shown in Figure 5-8. For example, to use a more recent version of Ant in Eclipse (Eclipse 2.1.1 comes with Ant 1.5.3, but the latest version of Ant, as of this writing, is 1.5.4, and Version 1.6 is out in beta; you can get alternate Ant versions directly from Apache at *http://ant.apache.org*), select the Runtime item and change the JAR entries you see in Figure 5-8 to the new versions of *ant.jar* and *optional.jar*. You can also set Ant variables like ANT_HOME in this dialog.

You can add new Ant tasks and types with the Tasks and Types tabs, which means that those tasks and types will be available to build files without having to use Ant taskdef or typedef elements. Eclipse also lets you set global Ant properties if you select the Properties tab in this dialog. To add a new global property, click the Add button in the Properties tab, and enter a name and value for the new property.

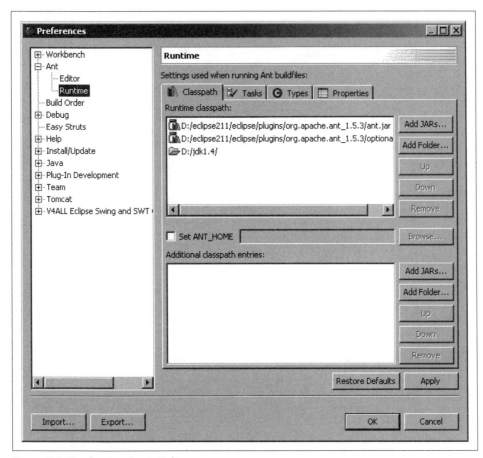

Figure 5-8. Configuring Ant in Eclipse

You also have limited control over the Ant editor's options using the Preferences dialog and selecting the Ant → Editor item. The Ant editor is actually little more than a simple XML editor, but you can specify such items as the colors used in syntax highlighting, or whether the editor shows an overview ruler, as you see in Figure 5-9.

The Ant editor also offers code assist. For example, if you enter < and then pause in typing, code assist will give you a list of possible Ant build file elements. Entering additional letters narrows down the list—for example, entering <p makes code assist give you the choice of <path>, <patternset>, and <property>. Code assist will also list possible attributes of Ant elements; just click inside the opening tag of an Ant element and press Ctrl+Space. Also, letting the mouse cursor rest on one of the items in the code assist list makes Eclipse display an explanation of what that item does. For example, the explanation for the property element is "Sets a property by name, or a set of properties (from file or resource) in the project."

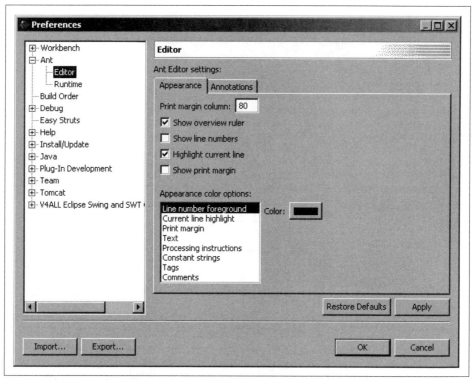

Figure 5-9. Configuring the Ant editor

You can also configure Ant when you're about to run it, before selecting an Ant target to build. Right-click *build.xml*, select Run Ant, and click the Main tab in the dialog that opens, as shown in Figure 5-10. You can set the location of the build file you want to use here, as well as the base directory for the build. You can also set Ant arguments in the Arguments field.

 You can also run Ant as an external tool: select Run → External Tools → External Tools, click Program, click New, and enter the name you want to give to the external version of Ant. To fill in the Location field, click Browse File System and find the correct file for your operating system (for example, *ant.bat* in the Ant *bin* folder in Windows). In the Working Directory field enter the directory of your build file, and click to execute your build file.

In addition, there's also an Ant view in Eclipse, which you open with Window → Show View → Other → Ant. This view provides an Ant-based overview of build files; to add a build file to this view, right-click the view, select Add Buildfile, and navigate to the build file you want to display. The view will display a breakdown of the build file, as you see in Figure 5-11, and you can run various Ant targets by right-clicking them and selecting Run.

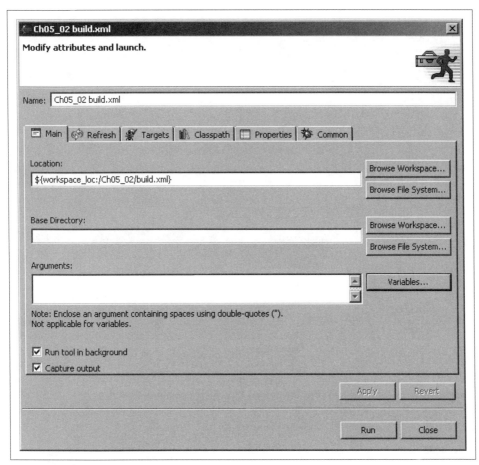

Figure 5-10. Setting the run configuration

Catching Errors in Build Files

Eclipse gives you some support for catching Ant errors before you run Ant, but not much. The Eclipse Ant editor doesn't handle syntax errors as the JDT editor does for Java—for example, if you misspell the project element's default attribute as deefault, the Ant editor won't have a problem. However, if the XML in your build file has syntax errors, such as missing a closing tag or improper nesting (in XML terms: if your XML is not *well-formed*), you'll see the same wavy red line and hollow red box you see in the JDT editor in the Ant editor, indicating a syntax error, as shown in Figure 5-12. You can determine what error occurred by looking at the wavy line's tooltip, as shown in the figure, where we haven't closed the mkdir element.

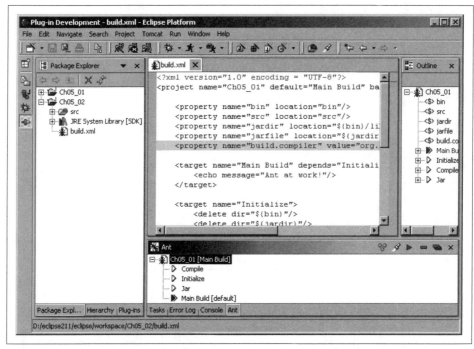

Figure 5-11. The Ant view

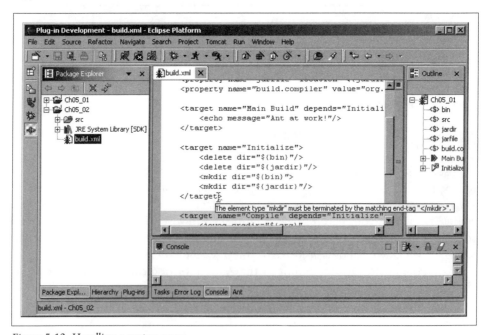

Figure 5-12. Handling a syntax error

If you miss an XML error like this in the editor, you'll see a message reminding you of it as soon as you try to run Ant to build the project. The Ant editor doesn't display non-XML syntax errors (like misspelling the project attribute as deefault), but you'll automatically see any syntax errors listed when you try to run Ant, as shown at the top of Figure 5-13.

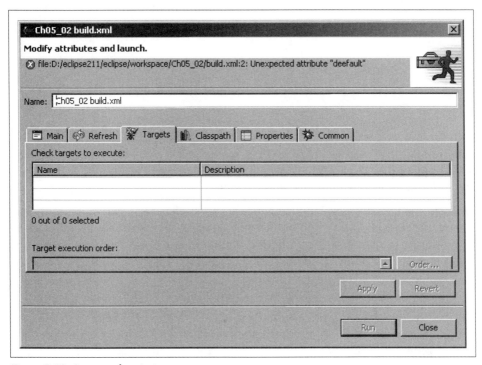

Figure 5-13. An error description

Unfortunately, that's as much support as Eclipse gives you for handling Ant errors—when Ant runs, it'll display its own errors in the Console view, and it's up to you to take it from there (although Eclipse does hyperlink errors to the associated lines in the build or Java file). Eclipse doesn't support interactive debugging of Ant scripts yet, which is a pity, given how complex those scripts can become. Perhaps we'll see that one day in Eclipse; in fact, given the popularity of Ant, it's possible that future versions of Eclipse may include an Ant wizard, invoked with File → New, that will let you set up build targets, directories, and Ant tasks as easily as creating a new Eclipse project.

CHAPTER 6

GUI Programming: From Applets to Swing

This chapter is all about creating GUIs with Java code in Eclipse. So far, our code has just displayed text in the console. In this chapter, we're going to start creating GUIs using applets, the Abstract Windowing Toolkit (AWT), and Swing. We'll also take a look at using an Eclipse plug-in to create Swing code.

Our first topic is all about building applets. Java applets were Java's first foray into the Internet, and they were popular for quite a while. Browsers first started stocking Java in order to support applets. In time, applets have become less popular because they're necessarily limited and have been superceded by glitzy packages like Flash and Java Web Start. Nonetheless, Eclipse has special provisions for developing and testing applets, so we'll take a brief look here at how that support works.

Creating an applet is much like creating any other Java project in Eclipse. In this case, our applet is just going to display the message "Hello from Eclipse!" Create a new Java project named Ch06_01, and give it a new class, Ch06_01, in the org.eclipsebook.ch06 package. To create an applet, we'll need to import java.applet.Applet and java.awt.*:

```
import java.applet.Applet;
import java.awt.*;
```

Then extend the Ch06_01 class from the Applet class:

```
public class Ch06_01 extends Applet {
    .
    .
    .
```

In an applet, the init method lets you initialize the applet, and we'll set the background color to white in that method. The start, stop, and destroy methods let you handle the associated events in the applet's life cycle. To draw our text in the applet's window, we'll use the Graphics object passed to the paint method. Here's the code to add:

```
public class Ch06_01 extends Applet {

    public void init()
    {
        setBackground(Color.white);
    }
```

```
    public void start( )
    {
    }

    public void paint(Graphics g)
    {
        g.drawString("Hello from Eclipse!", 60, 100);
    }

    public void stop( )
    {
    }

    public void destroy( )
    {
    }
}
```

And that's all you need for the applet's code. To test it, select Run As → Java Applet, and the applet should run. If Eclipse doesn't recognize your applet, you can specifically set the launch configuration for this code. To do that, select the Ch06_01 project in the Package Explorer and select Run → Run to open the Run dialog you see in Figure 6-1. Then double-click the Java Applet configuration in the Configurations box and the Ch06_01 project will automatically be added as an applet. Click the Run button to run the applet. After setting the launch configuration, you should be able to select Run As → Java Applet to run the applet.

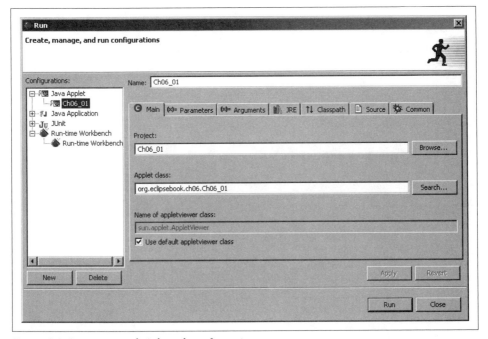

Figure 6-1. Setting an applet's launch configuration

You can see the results in the Java applet viewer in Figure 6-2. The applet is working as it should.

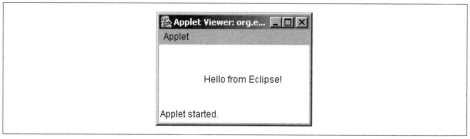

Figure 6-2. Running an applet

 To use this applet in a web page, use the generated class file, *Ch06_01. class*, together with the <APPLET> HTML tag, something like this:

```
<APPLET
    CODE = "Ch06_01.class"
    WIDTH = 300
    HEIGHT = 200
>
```

That's all it takes; the applet is complete. You can see the entire code for the applet in Example 6-1.

Example 6-1. A simple applet

```
package org.eclipsebook.ch06;

import java.applet.Applet;
import java.awt.*;

public class Ch06_01 extends Applet {
    public void init()
    {
        setBackground(Color.white);
    }

    public void start()
    {
    }

    public void paint(Graphics g)
    {
        g.drawString("Hello from Eclipse!", 60, 100);
    }

    public void stop()
    {
    }
```

Example 6-1. A simple applet (continued)
```
    public void destroy( )
    {
    }
}
```

When you launch them, Java applets appear in the Java applet viewer by default. That's fine as far as it goes, but there's more to GUIs than applets. The next step is going to be creating our own windowed applications.

Creating AWT Applications

The Abstract Windowing Toolkit, or AWT, was Java's early attempt at a GUI toolkit. It's still supported and used, so we'll take a look at an example here that will launch its own window. The original AWT package only took six weeks to write, and the controls, designed for use in applets, were modeled after HTML controls. Since that time, Swing has taken over the standard Java interface—but even Swing is built on top of AWT.

Our AWT example will just launch its own window and display the same message as our applet. To follow along, create a new project, Ch06_02, and give it a new class with a main method, Ch06_02, putting that class into the org.eclipsebook.ch06 package. We need to import java.awt.* for basic AWT support, and java.awt.event.* to handle the window-closing event, so add this code:
```
    import java.awt.*;
    import java.awt.event.*;
```
The actual window this example will display will be based on the AWT Frame class and will be called AppFrame, so add this code to *Ch06_02.java*:
```
    class AppFrame extends Frame
    {
            .
            .
            .
    }
```
As in our applet, we'll override the paint method and use the passed Graphics object to display the text we want in the new window:
```
    class AppFrame extends Frame
    {
        public void paint(Graphics g)
        {
            g.drawString("Hello from Eclipse!", 60, 100);
        }
    }
```

Now, in the `Ch06_02` class's main method, we'll create a new window of the `AppFrame` class and set its size:

```
public class Ch06_02 {

    public static void main(String [] args)
    {
       AppFrame f = new AppFrame( );

       f.setSize(200, 200);
         .
         .
         .
    }
}
```

All that's left is to add the standard code to handle the window-close event that occurs when the user clicks the X button in the window at the upper right, and to show the window using its `show` method:

```
public class Ch06_02 {

    public static void main(String [] args)
    {
       AppFrame f = new AppFrame( );

       f.setSize(200, 200);

       f.addWindowListener(new WindowAdapter( ) { public void
           windowClosing(WindowEvent e) {System.exit(0);}});

       f.show( );
    }
}
```

To run this application, select Run As → Java Application. This application will launch the AWT window, complete with the message you see in Figure 6-3.

Figure 6-3. Running a windowed AWT application

And that's it—the code for this application appears in Example 6-2.

Example 6-2. A basic AWT application

```
package org.eclipsebook.ch06;

import java.awt.*;
```

Example 6-2. A basic AWT application (continued)

```java
import java.awt.event.*;

public class Ch06_02 {

    public static void main(String [] args)
    {
        AppFrame f = new AppFrame( );

        f.setSize(200, 200);

        f.addWindowListener(new WindowAdapter( ) { public void
            windowClosing(WindowEvent e) {System.exit(0);}});

        f.show( );
    }
}

class AppFrame extends Frame
{
    public void paint(Graphics g)
    {
        g.drawString("Hello from Java!", 60, 100);
    }
}
```

As you can see, launching windowed applications this way is no problem from Eclipse—just set up your application to launch windows and run it. AWT is fine up to a point, but Swing is where the action is today.

Creating Swing Applications

Our first Swing application will be simple, and it will only mimic the applet and AWT applications we've seen by displaying the same message as they did. To put together this application, create a project named Ch06_03 and add the class Ch06_03 with a main method to the org.eclipsebook.ch06 package. We'll need these imports in this example:

```java
import java.awt.*;
import javax.swing.*;
import java.awt.event.*;
```

In this example, we'll derive a new class, Panel, from the Swing JPanel class to display the message in:

```java
class Panel extends JPanel
{
        .
        .
        .
}
```

The JPanel class has a method named paintComponent and we'll override that method to display the text message like this:

```
class Panel extends JPanel
{
    Panel( )
    {
        setBackground(Color.white);
    }

    public void paintComponent (Graphics g)
    {
        super.paintComponent(g);
        g.drawString("Hello from Eclipse!", 60, 100);
    }
}
```

The main class in this application, Ch06_03, will extend the Swing JFrame class:

```
public class Ch06_03 extends JFrame {
        .
        .
        .
```

In the Ch06_03 class constructor, we'll create an object of the Panel class and add it to the content pane of the current JFrame object:

```
Panel p;

public Ch06_03( )
{
    super("Swing application");

    Container contentPane = getContentPane( );
    p = new Panel( );
    contentPane.add(p);
}
```

All that's left is to create a new object of the Ch06_03 class in the main method, display that object with the setVisible method, and handle the window closing with the WindowAdapter class as we did in AWT. You can see how this works in the main method in Example 6-3.

Example 6-3. A simple Swing application

```
package org.eclipsebook.ch06;

import javax.swing.*;
import java.awt.*;
import java.awt.event.*;

public class Ch06_03 extends JFrame {

    Panel p;
```

Example 6-3. A simple Swing application (continued)

```java
    public Ch06_03( )
    {
        super("Swing application");

        Container contentPane = getContentPane( );
        p = new Panel( );
        contentPane.add(p);
    }

    public static void main(String args[])
    {
        final JFrame f = new Ch06_03( );

        f.setBounds(100, 100, 300, 300);
        f.setVisible(true);
        f.setDefaultCloseOperation(DISPOSE_ON_CLOSE);

        f.addWindowListener(new WindowAdapter( ) {
            public void windowClosing(WindowEvent e) {
                System.exit(0);
            }
        });
    }
}

class Panel extends JPanel
{
    Panel( )
    {
        setBackground(Color.white);
    }

    public void paintComponent (Graphics g)
    {
        super.paintComponent(g);
        g.drawString("Hello from Eclipse!", 60, 100);
    }
}
```

You can see the results when you run this application in a Swing window in Figure 6-4.

Figure 6-4. A Swing application

One of the original motivations behind Swing was to let developers tailor the "look-and-feel" of their applications to various operating systems. That's become a big issue in Eclipse, which comes with IBM's Standard Widget Toolkit (SWT), a replacement toolkit for AWT and Swing, built-in. SWT is the focus of the next two chapters, but before we get there, we'll take a look at what Swing has to offer for pluggable look-and-feels in a new example, Ch06_04.

To set a Swing program's look-and-feel, you use the UIManager class's setLookAndFeel method. In this example, we'll add three radio buttons to support the Metal (Sun's Java look-and-feel), Motif, and Windows look-and-feels. First, we'll derive the Ch06_04 class from the Swing JFrame class and create the radio buttons:

```
public class Ch06_04 extends JFrame {
    JRadioButton b1 = new JRadioButton("Metal"),
    b2 = new JRadioButton("Motif"),
    b3 = new JRadioButton("Windows");
```

As in the previous example, we'll use a JPanel object for display purposes. Here, we'll display an assortment of controls, buttons, text fields, labels, checkboxes, and so on, and we'll add an ActionListener to the Metal/Motif/Windows radio buttons:

```
class Panel extends JPanel implements ActionListener
{
    public Panel()
    {
        add(new JButton("JButton"));
        add(new JTextField("JTextField"));
        add(new JCheckBox("JCheckBox"));
        add(new JRadioButton("JRadioButton"));
        add(new JLabel("JLabel"));
        add(new JList(new String[] {
            "JList Item 1", "JList Item 2", "JList Item 3"}));
        add(new JScrollBar(SwingConstants.HORIZONTAL));

        ButtonGroup group = new ButtonGroup();
        group.add(b1);
        group.add(b2);
        group.add(b3);

        b1.addActionListener(this);
        b2.addActionListener(this);
        b3.addActionListener(this);

        add(b1);
        add(b2);
        add(b3);
        .
        .
        .
```

All that's left is to call the UIManager class's setLookAndFeel method inside the actionPerformed method to switch the look-and-feel as needed. You can see how that works in the full code, which appears in Example 6-4.

Example 6-4. The Ch06_04.java Swing application with pluggable look-and-feel

```java
package org.eclipsebook.ch06;

import java.awt.*;
import javax.swing.*;
import java.awt.event.*;

public class Ch06_04 extends JFrame {
    JRadioButton b1 = new JRadioButton("Metal"),
    b2 = new JRadioButton("Motif"),
    b3 = new JRadioButton("Windows");

    public Ch06_04() {
        super("Swing application");

        Container contentPane = getContentPane();
        contentPane.add(new Panel(), BorderLayout.CENTER);
    }

    public static void main(String args[])
    {
        final JFrame f = new Ch06_04();

        f.setBounds(100, 100, 300, 300);
        f.setVisible(true);
        f.setDefaultCloseOperation(DISPOSE_ON_CLOSE);

        f.addWindowListener(new WindowAdapter() {
            public void windowClosing(WindowEvent e) {
                System.exit(0);
            }
        });
    }

    class Panel extends JPanel implements ActionListener
    {
        public Panel()
        {
            add(new JButton("JButton"));
            add(new JTextField("JTextField"));
            add(new JCheckBox("JCheckBox"));
            add(new JRadioButton("JRadioButton"));
            add(new JLabel("JLabel"));
            add(new JList(new String[] {
                "JList Item 1", "JList Item 2", "JList Item 3"}));
            add(new JScrollBar(SwingConstants.HORIZONTAL));

            ButtonGroup group = new ButtonGroup();
            group.add(b1);
            group.add(b2);
            group.add(b3);
```

Example 6-4. The Ch06_04.java Swing application with pluggable look-and-feel (continued)

```
        b1.addActionListener(this);
        b2.addActionListener(this);
        b3.addActionListener(this);

        add(b1);
        add(b2);
        add(b3);
    }

    public void actionPerformed(ActionEvent e)
    {
        JRadioButton src = (JRadioButton)e.getSource( );

        try {
            if((JRadioButton)e.getSource( ) == b1)
                UIManager.setLookAndFeel(
                  "javax.swing.plaf.metal.MetalLookAndFeel");
            else if((JRadioButton)e.getSource( ) == b2)
                UIManager.setLookAndFeel(
                    "com.sun.java.swing.plaf.motif.MotifLookAndFeel");
            else if((JRadioButton)e.getSource( ) == b3)
                UIManager.setLookAndFeel(
                    "com.sun.java.swing.plaf.windows.WindowsLookAndFeel");
        }
        catch(Exception ex) {}

        SwingUtilities.updateComponentTreeUI(getContentPane( ));
    }
  }
}
```

When you run this application, you'll see a number of controls in the launched window, as seen in Figure 6-5. This figure shows the default "Metal" look that Sun developed as a cross-platform look.

Figure 6-5. The Metal look

On the other hand, selecting the Motif radio button changes the look-and-feel to Motif, as you see in Figure 6-6.

Figure 6-6. The Motif look

And selecting the Windows radio button displays the Windows look-and-feel, as you see in Figure 6-7.

Figure 6-7. The Windows look

As you can see, Swing makes an effort to stay up-to-date with various looks. Unfortunately, the various operating systems that Swing emulates have changed faster than Swing has, and Swing is substantially behind the times now, especially when it comes to Windows.

 We'll talk more on this issue in the next chapter when we start dealing with SWT.

Now that we're designing GUIs, you may be asking yourself, wouldn't it be great if Eclipse came with visual tools that would let you simply drag and drop controls into place? Many developers have asked for that, but it doesn't appear likely that Eclipse will include a drag-and-drop GUI toolbox soon. However, there are a number of Eclipse plug-ins that provide this functionality—some are commercial, some are free. Next, we'll take a look at a free plug-in that lets you build Swing applications.

Using Eclipse Plug-ins

Many Eclipse plug-ins are available, and many are free. You can find over 400 plug-ins at *http://www.eclipse-plugins.2y.net/eclipse/*, and the plug-in we'll use for Swing is available from that site. On the other hand, Eclipse plug-ins can change very frequently, so we can't base entire chapters on them—the plug-in you download would be different from the one written about in this book.

But we can look at what specific plug-ins have to offer in general terms, and we'll do that here. In this chapter, we'll take a look at the popular, free V4ALL plug-in to help us write some Swing code, available from *http://www.eclipse-plugins.2y.net/eclipse/*. Navigate to that page, click the *plugins* link, then the *categories* link, and then the *UI* link to find the Eclipse V4ALL Swing & SWT plug-in. Stop Eclipse if it's running and download that compressed plug-in file to Eclipse's *eclipse* directory (this is the directory that contains the *workspace* and *plugins* directories).

When you download plug-ins, you usually download them to the *eclipse* directory. They'll come zipped or tarred, and you usually uncompress them in the *eclipse* directory. When you uncompress them, the support files for plug-ins go automatically into the *plugins* and *features* directories, which are subdirectories of the *eclipse* directory.

 Plug-ins are not always designed to be uncompressed in the *eclipse* directory—if possible, check the plug-in's documentation first. When you're about to unzip a plug-in, open it in an unzip utility and see if it'll unzip files to the *plugins* directory. If so, unzipping it in the *eclipse* directory is the right thing to do. Some plug-ins should be uncompressed in the *plugins* directory directly, however.

Unzip or untar the V4ALL plug-in now, which should automatically load its files into the *plugins* and *features* directories. That's all the installation you need. Now start Eclipse again. Eclipse may display a dialog indicating that there are pending configuration changes and may ask you if Eclipse should restart. Restart Eclipse if you're asked.

Congratulations—you've just installed the V4ALL plug-in. It's time to put it to work.

Using the V4ALL Plug-in

The V4ALL plug-in gives you a palette of Swing components that you can drag to a "whiteboard" to design your application. To see how this works, we'll create a Swing application using this plug-in. Create a new Java project named Ch06_05, and give it a source folder, *src*, in the third pane of the New Project dialog as we've done before. Now create a new class, Ch06_05, in the org.eclipsebook.ch06 package.

Adding a V4ALL Editor to a Project

To add a new V4ALL editor to the project, right-click the `org.eclipsebook.ch06` package and select New → Other, opening the New dialog you see in Figure 6-8.

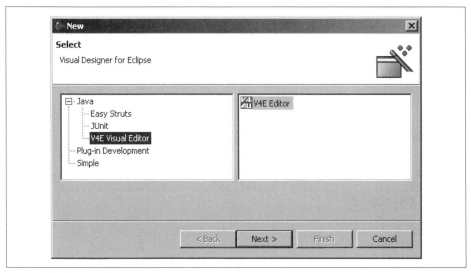

Figure 6-8. The New dialog

You should see V4E Visual Editor as one of the options; select that item and click Next to open the V4E dialog you see in Figure 6-9.

The V4E dialog lets you select the name of the V4ALL file that will contain the design information V4ALL will use. Keep the default name, *Gui_1.v4all*, and click Finish.

Designing the GUI

When you name your V4ALL file of design information and click Finish, the V4ALL perspective that you see in Figure 6-10 will open. You can see the new entry, *Gui_1.v4all*, in the Package Explorer at left. In the center, you see the V4ALL palette, from which you can drag Swing containers and components. You create your application in the whiteboard, which appears to the right of the palette. Under the palette is the properties view, which lets you set various properties of items in the whiteboard.

Our Swing example will display a button and a text field in a Swing frame, so find the `Frame` item in the Containers section of the palette and drag it to the whiteboard. You can see the results in Figure 6-10.

Next, drag a button and a text field from the Components section of the palette to the Swing frame, as you see in Figure 6-11 (note that we've also resized the frame to fit better around these two controls).

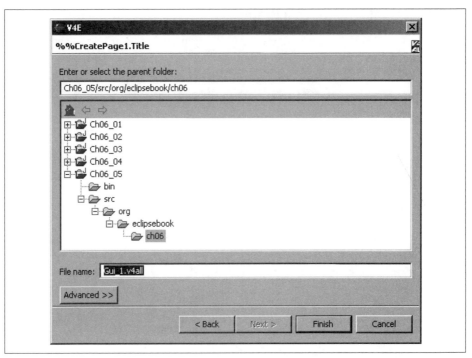

Figure 6-9. The V4E dialog

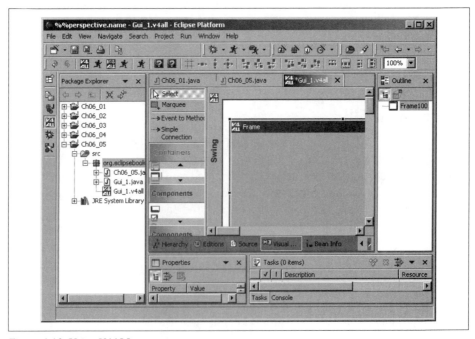

Figure 6-10. Using V4ALL

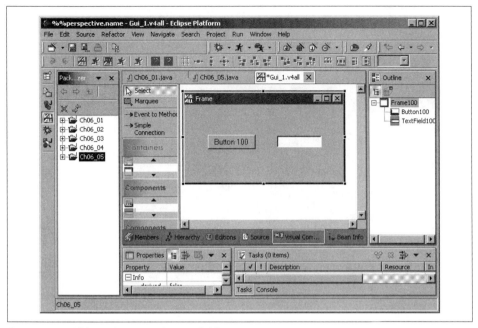

Figure 6-11. Adding a button and a text field

The default caption for the button is "Button 100"; to change that, select the button and click the Text property in the Properties view. Click the ellipsis ("...") button that appears in the Text property line, enter "Click Me" in the Text Input dialog that appears, and click OK.

Creating a Method

In this application, our goal is to display a message in the text field when the user clicks the button, so our next step is to create a method that will handle the button click. To create a new method, drag a method item from the palette Beans & Factories section (the method item's icon is a pair of parentheses) to the whiteboard. Double-click the new method item and edit its name to read processEvent( ), as you see in Figure 6-12.

To connect the Click Me button to this method, select the Event to Method item in the palette, then click the button. Next, move the mouse to the processEvent method item and click that item. This connects the button with the method visually using an arrow, as you see in Figure 6-12.

To indicate what event you want to handle, click Select at the top of the palette and click the arrow that extends from the button to the method. Then select the Action Performed item in the Events property in the Properties view. That's all it takes.

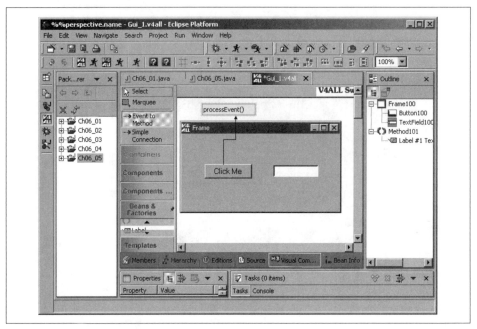

Figure 6-12. Creating a new method

Generating and Editing the Code

We're ready to generate some code. To do that, right-click the whiteboard and select the Code Generation → Generate Code for Swing context menu item (or click the leftmost V4ALL button in the second toolbar beneath the menu bar, which you can see in Figure 6-12). This creates *Gui_1.java*, which you can see opened in Figure 6-13.

This code was generated for us by V4ALL. The processEvent method we've created will be called when the Click Me button is clicked. If you open the processEvent method, you'll see this generated code:

```
public void processEvent(){
    // user code begin {1} Swing
    // user code end
    // user code begin {1} SWT
    // user code end
    // user code begin {1} HTML
    // user code end
    // user code begin {1} Eclipse
    // user code end
    // user code begin {1} C#
    // user code end
}
```

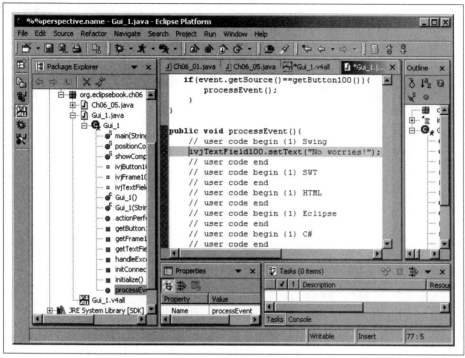

Figure 6-13. Working on V4ALL-generated code

As you can see by looking at the code, the text field is referred to as ivjTextField100, so we can use that object's setText method to display a message, "No worries!", like this (you can see this code entered in Figure 6-13):

```java
public void processEvent( ){
    // user code begin {1} Swing
    ivjTextField100.setText("No worries!");
    // user code end
    // user code begin {1} SWT
    // user code end
    // user code begin {1} HTML
    // user code end
    // user code begin {1} Eclipse
    // user code end
    // user code begin {1} C#
    // user code end
}
```

Running the Result

That's all we need. Save the *Gui_1.java* file now, select it in the Package Explorer, and select the Run As → Java Application menu item, launching the new Swing application, as you see in Figure 6-14. When you click the button, the text field shows the message, as we've designed it to do.

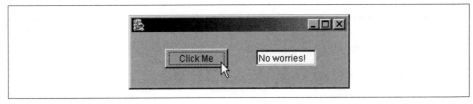

Figure 6-14. The new Swing application

And that's it—everything works as planned. You've created and launched a Swing application using the V4ALL plug-in.

Our V4ALL example is complete, as is our look at applets, AWT, and Swing in this chapter. In the next chapter, we're going to start working with the new GUI alternative, the Standard Widget Toolkit, that comes with Eclipse.

CHAPTER 7

SWT: Buttons, Text, Labels, Lists, Layouts, and Events

SWT, the Standard Widget Toolkit, was created by IBM as a replacement for both the Java Abstract Windowing Toolkit (AWT) and Swing. It's a big topic, and it comes with Eclipse, ready to use. Here's how the Eclipse documentation describes SWT:

> The Standard Widget Toolkit (SWT) is a widget toolkit for Java developers that provides a portable API and tight integration with the underlying native OS GUI platform.

Java Graphics

Graphics work in Java has a long and glorious past, and, let's hope, a similar future. It started with the very basic AWT, moved on through the powerful Swing package, and now stands on the threshold of the SWT age.

AWT

The AWT, Java's first attempt at a GUI toolkit, was written in a matter of weeks. It lets Java developers display windows with various controls like text boxes and buttons. AWT GUIs were easy to develop, and they used the underlying operating system's controls themselves—for example, in Windows, you'd see a Windows text box. On the Mac, you'd see a Mac text box. Some operating systems had a different control set from other operating systems, which meant that Sun only implemented those controls common to all operating systems Java was targeted to, and that limited AWT to a set of relatively simple controls.

Swing

To address the growing needs of developers, Java introduced Swing, which provides non-native implementations of higher level controls like trees, tables, and text. This provides a great deal of functionality, but it makes applications developed in Swing stand out as being different and very Java-specific.

Sun added a "look-and-feel" emulation (which we saw at work in the previous chapter) to help applications look more like the operating system they're running on, but they couldn't keep up with all the operating system releases (such as Windows ME, 2000, XP, and so on). In addition, because the GUI was implemented in Java and not natively in the operating system, Swing response time was poor compared to native applications.

SWT

SWT addresses many of the issues here by providing a set of *widgets* that make use of native controls (through the Java Native Interface, JNI) when such controls are available. Otherwise, SWT creates its own controls as needed for those that don't have an operating system counterpart. This does mean that native code is needed to support each operating system, but so far, IBM has been able to provide that and stay up-to-date. Additionally, SWT comes with Eclipse, so it is a fit topic for our discussion.

SWT is substantial and feature-rich, as you'd expect if it's intended to replace AWT and Swing. We're going to get an introduction to SWT in this and the next chapter, and it turns out that you really don't need in-depth SWT knowledge to create powerful and useful SWT applications. All you need to know about are widgets (the user-interface elements you use in SWT), SWT layouts (which let you position those widgets), and SWT events. We're going to see plenty of examples, starting immediately, to see how all these work in SWT.

 SWT is being ported to more and more graphical environments all the time. Currently supported are: Windows, Linux GTK, Linux Motif, Solaris Motif, AIX Motif, HPUX Motif, Photon QNX, and Mac OS X.

An SWT Example

Instead of talking about SWT in the abstract, let's get this show on the road and see some code at work. Coding an example is going to give us the SWT story and what it takes to put together an SWT application. Our first example will be a simple one, and it will just display the message "No worries!" in an SWT window.

To follow along, create a new project, Ch07_01, and add a class, Ch07_01, in the org. eclipsebook.ch07 package. To work with SWT and SWT widgets, you typically start with these two imports:

```
import org.eclipse.swt.widgets.*;
import org.eclipse.swt.*;
```

You'll need to include *swt.jar* in the build path to make these imports work. Remember that SWT is operating system–dependent, so there's going to be a different *swt.jar* for different operating systems. To add *swt.jar* to the Ch07_01 project, select that project in the Package Explorer, right-click it, and select Properties. In the Properties for Ch07_01 dialog that opens, select the Java Build Path item and click the Add

External JARs button. Then navigate to *swt.jar*, which you'll find in one of the following directories, depending on your operating system (note that *INSTALLDIR* is the Eclipse installation directory; also note that you'll have to update these paths for your version of Eclipse, such as changing 2.1.1 to 2.1.2 or some other value):

Win32
> *INSTALLDIR\eclipse\plugins\org.eclipse.swt.win32_2.1.1\ws\win32\swt.jar*

Linux GTK
> *INSTALLDIR/eclipse/plugins/org.eclipse.swt.gtk_2.1.1/ws/gtk/swt.jar*

Linux Motif
> *INSTALLDIR/eclipse/plugins/org.eclipse.swt.motif_2.1.1/ws/motif/swt.jar*

Solaris Motif
> *INSTALLDIR/eclipse/plugins/org.eclipse.swt.motif_2.1.1/ws/solaris/sparc/swt.jar*

AIX Motif
> *INSTALLDIR/eclipse/plugins/org.eclipse.swt.motif_2.1.1/ws/aix/ppc/swt.jar*

HPUX Motif
> *INSTALLDIR/eclipse/plugins/org.eclipse.swt.motif_2.1.1/ws/hpux/PA_RISC/swt.jar*

Photon QNX
> *INSTALLDIR/eclipse/plugins/org.eclipse.swt.photon_2.1.1/ws/photon/swt.jar*

Mac OS X
> *INSTALLDIR/eclipse/plugins/org.eclipse.swt.carbon_2.1.1/ws/carbon/swt.jar*

After locating *swt.jar*, click Open, and then click OK to add it to the project's build path.

> Some operating systems, such as Linux GTK, need more than one JAR to run SWT (in Linux GTK, you use *swt.jar* and *swt-pi.jar*). In such cases, you have to add all of the required JARs to the build path. (All the required JAR files will be in the same folder.)

In the code, the next step is to create a `Display` object, which represents an *SWT session*. This object acts as the connection between SWT and the operating system's GUI support. You use a `Display` object to start an event loop and control communication between the main user interface thread and other threads. Here's how we create the `Display` object in the main method of the `Ch07_01` class:

```
import org.eclipse.swt.widgets.*;
import org.eclipse.swt.*;

public class Ch07_01 {

    public static void main(String [] args) {
        Display display = new Display();
        .
        .
        .

}
```

Now that you've got a `Display` object, you can create the various windows you want to work with by creating `Shell` objects. In SWT, a shell is a window that is managed by the operating system's window manager. A top-level shell is one that is a direct child of the display and is a window the user can move, resize, minimize, and so on. You can also have secondary shells, which are children of another shell, such as dialogs or message boxes. Here's how we create and size the shell we'll be using—note that passing the display object to the `Shell` constructor makes the shell a child of the `display` object:

```
import org.eclipse.swt.widgets.*;
import org.eclipse.swt.*;

public class Ch07_01 {

    public static void main(String [] args) {
        Display display = new Display();
        Shell shell = new Shell(display);
        shell.setSize(300, 200);
        .
        .
        .
    }
}
```

We're ready to add some widgets to our application. You'll find that, in the SWT documentation, the term *widget* is used almost interchangeably with the terms *control* and *composite*. Technically speaking, the formal—and somewhat circular—definition of a *widget* in the SWT documentation is "the abstract class for any UI object that can be placed inside another widget." Practically speaking, *widget* is the general term for any UI element in SWT. *Composites* are widgets that are designed to have children, such as toolbars, trees, and canvases. *Controls* are widgets that have an operating system counterpart, such as buttons, lists, and labels. You can see all the SWT controls in Table 7-1. Note that we're also listing the possible styles and events for each control.

Table 7-1. SWT controls and options

Widget	Purpose	Styles	Events
Button	A standard push button.	BORDER, CHECK, PUSH, RADIO, TOGGLE, FLAT, LEFT, RIGHT, CENTER, ARROW (with UP, DOWN)	Dispose, FocusIn, FocusOut, Help, KeyDown, KeyUp, MouseDouble-Click, MouseDown, MouseEnter, MouseExit, MouseHover, MouseUp, MouseMove, Move, Paint, Resize, Selection
Canvas	A composite control that can contain other controls, and also is a drawing surface. Often the foundation of custom controls.	BORDER, H_SCROLL, V_SCROLL, NO_BACKGROUND, NO_FOCUS, NO_MERGE_PAINTS, NO_REDRAW_RESIZE, NO_RADIO_GROUP	Dispose, FocusIn, FocusOut, Help, KeyDown, KeyUp, MouseDouble-Click, MouseDown, MouseEnter, MouseExit, MouseHover, MouseUp, MouseMove, Move, Paint, Resize
Caret	The standard I-beam caret used to indicate the insertion point for text.		Dispose

Table 7-1. SWT controls and options (continued)

Widget	Purpose	Styles	Events
Combo	A standard combo box— that is, the combination of a text control and a drop-down list.	BORDER, DROP_DOWN, READ_ONLY, SIMPLE	Dispose, FocusIn, FocusOut, Help, KeyDown, KeyUp, MouseDouble-Click, MouseDown, MouseEnter, MouseExit, MouseHover, MouseUp, MouseMove, Move, Paint, Resize, DefaultSelection, Modify, Selection
Composite	Control that can contain other widgets.	BORDER, H_SCROLL, V_SCROLL	Dispose, FocusIn, FocusOut, Help, KeyDown, KeyUp, MouseDouble-Click, MouseDown, MouseEnter, MouseExit, MouseHover, MouseUp, MouseMove, Move, Paint, Resize
CoolBar	A composite control that allows users to reposition contained items dynamically.	BORDER	Dispose, FocusIn, FocusOut, Help, KeyDown, KeyUp, MouseDouble-Click, MouseDown, MouseEnter, MouseExit, MouseHover, MouseUp, MouseMove, Move, Paint, Resize
CoolItem	A UI element that represents a positionable area of a cool bar.	DROP_DOWN	Dispose
Group	A composite control that groups other widgets together. Can enclose them in an etched border and display a label.	BORDER, SHADOW_ETCHED_IN, SHADOW_ETCHED_OUT, SHADOW_IN, SHADOW_OUT, SHADOW_NONE	Dispose, FocusIn, FocusOut, Help, KeyDown, KeyUp, MouseDouble-Click, MouseDown, MouseEnter, MouseExit, MouseHover, MouseUp, MouseMove, Move, Paint, Resize
Label	The standard label control—displays text or an image.	BORDER, CENTER, LEFT, RIGHT, WRAP, SEPARATOR (with HORIZONTAL, SHADOW_IN, SHADOW_OUT, SHADOW_NONE, VERTICAL)	Dispose, FocusIn, FocusOut, Help, KeyDown, KeyUp, MouseDouble-Click, MouseDown, MouseEnter, MouseExit, MouseHover, MouseUp, MouseMove, Move, Paint, Resize
List	The standard list control—allows the user to choose items from a list of items.	BORDER, H_SCROLL, V_SCROLL, SINGLE, MULTI	Dispose, FocusIn, FocusOut, Help, KeyDown, KeyUp, MouseDouble-Click, MouseDown, MouseEnter, MouseExit, MouseHover, MouseUp, MouseMove, Move, Paint, Resize, Selection, DefaultSelection
Menu	The standard menu control—contains selectable menu items.	BAR, DROP_DOWN, NO_RADIO_GROUP, POP_UP	Dispose, Help, Hide, Show
MenuItem	UI object that represents an item in a menu.	CHECK, CASCADE, PUSH, RADIO, SEPARATOR	Dispose, Arm, Help, Selection
ProgressBar	The standard progress bar—displays progress of a task to the user, usually as a bar graph.	BORDER, INDETERMINATE, SMOOTH, HORIZONTAL, VERTICAL	Dispose, FocusIn, FocusOut, Help, KeyDown, KeyUp, MouseDouble-Click, MouseDown, MouseEnter, MouseExit, MouseHover, MouseUp, MouseMove, Move, Paint, Resize

Table 7-1. SWT controls and options (continued)

Widget	Purpose	Styles	Events
Sash	Allows the user to drag a "rubber-banded" outline of the sash within the parent window to allow users to resize child widgets by moving their dividing lines.	BORDER, HORIZONTAL, VERTICAL	Dispose, FocusIn, FocusOut, Help, KeyDown, KeyUp, MouseDouble-Click, MouseDown, MouseEnter, MouseExit, MouseHover, MouseUp, MouseMove, Move, Paint, Resize, Selection
Scale	Control that represents a range of numeric values.	BORDER, HORIZONTAL, VERTICAL	Dispose, FocusIn, FocusOut, Help, KeyDown, KeyUp, MouseDouble-Click, MouseDown, MouseEnter, MouseExit, MouseHover, MouseUp, MouseMove, Move, Paint, Resize, Selection
ScrollBar	The standard scrollbar—represents a range of positive numeric values.	HORIZONTAL, VERTICAL	Dispose, Selection
Shell	A window that is managed by the operating system window manager.	BORDER, H_SCROLL, V_SCROLL, CLOSE, MIN, MAX, NO_TRIM, RESIZE, TITLE (see also SHELL_TRIM, DIALOG_TRIM)	Dispose, FocusIn, FocusOut, Help, KeyDown, KeyUp, MouseDouble-Click, MouseDown, MouseEnter, MouseExit, MouseHover, MouseUp, MouseMove, Move, Paint, Resize, Activate, Close, Deactivate, Deiconify, Iconify
Slider	Control that represents a range of numeric values, which the user can select by positioning a draggable thumb.	BORDER, HORIZONTAL, VERTICAL	Dispose, FocusIn, FocusOut, Help, KeyDown, KeyUp, MouseDouble-Click, MouseDown, MouseEnter, MouseExit, MouseHover, MouseUp, MouseMove, Move, Paint, Resize, Selection
TabFolder	Composite control that groups controls into pages that the user can select using labeled tabs.	BORDER	Dispose, FocusIn, FocusOut, Help, KeyDown, KeyUp, MouseDouble-Click, MouseDown, MouseEnter, MouseExit, MouseHover, MouseUp, MouseMove, Move, Paint, Resize, Selection
TabItem	Control corresponding to a tab in a tab folder.		Dispose
Table	Control that displays a list of table items.	BORDER, H_SCROLL, V_SCROLL, SINGLE, MULTI, CHECK, FULL_SELECTION, HIDE_SELECTION	Dispose, FocusIn, FocusOut, Help, KeyDown, KeyUp, MouseDouble-Click, MouseDown, MouseEnter, MouseExit, MouseHover, MouseUp, MouseMove, Move, Paint, Resize, Selection, DefaultSelection
TableColumn	UI object that represents a column in a table.	LEFT, RIGHT, CENTER	Dispose, Move, Resize, Selection
TableItem	UI object that represents an item in a table.		Dispose

Table 7-1. SWT controls and options (continued)

Widget	Purpose	Styles	Events
Text	The standard text control, which allows the user to type text into it.	BORDER, SINGLE, READ_ONLY, LEFT, CENTER, RIGHT, WRAP, MULTI (with H_SCROLL, V_SCROLL)	Dispose, FocusIn, FocusOut, Help, KeyDown, KeyUp, MouseDouble-Click, MouseDown, MouseEnter, MouseExit, MouseHover, MouseUp, MouseMove, Move, Paint, Resize, DefaultSelection, Modify, Verify
ToolBar	The standard toolbar—a composite control that contains toolbar items.	BORDER, FLAT, WRAP, RIGHT, SHADOW_OUT HORIZONTAL, VERTICAL	Dispose, FocusIn, FocusOut, Help, KeyDown, KeyUp, MouseDouble-Click, MouseDown, MouseEnter, MouseExit, MouseHover, MouseUp, MouseMove, Move, Paint, Resize
ToolItem	UI object that represents an item in a toolbar.	PUSH, CHECK, RADIO, SEPARATOR, DROP_DOWN	Dispose, Selection
Tracker	UI object that implements "rubber-banding" rectangles.	LEFT, RIGHT, UP, DOWN, RESIZE	Dispose, Move, Resize
Tree	Control that displays a hierarchical list of tree items.	BORDER, H_SCROLL, V_SCROLL, SINGLE, MULTI, CHECK	Dispose, FocusIn, FocusOut, Help, KeyDown, KeyUp, MouseDouble-Click, MouseDown, MouseEnter, MouseExit, MouseHover, MouseUp, MouseMove, Move, Paint, Resize, Selection, DefaultSelection, Collapse, Expand
TreeItem	UI object that represents a tree item in a tree.		Dispose

In this example, we're going to use an SWT label to display our "No worries!" message. You can see the possible styles for labels and all SWT controls in Table 7-1; here are more details for the label styles:

SWT.BORDER
    Adds a border

SWT.CENTER
    Centers text

SWT.LEFT
    Left-justifies text

SWT.RIGHT
    Right-justifies text

SWT.WRAP
    Wraps text

SWT.SEPARATOR
    Supports a separator

Here's how we create a label and set its text as appropriate—note that we're center-ing the label by setting its style to SWT.CENTER and setting the bounds of the label to correspond to the entire client area of the shell:

```
import org.eclipse.swt.widgets.*;
import org.eclipse.swt.*;

public class Ch07_01 {

    public static void main(String [] args) {
        Display display = new Display();
        Shell shell = new Shell(display);
        shell.setSize(300, 200);
        Label label = new Label(shell, SWT.CENTER);
        label.setText("No worries!");
        label.setBounds(shell.getClientArea());
            .
            .
            .
    }
```

Finally, you open the shell to display it and add the event-dispatching loop. That loop usually keeps going until the user closes the main window. In the body of the loop, we check if the display object needs to dispatch a message, and then make that object sleep for a while. After the loop terminates, we dispose of the display object, as you can see in the final listing for Example 7-1.

Example 7-1. The first SWT application, Ch07_01.java

```
import org.eclipse.swt.widgets.*;
import org.eclipse.swt.*;

public class Ch07_01 {

    public static void main(String [] args) {
        Display display = new Display();
        Shell shell = new Shell(display);
        shell.setSize(300, 200);
        Label label = new Label(shell, SWT.CENTER);
        label.setText("No worries!");
        label.setBounds(shell.getClientArea());
        shell.open();
        while(!shell.isDisposed()) {
            if(!display.readAndDispatch()) display.sleep();
        }
        display.dispose();
    }
}
```

Note, in particular, that when we're done with the display object, we dispose of it with its dispose method. Disposing of resources like this is not necessary in AWT or Swing, but it is in SWT because the operating systems under SWT require the explicit allocation and disposing of resources. The upshot is that SWT requires you to free any operating system resources that you have allocated, and you can use the *widget*.dispose method to do that.

That completes the code, but this example is not yet ready to run; the next step is to add the native code support JNI library in the path so the Java virtual machine can find that native code. Recall that SWT uses native code support for display, which means that you had to use some JNI code. To do that, select the class that you want to run (Ch07_01 here) in the Package Explorer, and select Run → Run to set up a launch configuration.

In the Launch Configurations dialog that appears, select Java Application and click the New button. The Name, Project, and Main class boxes should be filled in; if they're not, fill them in now. Then click the Arguments tab, and in the VM Arguments box, insert the location of the SWT library, which depends on your operating system (you'll have to update these paths for your version of Eclipse, such as changing 2.1.1 to 2.1.2 or something similar):

Win32

-Djava.library.path=INSTALLDIR\plugins\org.eclipse.swt.win32_2.1.1\os\win32\x86

Linux GTK

-Djava.library.path=INSTALLDIR/eclipse/plugins/org.eclipse.swt.gtk_2.1.1/os/linux/x86

Linux Motif

-Djava.library.path=INSTALLDIR/eclipse/plugins/org.eclipse.swt.motif_2.1.1/os/linux/x86

Solaris Motif

-Djava.library.path=INSTALLDIR/eclipse/plugins/org.eclipse.swt.motif_2.1.1/os/solaris/sparc

AIX Motif

-Djava.library.path=INSTALLDIR/eclipse/plugins/org.eclipse.swt.motif_2.1.1/os/aix/ppc

HPUX Motif

-Djava.library.path=INSTALLDIR/eclipse/plugins/org.eclipse.swt.motif_2.1.1/os/hpux/PA_RISC

Photon QNX

-Djava.library.path=INSTALLDIR/eclipse/plugins/org.eclipse.swt.photon_2.1.1/os/qnx/x86

Mac OS X

-Djava.library.path=INSTALLDIR/eclipse/plugins/org.eclipse.swt.carbon_2.1.1/os/macosx/ppc

Then click the Apply button, followed by the Run button. You should see this new example at work, as in Figure 7-1.

Figure 7-1. The first SWT application

That's our first SWT application—not too involved, but now we've got the basics of SWT applications down.

Working with Buttons

Our next step is going to be adding interactive widgets to SWT applications. In this case, we're going to add a button that, when clicked, will display text in a text control. We start off as before, except this time, we also import `org.eclipse.swt.events.*` to handle button clicks and `org.eclipse.swt.layout.*` to set the layout of our controls. And we can also embellish our example a little more by setting the text that should appear in the shell's titlebar, using the `setText` method:

```
package org.eclipsebook.ch07;

import org.eclipse.swt.widgets.*;
import org.eclipse.swt.SWT;
import org.eclipse.swt.events.*;
import org.eclipse.swt.layout.*;

    public static void main(String [] args) {
        Display display = new Display();
        Shell shell = new Shell(display);
        shell.setSize(300, 200);
        shell.setText("Button Example");
        .
        .
        .
```

Now we're dealing with multiple controls, and we're also going to set the SWT layout of our shell to the *row layout*, which displays controls in rows:

```
public class Ch07_02 {

    public static void main(String [] args) {
        Display display = new Display();
        Shell shell = new Shell(display);
        shell.setSize(300, 200);
        shell.setText("Button Example");
        shell.setLayout(new RowLayout());
        .
        .
        .
```

The row layout is only one of several layouts that lets you specify how controls are arranged; we'll see the others in the next section. Now we'll add the button using the Button class and the text control using the Text class. Here are the possible styles for buttons:

SWT.BORDER
    Adds a border

SWT.CHECK
    Creates a check button

SWT.PUSH
    Creates a push button

SWT.RADIO
    Creates a radio button

SWT.TOGGLE
    Creates a toggle button

SWT.FLAT
    Creates a flat button

SWT.LEFT
    Sets left alignment

SWT.RIGHT
    Sets right alignment

SWT.CENTER
    Sets center alignment

SWT.ARROW
    Creates an arrow button

And here are the possible styles for text controls:

SWT.BORDER
    Adds a border

SWT.SINGLE
    Allows single selections

SWT.READ_ONLY
    Supports only read-only text

SWT.LEFT
    Sets left-alignment

SWT.CENTER
    Sets center alignment

SWT.RIGHT
    Sets right alignment

SWT.WRAP
    Allows text to wrap

SWT.MULTI
    Allows multiple selections

Here's how we add the button and text control in code:

```
public class Ch07_02 {

    public static void main(String [] args) {
        Display display = new Display();
        Shell shell = new Shell(display);
        shell.setSize(300, 200);
        shell.setText("Button Example");
        shell.setLayout(new RowLayout());

        final Button button = new Button(shell, SWT.PUSH);
        button.setText("Click Me");

        final Text text = new Text(shell, SWT.SHADOW_IN);
            .
            .
            .
```

To handle button clicks, you add a SelectionListener to the button, which you can do with the addSelectionListener method. Listeners in SWT are much like listeners in AWT; here are some of the most popular:

ControlListener
  Handles moving and resizing

FocusListener
  Handles the getting and losing of the focus

KeyListener
  Handles key strokes

MouseListener, MouseMoveListener, MouseTrackListener
  Handles the mouse

SelectionListener
  Handles widget selections (including button clicks)

The SelectionListener interface has two methods that you have to implement: widgetSelected, when a selection occurs in a control, and widgetDefaultSelected, when a default selection is made in a control. Here, we're just going to display the text "No worries!" in a text control using an anonymous inner class:

```
button.addSelectionListener(new SelectionListener()
{
    public void widgetSelected(SelectionEvent event)
    {
        text.setText("No worries!");
    }

    public void widgetDefaultSelected(SelectionEvent event)
    {
        text.setText("No worries!");
    }
});
```

All that's left is to display the shell and implement the event loop, as you see in Example 7-2.

Example 7-2. Using SWT buttons

```
package org.eclipsebook.ch07;

import org.eclipse.swt.widgets.*;
import org.eclipse.swt.SWT;
import org.eclipse.swt.events.*;
import org.eclipse.swt.layout.*;

public class Ch07_02 {

    public static void main(String [] args) {
        Display display = new Display();
        Shell shell = new Shell(display);
        shell.setSize(300, 200);
        shell.setLayout(new RowLayout());
        shell.setText("Button Example");

        final Button button = new Button(shell, SWT.PUSH);
        button.setText("Click Me");

        final Text text = new Text(shell, SWT.SHADOW_IN);

        button.addSelectionListener(new SelectionListener()
        {

            public void widgetSelected(SelectionEvent event)
            {
                text.setText("No worries!");
            }

            public void widgetDefaultSelected(SelectionEvent event)
            {
                text.setText("No worries!");
            }
        });

        shell.open();
        while(!shell.isDisposed()) {
            if(!display.readAndDispatch()) display.sleep();
        }
        display.dispose();
    }
}
```

You can see the results in Figure 7-2; when the user clicks the button, the text message appears in the text control.

Although we've used a row layout here, you can also directly set the bounds of controls with the setBounds(*x, y, width, height*) method. For example, if you want to explicitly set the location and sizes of the button and text control here, you might

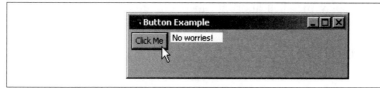

Figure 7-2. Using a button and text control

omit the call to shell.setLayout(new RowLayout( )) and use the setBounds method instead, like this:

```
public static void main (String [] args) {
    Display display = new Display ( );
    Shell shell = new Shell (display);
    shell.setSize(300, 200);
    shell.setText("Button Example");

    final Button button = new Button(shell, SWT.PUSH);
    button.setText("Click Me");
    button.setBounds(80, 80, 90, 20);

    final Text text = new Text (shell, SWT.SHADOW_IN);
    text.setBounds(180, 80, 90, 20);
```

Also, now that you're adding interactive widgets to your applications, you should know more about how widgets are handled with threads in SWT applications. In an SWT application, the main thread, the *UI thread*, is responsible for handling events and dispatching them to the correct widget. In AWT and Swing, you don't have to deal with the UI thread, but in SWT, the UI thread acts like a message pump that dispatches events to widgets as needed (setting things up this way makes it possible to use SWT plug-ins in Eclipse). The UI thread is the application's main thread, so if you want to perform a lot of heavy lifting, you should start other worker threads to do the work. The UI thread is also the only thread that can interact with widgets and not throw an SWTException exception.

If you do start other threads, you can update the user interface when their tasks are done with the asyncExec and syncExec methods. You pass these methods a new Runnable object that does the updating you want. For example, in a worker thread, you could get the current Display object using the Display.getDefault method and set the text in a label, like this:

```
Display.getDefault().asyncExec(new Runnable( )
{
    public void run( )
    {
        label.setText("No worries!");
    }
});
```

Working with Composites and Layouts

Selecting a layout lets you specify how to arrange your controls; there are four layout classes built into SWT:

FillLayout
> Lets you fill a shell's client area.

GridLayout
> Lays out control children in a grid.

RowLayout
> Lays out controls in either horizontal rows or vertical columns.

FormLayout
> Lets you position controls relative to the parent composite or another control. It is the most precise of all the layouts.

For example, here's how the grid layout works. We're going to create a grid layout with four columns and fill it with buttons. In this case, we'll create a new Composite control, which can contain other controls, and fill the composite with buttons. To start, we create a new shell and use a row layout to display our composite control. Then we create the composite control and a grid layout in it with four columns (the SWT.NONE constant means we're not setting any nondefault styles here):

```java
public static void main (String [] args) {
    Display display = new Display ();
    final Shell shell = new Shell (display);
    shell.setSize(300, 200);
    shell.setLayout(new RowLayout());

    final Composite composite = new Composite(shell, SWT.NONE);
    GridLayout gridLayout = new GridLayout();
    gridLayout.numColumns = 4;
    composite.setLayout(gridLayout);
    .
    .
    .
```

All that's left is to add the buttons to the composite control using a loop and to add the event loop itself, as you see in Example 7-3.

Example 7-3. Using SWT layouts, Ch07_03.java

```java
package org.eclipsebook.ch07;

import org.eclipse.swt.*;
import org.eclipse.swt.layout.*;
```

Example 7-3. Using SWT layouts, Ch07_03.java (continued)

```java
import org.eclipse.swt.widgets.*;

public class Ch07_03 {

    public static void main (String [] args) {
        Display display = new Display ();
        final Shell shell = new Shell (display);
        shell.setSize(300, 200);
        shell.setLayout(new GridLayout());

        final Composite composite = new Composite(shell, SWT.NONE);
        GridLayout gridLayout = new GridLayout();
        gridLayout.numColumns = 4;
        composite.setLayout(gridLayout);

        for (int loopIndex = 0; loopIndex < 18; loopIndex++) {
            Button button = new Button(composite, SWT.PUSH);
            button.setText("Button " + loopIndex);
        }

        shell.open ();
        while (!shell.isDisposed()) {
            if (!display.readAndDispatch()) display.sleep();
        }
        display.dispose ();
    }
}
```

You can see the results in Figure 7-3, where we've arranged our buttons using a grid layout.

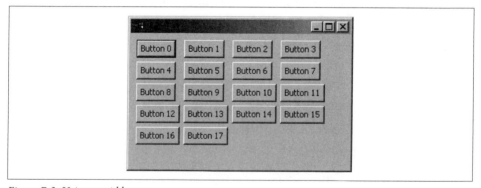

Figure 7-3. Using a grid layout

The form layout is relatively new and very powerful because it allows you to position controls where you want them relative to other controls or the container.

Working with Lists

Another popular control is the list control, represented by the SWT List class. We'll take a look at an example using this control and how to recover selections made in the control. Here are the styles you can use with lists:

SWT.BORDER
> Adds a border

SWT.H_SCROLL
> Adds a horizontal scrollbar

SWT.V_SCROLL
> Adds a vertical scrollbar

SWT.SINGLE
> Allows single selections

SWT.MULTI
> Allows multiple selections

In this case, we're going to fill the entire shell with a list control, using the fill layout. Here's what that looks like—note that we're also using the List class's add method to add items to the list:

```java
public class Ch07_04 {

    public static void main (String [] args) {
        Display display = new Display ();
        Shell shell = new Shell (display);
        shell.setText("List Example");
        shell.setSize(300, 200);
        shell.setLayout(new FillLayout(SWT.VERTICAL));

        final List list = new List (shell, SWT.BORDER | SWT.MULTI | SWT.V_SCROLL);

        for (int loopIndex = 0; loopIndex < 100; loopIndex++){
            list.add("Item " + loopIndex);
        }
        .
        .
        .
```

Now we can recover the selected items using a selection listener and the getSelectionIndices method. This method returns an int array of the selected indices in the list control, and we can display those indices in the console, as you see in Example 7-4.

Example 7-4. Using lists

```
package org.eclipsebook.ch07;

import org.eclipse.swt.*;
import org.eclipse.swt.widgets.*;
import org.eclipse.swt.layout.*;
import org.eclipse.swt.events.*;

public class Ch07_04 {

    public static void main (String [] args) {
        Display display = new Display ();
        Shell shell = new Shell (display);
        shell.setText("List Example");
        shell.setSize(300, 200);
        shell.setLayout(new FillLayout(SWT.VERTICAL));

        final List list = new List (shell, SWT.BORDER | SWT.MULTI | SWT.V_SCROLL);

        for (int loopIndex = 0; loopIndex < 100; loopIndex++){
            list.add("Item " + loopIndex);
        }

        list.addSelectionListener(new SelectionListener( )
        {

            public void widgetSelected(SelectionEvent event)
            {
                int [] selections = list.getSelectionIndices ();
                String outText = "";
                for (int loopIndex = 0; loopIndex < selections.length;
                    loopIndex++) outText += selections[loopIndex] + " ";
                System.out.println ("You selected: " + outText);
            }

            public void widgetDefaultSelected(SelectionEvent event)
            {
              int [] selections = list.getSelectionIndices ();
              String outText = "";
              for (int loopIndex = 0; loopIndex < selections.length; loopIndex++)
                  outText += selections[loopIndex] + " ";
              System.out.println ("You selected: " + outText);
            }
        });

        shell.open ();
        while (!shell.isDisposed ()) {
            if (!display.readAndDispatch ()) display.sleep ();
        }
        display.dispose ();
    }
}
```

You can see the results in Figure 7-4, where we're displaying the selections the user made in the list control.

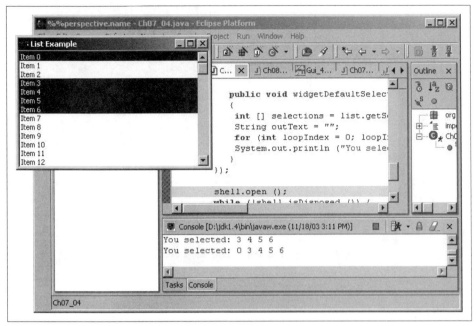

Figure 7-4. Selecting items in a list

Using V4ALL with SWT

You can also use plug-ins like V4ALL to create SWT code, which can make things a little easier because you can drag controls where you want them. In Figure 7-5, you can see an example that works much as our Swing example worked in the previous chapter. In this case, we've created a new V4ALL editor in a project named Ch07_05, just as we did in Chapter 6—but here, we're going to generate code for SWT, not Swing.

After creating the new V4ALL editor, add a button and a label to the new window, change the caption of the button to Click Me, and clear the caption of the label. Next, drag a method to the whiteboard, and name that method processEvent as you see in Figure 7-5. Connect that method to the button and, using the properties view as we did in Chapter 6, connect the processEvent method to the button's Action Performed event.

To generate the code for an SWT application, start by adding *swt.jar* to the build path, and select the Code Generation → Generate Code for SWT menu item, creating *Gui_1.java*. In that file, Eclipse may have marked two imports as never used, so remove those two imports:

```
import org.eclipse.swt.*;
import org.eclipse.swt.graphics.*;
import org.eclipse.swt.widgets.*;
```

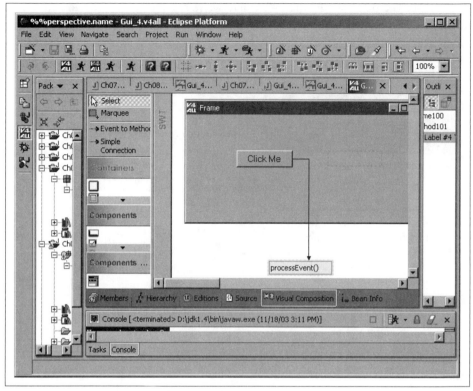

Figure 7-5. Designing an SWT application with V4ALL

```
import org.eclipse.swt.custom.*;
import org.eclipse.swt.layout.*;
```

Then add the code to the processEvent method to set the text in the label to "No worries." when the user clicks the button:

```
public void processEvent(){
// user code begin {1} Swing
// user code end
// user code begin {1} SWT
    ivjLabel100.setText("No worries.");
// user code end
// user code begin {1} HTML
// user code end
// user code begin {1} Eclipse
// user code end
// user code begin {1} C#
// user code end
}
```

Finally, create a launch configuration for the Gui_1 class in *Gui_1.java*, setting the VM arguments to -Djava.library.path="d:\eclipse211\eclipse\plugins\org.eclipse. swt.win32_2.1.1\os\win32\x86" as we've done throughout this chapter. And that's it—when you run this new SWT application, you should see the results in Figure 7-6, where you can click the button and the text message will appear in the label.

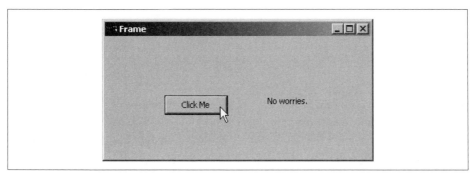

Figure 7-6. Running the V4ALL SWT application

That completes our first chapter on SWT; we got our start with SWT and several important controls. There's a lot more to SWT, however, and we're going to continue our exploration in the next chapter with new controls, such as menus and sliders.

CHAPTER 8

SWT: Menus, Toolbars, Sliders, Trees, and Dialogs

SWT supports many more widgets than we had a chance to work with in the previous chapter, and we'll get the details on a number of the most central SWT controls here: menus, toolbars, sliders, trees, and custom dialogs.

Working with Menus

As you'd expect, SWT supports menus, as any GUI builder should. The process of creating and supporting menus in your SWT applications is not necessarily easy, but it's not unduly difficult. To make this work in an example, we're going to create a menu system with a File menu and a Help menu and react to various menu selections, displaying text in a label to match the selected items.

To create a menu system in SWT, you create a Menu object, corresponding to the top level of the menu system. As with all the SWT controls, you can see the allowed styles back in Table 7-1; here are the possible styles for menus:

SWT.BAR
> Sets menu bar behavior

SWT.DROP_DOWN
> Creates a drop-down menu

SWT.POP_UP
> Creates a pop-up menu

SWT.NO_RADIO_GROUP
> Prevents the use of radio groups

SWT.LEFT_TO_RIGHT
> Sets left-to-right orientation

SWT.RIGHT_TO_LEFT
> Sets right-to-left orientation

The File and Help menus are MenuItem objects associated with the Menu object, and here are the possible styles for menu items:

SWT.CHECK
    Creates a checkbox

SWT.CASCADE
    Creates a cascading submenu

SWT.PUSH
    Creates a push button

SWT.RADIO
    Creates a radio button

SWT.SEPARATOR
    Creates a menu separator

 Note, in particular, how easy it is to add a menu separator to a menu—just create a new menu item using the SWT.SEPARATOR style.

We begin by creating the File menu and setting its text this way—as in other GUI support packages, the "&" before the "F" in File sets the shortcut for this menu (allowing you, for example, to open the menu by pressing Alt+F in Windows, or Apple+F in Mac OS X):

```
menuBar = new Menu(shell, SWT.BAR);
fileMenuHeader = new MenuItem(menuBar, SWT.CASCADE);
fileMenuHeader.setText("&File");
```

That adds the File menu item to the menu bar. The next step is to create a drop-down menu that will display the File menu's items, which works like this:

```
menuBar = new Menu(shell, SWT.BAR);
fileMenuHeader = new MenuItem(menuBar, SWT.CASCADE);
fileMenuHeader.setText("&File");

fileMenu = new Menu(shell, SWT.DROP_DOWN);
fileMenuHeader.setMenu(fileMenu);
```

In this example, we're going to give the File menu two items, Save and Exit, and we only have to create two new MenuItem objects to do that:

```
menuBar = new Menu(shell, SWT.BAR);
fileMenuHeader = new MenuItem(menuBar, SWT.CASCADE);
fileMenuHeader.setText("&File");

fileMenu = new Menu(shell, SWT.DROP_DOWN);
fileMenuHeader.setMenu(fileMenu);

fileSaveItem = new MenuItem(fileMenu, SWT.PUSH);
fileSaveItem.setText("&Save");
```

```
fileExitItem = new MenuItem(fileMenu, SWT.PUSH);
fileExitItem.setText("E&xit");
```

The File → Save and File → Exit items are handled with listeners. Here's how you connect those items to the SelectionListener objects fileSaveItemListener and fileExitItemListener:

```
fileSaveItem.addSelectionListener(new fileSaveItemListener());
fileExitItem.addSelectionListener(new fileExitItemListener());
```

When the File → Save item is selected, we're going to display the message "Saved" in a label:

```
class fileSaveItemListener implements SelectionListener
{
    public void widgetSelected(SelectionEvent event)
    {
     label.setText("Saved");
    }

    public void widgetDefaultSelected(SelectionEvent event)
    {
     label.setText("Saved");
    }
}
```

On the other hand, when the user selects the File → Exit item, we want to exit the application. You do that by closing the shell and disposing of the display object:

```
class fileExitItemListener implements SelectionListener
{
    public void widgetSelected(SelectionEvent event)
    {
        shell.close();
        display.dispose();
    }

    public void widgetDefaultSelected(SelectionEvent event)
    {
        shell.close();
        display.dispose();
    }
}
```

When you've got the menu system configured as you want it, you add the menuBar object to the current shell with the setMenuBar method, and display the shell as usual:

```
shell.setMenuBar(menuBar);

shell.open();
while(!shell.isDisposed()) {
    if(!display.readAndDispatch()) display.sleep();
}
display.dispose();
```

That's all it takes for the File menu. In this example, we also want to add the Help → Get Help menu item; the additional code for the listing appears in Example 8-1.

Example 8-1. Using SWT menus

```
package org.eclipsebook.ch08;

import org.eclipse.swt.widgets.*;
import org.eclipse.swt.SWT;
import org.eclipse.swt.events.*;

public class Ch08_01 {

    Display display;
    Shell shell;
    Menu menuBar, fileMenu, helpMenu;
    MenuItem fileMenuHeader, helpMenuHeader;
    MenuItem fileExitItem, fileSaveItem, helpGetHelpItem;
    Label label;

    public Ch08_01(){

        display = new Display();
        shell = new Shell(display);
        shell.setText("Menu Example");
        shell.setSize(300, 200);

        label = new Label(shell, SWT.CENTER);
        label.setBounds(shell.getClientArea());

        menuBar = new Menu(shell, SWT.BAR);
        fileMenuHeader = new MenuItem(menuBar, SWT.CASCADE);
        fileMenuHeader.setText("&File");

        fileMenu = new Menu(shell, SWT.DROP_DOWN);
        fileMenuHeader.setMenu(fileMenu);

        fileSaveItem = new MenuItem(fileMenu, SWT.PUSH);
        fileSaveItem.setText("&Save");

        fileExitItem = new MenuItem(fileMenu, SWT.PUSH);
        fileExitItem.setText("E&xit");

        helpMenuHeader = new MenuItem(menuBar, SWT.CASCADE);
        helpMenuHeader.setText("&Help");

        helpMenu = new Menu(shell, SWT.DROP_DOWN);
        helpMenuHeader.setMenu(helpMenu);

        helpGetHelpItem = new MenuItem(helpMenu, SWT.PUSH);
        helpGetHelpItem.setText("&Get Help");

        fileExitItem.addSelectionListener(new fileExitItemListener());
        fileSaveItem.addSelectionListener(new fileSaveItemListener());
        helpGetHelpItem.addSelectionListener(new helpGetHelpItemListener());
```

Example 8-1. Using SWT menus (continued)

```
        shell.setMenuBar(menuBar);
        shell.open( );
        while(!shell.isDisposed( )) {
            if(!display.readAndDispatch( )) display.sleep( );
        }
        display.dispose( );
    }

    class fileExitItemListener implements SelectionListener
    {
        public void widgetSelected(SelectionEvent event)
        {
            shell.close( );
            display.dispose( );
        }

        public void widgetDefaultSelected(SelectionEvent event)
        {
            shell.close( );
            display.dispose( );
        }
    }

    class fileSaveItemListener implements SelectionListener
    {
        public void widgetSelected(SelectionEvent event)
        {
         label.setText("Saved");
        }

        public void widgetDefaultSelected(SelectionEvent event)
        {
         label.setText("Saved");
        }
    }

    class helpGetHelpItemListener implements SelectionListener
    {
        public void widgetSelected(SelectionEvent event)
        {
            label.setText("No worries!");
        }

        public void widgetDefaultSelected(SelectionEvent event)
        {
         label.setText("No worries!");
        }
    }

    public static void main(String [] args) {
        Ch08_01 menuExample = new Ch08_01( );
    }
}
```

You can see the results in Figures 8-1 and 8-2; when the user selects the File → Save item, the application catches the menu selection and displays the result in the label that's been added to the shell.

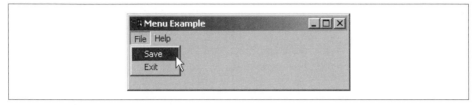

Figure 8-1. Selecting an SWT menu item

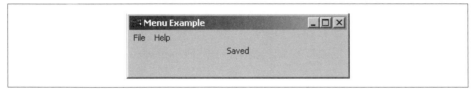

Figure 8-2. The results of selecting a menu item

 One of the most common items to support with menu systems is an About dialog for the application, selected with Help → About. To support a Help → About item in your application, take a look at the work we do with dialog boxes later in this chapter. All you've got to do is launch a dialog box when this menu item is selected; the dialog can contain all the controls you need to display application info.

Working with Toolbars

SWT also supports toolbars, using the `Toolbar` class. To create a toolbar, you just associate the toolbar with the shell you're working with and set its style:

`SWT.BORDER`
Creates a toolbar with a border

`SWT.FLAT`
Creates a flat toolbar

`SWT.WRAP`
Creates a wrappable toolbar

`SWT.RIGHT`
Aligns the toolbar on the right

`SWT.SHADOW_OUT`
Adds a shadow to the toolbar

`SWT.HORIZONTAL`
Creates a horizontal toolbar

`SWT.VERTICAL`

>   Creates a vertical toolbar

Here's how we'll create a new toolbar (the constant `SWT.NONE` indicates we're not setting a custom style):

```
ToolBar toolbar = new ToolBar(shell, SWT.NONE);
```

Each item in the toolbar is a `ToolItem` object, and we'll create four push buttons in an example next, using the `SWT.PUSH` style and the `ToolItem` class. Here are the possible styles for tool items:

`SWT.PUSH`

>   A push button

`SWT.CHECK`

>   A checkbox

`SWT.RADIO`

>   A radio button

`SWT.SEPARATOR`

>   A toolbar separator

`SWT.DROP_DOWN`

>   A drop-down item

You can set the text that will appear in the four buttons—in this case, the text will be Now, is, the, time—this way:

```
ToolBar toolbar = new ToolBar(shell, SWT.NONE);
ToolItem item1 = new ToolItem(toolbar, SWT.PUSH);
item1.setText("Now");
ToolItem item2 = new ToolItem(toolbar, SWT.PUSH);
item2.setText("is");
ToolItem item3 = new ToolItem(toolbar, SWT.PUSH);
item3.setText("the");
ToolItem item4 = new ToolItem(toolbar, SWT.PUSH);
item4.setText("time");
```

If you want to, you can also display images, disabled images, and hot images (displayed when the mouse moves over a toolbar item) in a toolbar item using an SWT Image object:

```
ToolItem item1 = new ToolItem(toolbar, SWT.PUSH);
item1.setImage(image);
item1.setDisabledImage(disabledImage);
item1.setHotImage(hotImage);
```

We're also going to set the bounds of the toolbar in the shell and create a text control to display text matching the button the user has clicked:

```
toolbar.setBounds(0, 0, 200, 70);

final Text text = new Text(shell, SWT.BORDER);
text.setBounds(0, 100, 200, 25);
```

You need to connect the various toolbar items to a listener to handle their events, and, in this case, we're going to use a generic `Listener` object. You can handle events from toolbar items with the `Listener` class's handleEvent method:

```
Listener listener = new Listener() {
    public void handleEvent(Event event) {
        .
        .
        .
    }
};
```

This method is passed an event object, and you can extract the widget that actually caused the event with this object's `widget` member. To determine which toolbar item you've retrieved, you can recover the text in the toolbar item with the getText method, which retrieves the text from any widget, from text controls to toolbar buttons:

```
Listener listener = new Listener() {
    public void handleEvent(Event event) {
        ToolItem item = (ToolItem)event.widget;
        String string = item.getText();
        .
        .
        .
    }
};
```

To complete the listener, check what toolbar item was selected and display an appropriate message in text control—note that when you have recovered the text from the button's caption, you know which button was clicked:

```
Listener listener = new Listener() {
    public void handleEvent(Event event) {
        ToolItem item =(ToolItem)event.widget;
        String string = item.getText();
        text.setText("You selected:" + string);
    }
};
```

That completes the listener, which you can add to each toolbar item with the addListener method. In this case, we're going to indicate that we want to handle the SWT.Selection event, as you see in the listing for Example 8-2.

Example 8-2. Using SWT toolbars

```
package org.eclipse.ch08;

import org.eclipse.swt.*;
import org.eclipse.swt.widgets.*;

public class Ch08_02 {

    public static void main(String [] args) {
```

Example 8-2. Using SWT toolbars (continued)

```
Display display = new Display();
final Shell shell = new Shell(display);
shell.setSize(300, 200);

ToolBar toolbar = new ToolBar(shell, SWT.NONE);
ToolItem item1 = new ToolItem(toolbar, SWT.PUSH);
item1.setText("Now");
ToolItem item2 = new ToolItem(toolbar, SWT.PUSH);
item2.setText("is");
ToolItem item3 = new ToolItem(toolbar, SWT.PUSH);
item3.setText("the");
ToolItem item4 = new ToolItem(toolbar, SWT.PUSH);
item4.setText("time");

 toolbar.setBounds(0, 0, 200, 70);

final Text text = new Text(shell, SWT.BORDER);
text.setBounds(0, 100, 200, 25);

Listener listener = new Listener() {
    public void handleEvent(Event event) {
        ToolItem item =(ToolItem)event.widget;
        String string = item.getText();
        text.setText("You selected:" + string);                 }
};

item1.addListener(SWT.Selection, listener);
item2.addListener(SWT.Selection, listener);
item3.addListener(SWT.Selection, listener);
item4.addListener(SWT.Selection, listener);

shell.open();

while (!shell.isDisposed()) {
    if (!display.readAndDispatch())
        display.sleep();
}
display.dispose();
    }
}
```

The results appear in Figure 8-3. Although the toolbar appears at the upper left, it's still a widget like any other. You can position the toolbar where you want it by using the setBounds method or by using one of the SWT layouts.

That's all you need—when the user clicks an item in the toolbar, the application reports which items were clicked correctly, as you see in Figure 8-4.

It's worth noting that you can elaborate toolbars to support other controls as well—for example, to add a combo box to a toolbar, you can use this code:

```
Combo combo = new Combo(toolbar, SWT.READ_ONLY);
```

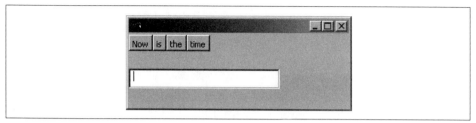

Figure 8-3. A new toolbar

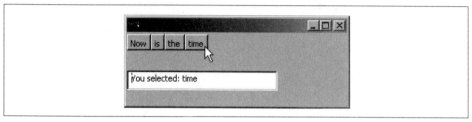

Figure 8-4. Recovering a toolbar event

As with any serious GUI package, toolbars can also display drop-down menus. In SWT, however, you support toolbar menus with context menus, setting their location and making them visible as needed using code like this:

```
menu.setLocation(point.x, point.y);
menu.setVisible(true);
```

Working with Sliders

Another handy SWT control is the slider, which lets the user select a value from a continuous numeric range. Sliders are easy to use; this next example will recover a slider's new position when the user moves the slider's thumb (also called the slider's scrollbox). Here are the styles you can use when creating sliders:

SWT.BORDER
 Adds a border

SWT.HORIZONTAL
 Creates a horizontal slider

SWT.VERTICAL
 Creates a vertical slider

We'll add a prompt to the user in a label ("Move the slider"), a horizontal slider using the style SWT.HORIZONTAL (use SWT.VERTICAL to create a vertical slider instead), and a text control to display the new position of the slider:

```
final Label label = new Label(shell, SWT.NONE);
label.setText("Move the slider");
label.setBounds(0, 20, 150, 15);
```

```
final Slider slider = new Slider(shell, SWT.HORIZONTAL);
slider.setBounds(0, 40, 200, 20);

final Text text = new Text(shell, SWT.BORDER);
text.setBounds(0, 100, 200, 25);
```

That adds the slider; the next step is to handle user actions. Sliders support a number of events, each of which is given by an SWT constant:

SWT.ARROW_DOWN
> The down/right arrow button was clicked.

SWT.ARROW_UP
> The up/left arrow button was clicked.

SWT.DRAG
> The thumb was dragged.

SWT.END
> The slider reached the end of its range.

SWT.HOME
> The slider reached the beginning of its range.

SWT.PAGE_DOWN
> The down/right scrollbar was clicked.

SWT.PAGE_UP
> The up/left scrollbar was clicked.

You use the event object's `detail` member to determine which of these events occurred, as here in a `switch` statement, where we're displaying what event occurred in the application's text control:

```
slider.addListener(SWT.Selection, new Listener() {
    public void handleEvent(Event event) {
        String outString = "Event: SWT.NONE";
        switch(event.detail) {
            case SWT.ARROW_DOWN: outString = "Event: SWT.ARROW_DOWN";
            break;
            case SWT.ARROW_UP: outString = "Event: SWT.ARROW_UP";
            break;
            case SWT.DRAG: outString = "Event: SWT.DRAG";
            break;
            case SWT.END: outString = "Event: SWT.END";
            break;
            case SWT.HOME: outString = "Event: SWT.HOME";
            break;
            case SWT.PAGE_DOWN: outString = "Event: SWT.PAGE_DOWN";
            break;
            case SWT.PAGE_UP: outString = "Event: SWT.PAGE_UP";
            break;
        }
```

```
            .
            .
            .
        }
    });
```

To determine the slider's current position, you use the getSelection method, as you see in the listing for Example 8-3.

Example 8-3. Using SWT sliders

```
package org.eclipsebook.ch08;

import org.eclipse.swt.*;
import org.eclipse.swt.widgets.*;

public class Ch08_03 {

    public static void main(String [] args) {
        Display display = new Display();
        Shell shell = new Shell(display);
        shell.setText("Sliders");
        shell.setSize(300, 200);

        final Label label = new Label(shell, SWT.NONE);
        label.setText("Move the slider");
        label.setBounds(0, 20, 150, 15);

        final Slider slider = new Slider(shell, SWT.HORIZONTAL);
        slider.setBounds(0, 40, 200, 20);

        final Text text = new Text(shell, SWT.BORDER);
        text.setBounds(0, 100, 200, 25);

        slider.addListener(SWT.Selection, new Listener() {
            public void handleEvent(Event event) {
                String outString = "Event: SWT.NONE";
                switch(event.detail) {
                    case SWT.ARROW_DOWN: outString = "Event: SWT.ARROW_DOWN";
                    break;
                    case SWT.ARROW_UP: outString = "Event: SWT.ARROW_UP";
                    break;
                    case SWT.DRAG: outString = "Event: SWT.DRAG";
                    break;
                    case SWT.END: outString = "Event: SWT.END";
                    break;
                    case SWT.HOME: outString = "Event: SWT.HOME";
                    break;
                    case SWT.PAGE_DOWN: outString = "Event: SWT.PAGE_DOWN";
                    break;
                    case SWT.PAGE_UP: outString = "Event: SWT.PAGE_UP";
                    break;
                }
```

Example 8-3. Using SWT sliders (continued)

```
                outString += " Position: " + slider.getSelection( );
                text.setText(outString);
            }
        });

        shell.open( );
        while(!shell.isDisposed( )) {
            if(!display.readAndDispatch( )) display.sleep( );
        }
        display.dispose( );
    }
}
```

You can see the results in Figure 8-5, where the user is dragging the thumb in the slider and the code is indicating that a drag event has occurred and the new location of the slider thumb.

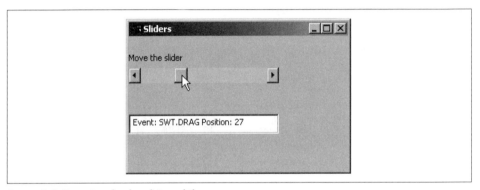

Figure 8-5. Dragging the thumb in a slider

When the user clicks the scrollbar, a page up or page down event occurs, as shown in Figure 8-6, and the thumb moves to a new position (the thumb's page increment is set to 10 by default).

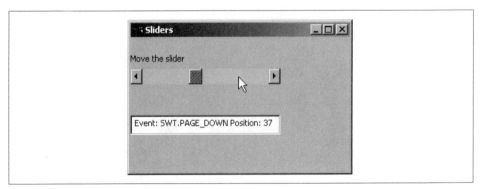

Figure 8-6. Creating a page down event

Besides using getSelection as we've done here, you can also use the setSelection method to set the current location of the slider. For example, if the user selects a page they want to jump to in a document, you can move the slider's position to match with the setSelection method.

 By default, the slider range extends from 0 to 100 minus the thumb's width (which is 10 pixels by default). You can set the maximum and minimum values for the slider range with the slider's setMinimum and setMaximum methods, the increment for the slider's position when the arrow buttons are clicked with the setIncrement method, and the page increment when the scrollbar is clicked with the setPageIncrement method. You can also set the current position in the slider with the setPosition method.

Working with Trees

Trees are another standard SWT element; you use the Tree class to create trees and the TreeItem class to add nodes to the tree. Here are the possible SWT styles for trees:

SWT.BORDER
    Adds a border

SWT.H_SCROLL
    Adds a horizontal scrollbar

SWT.V_SCROLL
    Adds a vertical scrollbar

SWT.SINGLE
    Supports single selections

SWT.MULTI
    Supports multiple selections

SWT.CHECK
    Supports checkboxes

In this example, we'll create a new tree with a border:

```
final Tree tree = new Tree(shell, SWT.BORDER);
tree.setSize(290, 290);
shell.setSize(300, 300);
```

To add nodes to the tree, use the TreeItem class, passing the tree object to the TreeItem constructor. In this example, we'll add five top-level items to the tree:

```
final Tree tree = new Tree(shell, SWT.BORDER);
tree.setSize(290, 290);
shell.setSize(300, 300);
```

```
for(int loopIndex1 = 0; loopIndex1 < 5; loopIndex1++) {
    TreeItem item0 = new TreeItem(tree, 0);
    item0.setText("Level 0 Item " + loopIndex1);
    .
    .
    .

}
```

Each tree node can have subnodes, and those subnodes can themselves have subnodes, and so on; you just pass the node you're adding children to to the TreeItem
constructor. For example, here's how we add five children to every node and five
children to each of those children in turn:

```
for(int loopIndex1 = 0; loopIndex1 < 5; loopIndex1++) {
    TreeItem item0 = new TreeItem(tree, 0);
    item0.setText("Level 0 Item " + loopIndex1);
    for(int loopIndex2 = 0; loopIndex2 < 5; loopIndex2++) {
        TreeItem item1 = new TreeItem(item0, 0);
        item1.setText("Level 1 Item " + loopIndex2);
        for(int loopIndex3 = 0; loopIndex3 < 5; loopIndex3++) {
            TreeItem item2 = new TreeItem(item1, 0);
            item2.setText("Level 2 Item " + loopIndex3);
        }
    }
}
```

That creates the tree; all that's left is to display the shell. You can see the whole listing in Example 8-4.

Example 8-4. Using SWT trees

```
package org.eclipse.ch08;

import org.eclipse.swt.*;
import org.eclipse.swt.widgets.*;

public class Ch08_04 {

    public static void main(String [] args) {
        Display display = new Display();
        Shell shell = new Shell(display);
        shell.setText("Trees");

        final Tree tree = new Tree(shell, SWT.BORDER);
        tree.setSize(290, 290);
        shell.setSize(300, 300);

        for(int loopIndex1 = 0; loopIndex1 < 5; loopIndex1++) {
            TreeItem item0 = new TreeItem(tree, 0);
            item0.setText("Level 0 Item " + loopIndex1);
            for(int loopIndex2 = 0; loopIndex2 < 5; loopIndex2++) {
                TreeItem item1 = new TreeItem(item0, 0);
                item1.setText("Level 1 Item " + loopIndex2);
                for(int loopIndex3 = 0; loopIndex3 < 5; loopIndex3++) {
```

Example 8-4. Using SWT trees (continued)

```
                TreeItem item2 = new TreeItem(item1, 0);
                item2.setText("Level 2 Item " + loopIndex3);
            }
        }
    }

    shell.open();
    while(!shell.isDisposed()) {
        if(!display.readAndDispatch()) display.sleep();
    }
    display.dispose();
    }
}
```

When the shell first opens, you can see the five top-level nodes in the tree, as in Figure 8-7.

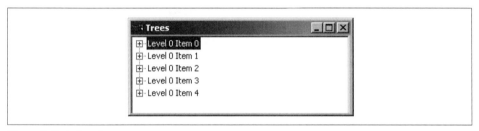

Figure 8-7. A closed tree

Clicking any of the + boxes opens the corresponding node, as you see in Figure 8-8.

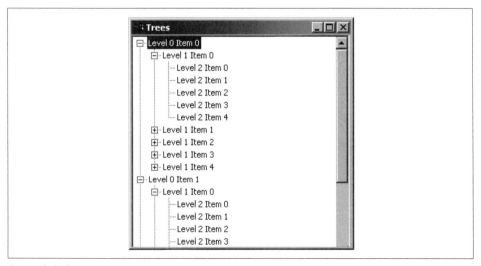

Figure 8-8. Opening a tree

As you can see, it's relatively easy to add nodes to a tree. Trees are substantial controls—you can also support checkmarks with the setChecked and getChecked methods, as well as images with the setImage method. You can handle selection events in trees as well—TreeItem objects can handle selection events just as the ToolbarItem objects we saw earlier; just add a selection listener to them.

Working with Dialogs

As our final SWT example, we'll take a look at creating new SWT dialogs and recovering data that the user entered in them. SWT comes with a number of prebuilt dialog classes, such as the FileDialog and DirectoryDialog classes, but in this example we're going to create our own custom dialog. We'll display a custom dialog with the message "OK to proceed?" along with OK and Cancel buttons and determine which button the user clicked.

In the main application shell, we'll display a button named opener that the user can click to display the dialog, and a text control to display the selection the user made:

```
final Button opener = new Button(shell, SWT.PUSH);
opener.setText("Click Me");
opener.setBounds(20, 20, 50, 25);

final Text text = new Text(shell, SWT.SHADOW_IN);
text.setBounds(80, 20, 100, 25);
```

The dialog will also be a Shell object. Here are the styles you can use:

SWT.APPLICATION_MODAL
: Makes a dialog box application modal

SWT.BORDER
: Adds a border

SWT.H_SCROLL
: Adds a horizontal scrollbar

SWT.V_SCROLL
: Adds a vertical scrollbar

SWT.CLOSE
: Adds a close button

SWT.DIALOG_TRIM
: Styles a dialog box

SWT.MIN
: Adds a minimize button

SWT.MAX
: Adds a maximize button

SWT.NO_TRIM
: Ensures no trimmings are used

SWT.RESIZE
  Handles moving and resizing

SWT.TITLE
  Allows space for a title

To create our dialog, we'll use the styles SWT.APPLICATION_MODAL | SWT.DIALOG_TRIM when creating it. Making it application modal means that the user must dismiss the dialog before working with any other window in the application:

```
final Shell dialog = new Shell(shell, SWT.APPLICATION_MODAL |
    SWT.DIALOG_TRIM);
dialog.setText("Dialog");
dialog.setSize(150, 100);
```

In this example, the dialog is designed to display a prompt to the user ("OK to proceed?") in a label and two buttons, OK and Cancel. We'll add these with this code:

```
final Label label = new Label(dialog, SWT.NONE);
label.setText("OK to proceed?");
label.setBounds(35, 5, 100, 20);

final Button okButton = new Button(dialog, SWT.PUSH);
okButton.setBounds(20, 35, 40, 25);
okButton.setText("OK");

Button cancelButton = new Button(dialog, SWT.PUSH);
cancelButton.setBounds(70, 35, 40, 25);
cancelButton.setText("Cancel");
```

To handle the OK and Cancel buttons, we'll use a Listener object, creating that object with an anonymous inner class, as usual. The difficulty here is in letting the code in that inner class indicate which selection the user made, because it's illegal for inner class code to set the value of a variable in the enclosing class. However, you *can* let code in an inner class set data in an array in the enclosing class, which is what we'll do here. Here's how we determine which button was clicked and set the Boolean response[0] accordingly in the application's main code—note that we also close the dialog here because the user clicked either the OK or Cancel button:

```
final boolean [] response = new boolean[1];
response[0] = true;

Listener listener = new Listener( ) {
    public void handleEvent(Event event) {
        if(event.widget == okButton){
            response[0] = true;
        }else{
            response[0] = false;
        }
        dialog.close( );
    }
};
```

Now you can assign this listener to the OK and Cancel buttons. We also need to assign a listener to the opener button to open and display the dialog in the first place:

```
okButton.addListener(SWT.Selection, listener);
cancelButton.addListener(SWT.Selection, listener);

Listener openerListener = new Listener( ) {
    public void handleEvent(Event event) {
        dialog.open( );
    }
};

opener.addListener(SWT.Selection, openerListener);
```

We also need a message loop for the dialog, which we'll add as well. Finally, when the dialog is closed, we'll check the return value in response[0] and display a message to indicate which button the user clicked:

```
while(!dialog.isDisposed( )) {
    if(!display.readAndDispatch( )) display.sleep( );
}

if(response[0]){
    text.setText("You clicked OK");
} else {
    text.setText("You clicked Cancel");
}
```

That completes the code; you can see the full listing in Example 8-5.

Example 8-5. Creating SWT dialogs

```
package org.eclipse.ch08;

import org.eclipse.swt.*;
import org.eclipse.swt.widgets.*;

public class Ch08_05 {

    public static void main(String [] args) {
        Display display = new Display( );
        Shell shell = new Shell(display);
        shell.setSize(200, 200);
        shell.setText("Dialogs");
        shell.open( );

        final Button opener = new Button(shell, SWT.PUSH);
        opener.setText("Click Me");
        opener.setBounds(20, 20, 50, 25);

        final Text text = new Text(shell, SWT.SHADOW_IN);
        text.setBounds(80, 20, 100, 25);
```

Example 8-5. Creating SWT dialogs (continued)

```
final Shell dialog = new Shell(shell, SWT.APPLICATION_MODAL |
    SWT.DIALOG_TRIM);
dialog.setText("Dialog");
dialog.setSize(150, 100);

final Label label = new Label(dialog, SWT.NONE);
label.setText("OK to proceed?");
label.setBounds(35, 5, 100, 20);

final Button okButton = new Button(dialog, SWT.PUSH);
okButton.setBounds(20, 35, 40, 25);
okButton.setText("OK");

Button cancelButton = new Button(dialog, SWT.PUSH);
cancelButton.setBounds(70, 35, 40, 25);
cancelButton.setText("Cancel");

final boolean [] response = new boolean[1];
response[0] = true;

Listener listener = new Listener() {
    public void handleEvent(Event event) {
        if(event.widget == okButton){
            response[0] = true;
        }else{
            response[0] = false;
        }
        dialog.close();
    }
};

okButton.addListener(SWT.Selection, listener);
cancelButton.addListener(SWT.Selection, listener);

Listener openerListener = new Listener() {
    public void handleEvent(Event event) {
        dialog.open();
    }
};

opener.addListener(SWT.Selection, openerListener);

while(!dialog.isDisposed()) {
    if(!display.readAndDispatch()) display.sleep();
}

if(response[0]){
    text.setText("You clicked OK");
} else {
    text.setText("You clicked Cancel");
}
```

Example 8-5. Creating SWT dialogs (continued)

```
        while(!shell.isDisposed()) {
            if(!display.readAndDispatch()) display.sleep();
        }
        display.dispose();
    }
}
```

Running this example displays the shell you see in Figure 8-9, with the button the user can click to display the dialog and the text control to display the results.

Figure 8-9. The Ch08_05 application

When you click the button, the dialog appears, as shown in Figure 8-10. Because we're creating a dialog here, there's no maximize or minimize buttons in the dialog, and its border is not resizeable. The OK button is highlighted, making it the default button; if the user closes the dialog by pressing Enter, the OK button is selected by default.

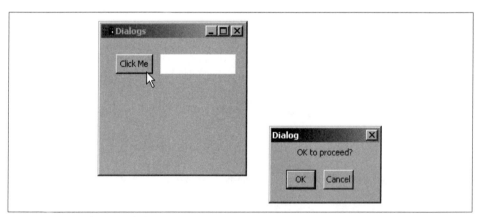

Figure 8-10. Displaying a dialog

Clicking one of the buttons in the dialog closes the dialog and displays the button you've clicked in the text control in the main window, as you see in Figure 8-11. In this way, we've been able to communicate between windows, catching the user's response and displaying it.

Figure 8-11. Recovering the result from a dialog

Opening Internet Explorer in an SWT Window

As you can see, SWT is dedicated to covering the bases when it comes to GUI development, giving you the controls you'd expect to find in standard GUIs. That also means SWT work can be pretty pedestrian, as you stock your GUI with standard controls like sliders, text controls, and so on. So we'll end the SWT discussion with an SWT example that's cooler than most—in this case, we'll see how to open Internet Explorer *inside* an SWT window and browse to a URL of our selection.

For example, the user may want to search for information on the Internet, in which case you could open a search engine. In our example, we'll assume the user needs some good computer books, so we'll browse to the site *http://www.oreilly.com*.

In this new project, Ch08_06, we'll use Object Linking and Embedding (OLE) to open Internet Explorer in an SWT window, which means this example will be Windows-only. Unfortunately, there is no counterpart in Linux or Mac OS X—yet. Still, it's worth looking at how this works in Windows because it's impressive.

On the other hand, browser widgets *will* be coming built-in to SWT in Eclipse 3.0—see the discussion in Chapter 13.

To work with OLE, you import the org.eclipse.swt.ole.win32.* packages and create an SWT OleControlSite object in the main method:

```
package org.eclipsebook.ch08;

import org.eclipse.swt.*;
import org.eclipse.swt.layout.*;
import org.eclipse.swt.widgets.*;
import org.eclipse.swt.ole.win32.*;

public class Ch08_06 {

    public static void main(String[] args) {

        final Display display = new Display();
```

```
Shell shell = new Shell(display);
shell.setSize(600, 400);
shell.setLayout(new FillLayout());

OleControlSite oleControlSite;
    .
    .
    .
```

The window we'll create will be an SWT OleFrame object, and we'll have Internet Explorer in place in that window. To do that, we'll customize the OleControlSite object to work with Internet Explorer, create a new OleFrame object, then execute the OLE verb OLE.OLEIVERB_INPLACEACTIVATE to start Internet Explorer. We'll also configure an OleAutomation object we'll call browser to let us interact with Internet Explorer:

```
OleControlSite oleControlSite;

OleFrame oleFrame = new OleFrame(shell, SWT.NONE);
oleControlSite = new OleControlSite(oleFrame, SWT.NONE, "Shell.Explorer");
oleControlSite.doVerb(OLE.OLEIVERB_INPLACEACTIVATE);
shell.open();

final OleAutomation browser = new OleAutomation(oleControlSite);
```

To work with the browser object, you can use the getIDsOfNames method to get the OLE IDs for the browser's navigation verb, and you simply invoke that verb to navigate to *http://www.oreilly.com*, as you see in Example 8-6.

Example 8-6. Opening Internet Explorer, Ch08_06.java

```
package org.eclipsebook.ch08;

import org.eclipse.swt.*;
import org.eclipse.swt.layout.*;
import org.eclipse.swt.widgets.*;
import org.eclipse.swt.ole.win32.*;

public class Ch08_06 {

    public static void main(String[] args) {

        final Display display = new Display();
        Shell shell = new Shell(display);
        shell.setSize(600, 400);
        shell.setLayout(new FillLayout());

        OleControlSite oleControlSite;

        OleFrame oleFrame = new OleFrame(shell, SWT.NONE);
        oleControlSite = new OleControlSite(oleFrame, SWT.NONE, "Shell.Explorer");
        oleControlSite.doVerb(OLE.OLEIVERB_INPLACEACTIVATE);
        shell.open();
```

Example 8-6. Opening Internet Explorer, Ch08_06.java (continued)

```java
        final OleAutomation browser = new OleAutomation(oleControlSite);

        int[] browserIDs = browser.getIDsOfNames(new String[]{"Navigate", "URL"});
        Variant[] address = new Variant[] {new Variant("http://www.oreilly.com")};
        browser.invoke(browserIDs[0], address, new int[]{browserIDs[1]});

        while (!shell.isDisposed()) {
            if (!display.readAndDispatch())
                display.sleep();
        }

        browser.dispose();
        display.dispose();
    }
}
```

You can see the results in Figure 8-12, where we've opened Internet Explorer and used it to navigate to *http://www.oreilly.com*. Pretty cool.

Figure 8-12. Using Internet Explorer in an SWT window

That completes this example, and it completes our look at SWT in these two chapters. There's a great deal more to the topic, of course, more than we could cover here. But these two chapters give you a good handle on SWT and give you the technology you need to master the topic.

The general technique is pretty simple: you create a `Display` object and `Shell` objects for the various windows you want to display, stock those shell objects with control, display the windows, and set up a message loop to handle events. It's a powerful GUI builder that's gaining popularity every day. For more on individual controls and how to work with them, take a look at the SWT documentation that comes with Eclipse.

CHAPTER 9

Web Development

Java has arrived on the Web with a vengeance in the form of JavaServer Pages (JSP) and servlets, and we'll take a look at how to create these using Eclipse in this chapter. To do that, we're going to use the Tomcat web server, which is the Sun Microsystems reference implementation for both JSP and servlets—and it's free for the downloading.

 Even though we're going to use Tomcat in this chapter, the Java code we write and the XML files we edit are not Tomcat-specific. JSP and servlets both must adhere to their respective specifications, which means you can use what we develop here with other JSP/servlet web containers.

Installing and Testing Tomcat

You can get the Tomcat web server at *http://jakarta.apache.org/tomcat/*; the current release version as of this writing is 4.1.29. Downloading and installing Tomcat isn't hard—just unzip or untar it, which creates this directory structure:

```
jakarta-tomcat-4.1.29
|__bin                  Binary executable files
|__common               Classes available to internal classes and web apps
|   |__classes          Common Java classes
|   |__endorsed         Endorsed Java classes
|   |__lib              Common Java classes in Java Archive (JAR) format
|__conf                 Configuration files (such as passwords)
|__logs                 The server's log files
|__server               Internal Tomcat classes
|__shared               Shared files
|__temp                 Temporary files
|__webapps              Directory for Web applications
|__work                 Scratch directory for holding temporary files
```

For web developers, the most important directory here is the *webapps* directory, which is where you store files to make them accessible to client browsers. We're going to see that directory at work throughout this chapter.

As we develop our web applications, we're going to start by running Tomcat outside Eclipse; later in this chapter, we'll take a look at how to launch it while working inside Eclipse. Our first goal is to get Tomcat working. Before running Tomcat from the command line, you must set these two environment variables:

JAVA_HOME

> Set to the installation directory of Java, the parent directory of the Java *bin* directory. For example, this might be *C:\jdk1.4* in Windows.

CATALINA_HOME

> Set to the installation directory of Tomcat, the parent directory of the Tomcat *bin* directory. For example, this might be */usr/local/jakarta-tomcat-4.1.29* in Linux.

You can set these environment variables from the command prompt as in this example: set JAVA_HOME=C:\jdk1.4. (In the Unix tcsh shell, use setenv instead.) On most operating systems, you can also set environment variables in a more permanent way using control panel dialogs or by setting configurations.

> You can find good instructions on setting environment variables for all operating systems that run Java from the Java download page in the installation notes. Here's the URL with links for various operating systems: *http://java.sun.com/j2se/1.4/install.html* (for example, for Windows, the URL is *http://java.sun.com/j2se/1.4/install-windows.html*), These notes are all about setting the PATH environment variable, but you can use them to set any environment variable.

After setting these two environment variables, you can run Tomcat by changing directories to Tomcat's *bin* directory and typing startup in Windows, or by running startup.sh in Unix. In Windows, a new DOS window will open, displaying initialization messages. When you want to shut Tomcat down, type shutdown in Windows or run shutdown.sh in Unix.

> You'll find the specific directions for starting Tomcat in the *running.txt* document that comes with Tomcat.

Now that Tomcat is running, open a browser and navigate to *http://localhost:8080*, which should open Tomcat's Welcome page, as you see in Figure 9-1. The "localhost" part of this URL is what you use for local web servers (and it corresponds to an IP address of 127.0.0.1), and 8080 is the port number; web servers usually use port 80, but Tomcat uses 8080 to avoid conflicts with other servers.

Figure 9-1. The Tomcat Welcome page

Creating a JSP

The web server is running and now it's time to put it to use. At its simplest, you can use Eclipse to write JSP files, which don't require compilation. These files can enclose Java code in *scriptlet*, *declaration*, and *expression* elements. The most general of these are scriptlets, which can enclose multiline Java code. Scriptlets are enclosed with the markup <% and %>, as you can see in Example 9-1. You can use the out object's `println` method to send text back to the browser; in this case, we're simply sending the text "Using JSP" back to the browser in this JSP.

Example 9-1. A sample JSP

```
<HTML>
  <HEAD>
    <TITLE>A Web Page</TITLE>
  </HEAD>

  <BODY>
    <H1>Working With JSP</H1>
    <% out.println("Using JSP"); %>
  </BODY>
</HTML>
```

An easy way to create this JSP file is just to enter it into Eclipse, as you can see in Figure 9-2, where we've created a new project, Ch09_01, and a new file, *Ch09_01.jsp*, to hold the JSP code. There's no syntax checking going on here; Eclipse is just using its standard default editor.

 If you do want to check syntax of JSP documents, give the free XML editor XML Buddy a try (available at *http://www.xmlbuddy.com*).

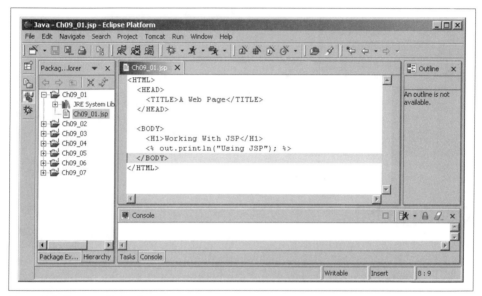

Figure 9-2. Entering JSP code

How can you install *Ch09_01.jsp* so Tomcat can serve it to client browsers? To handle the examples from this chapter, we're going to create a subdirectory of the Tomcat *webapps* directory, *Ch09*. This new directory must itself have a subdirectory named *WEB-INF*, which must have two subdirectories, *classes* and *lib*:

```
webapps
|__Ch09                     The folder for Chapter 9 examples
   |__WEB-INF               Information about Chapter 9's web applications
      |__classes            Java classes used by Chapter 9's web applications
      |__lib                JAR files used by Chapter 9's web applications
```

At this point, the *WEB-INF*, *classes*, and *lib* directories are empty—but they must exist, or Tomcat won't consider *Ch09* a valid directory for storing web documents. After creating these directories, store *Ch09_01.jsp* in the *Ch09* directory. Then shut down Tomcat (if it's running) and restart it.

When you add a new directory to the *webapps* directory, or install *.class* files anywhere in the *webapps* directory, you should shut down Tomcat and start it again. By default, Tomcat copies over what's in the *webapps* directory to the *work* directory and actually uses what's in the *work* directory to run, which means you should restart Tomcat when you make major changes in the *webapps* directory. Tomcat can be configured to detect those changes so it won't need to be restarted, but we're not going to do that here.

To see the JSP document at work, navigate to *http://localhost:8080/Ch09/Ch09_01.jsp* in a browser, as you see in Figure 9-3. Tomcat translates the Java code in the JSP into servlet form, compiles it, and runs it, and you can see the results in the figure.

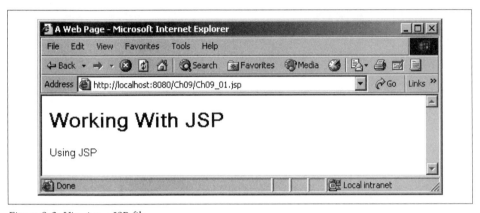

Figure 9-3. Viewing a JSP file

That got us started with Tomcat and our first JSP, but as you can see, Eclipse wasn't very deeply involved. We created *Ch09_01.jsp* using Eclipse, but not much more. It's time to bring Eclipse to the forefront.

Creating a Servlet

JSPs were introduced to make Java web programming more appealing for the novice, letting you mix HTML and Java code. JSPs are actually based on Java servlets (they're translated into servlets before being run), which are pure Java code, and which we're going to focus on for the most part in this chapter. You can see an example servlet in Example 9-2.

Example 9-2. A sample servlet

```
import java.io.*;
import javax.servlet.*;
import javax.servlet.http.*;
```

Example 9-2. A sample servlet (continued)

```java
public class ch09_02 extends HttpServlet
{
    public void doGet(HttpServletRequest request,
        HttpServletResponse response)
        throws IOException, ServletException
    {
        response.setContentType("text/html");
        PrintWriter out = response.getWriter( );

        out.println("<HTML>");
        out.println("<HEAD>");
        out.println("<TITLE>");
        out.println("A Servlet Example");
        out.println("</TITLE>");
        out.println("</HEAD>");
        out.println("<BODY>");
        out.println("<H1>");
        out.println("Working With Servlets");
        out.println("</H1>");
        out.println("Using servlets");
        out.println("</BODY>");
        out.println("</HTML>");
    }
}
```

Servlets like this one are based on the javax.servlet.http.HttpServlet class, and they often simply override the doGet method, which is passed a request object that holds data from the browser (including the browser type and the data from any HTML controls) and a response object that lets you tailor your response to the client browser.

 You override the doGet method to handle HTTP GET requests (as when the METHOD attribute in an HTML form is set to GET) or default servlet accesses. The doPost method, which takes the same arguments, handles the POST method (as when the METHOD attribute in an HTML form is set to POST). To handle either GET or POST requests, you can override the servlet service method, which also takes the same arguments (and is actually the method responsible for calling doGet or doPost).

In this case, we're tailoring our response to the browser by using the response object's getWriter method to get a PrintWriter object, and we're using that object's println method to send HTML back to the browser. In this case, we're just sending back an HTML page with the text "Using servlets" in it.

To follow along, create a new project, Ch09_02, and enter the code in *Ch09_02.java* into a new class, Ch09_02, in that project, using the package name *org.eclipsebook.ch09*. To satisfy the imports we need for this code, include *servlet.jar*, which comes with Tomcat, in the build path. You can find *servlet.jar* at *jakarta-tomcat-4.1.29\common\ lib\servlet.jar*; right-click the Ch09_02 project in the Package Explorer, select Properties, and then add *servlet.jar* to the build path.

At this point, you should be able to build the servlet by selecting the Ch09_02 project in the Package Explorer and selecting Project → Build Project, creating *Ch09_02.class*. Class files like this go into the Tomcat *classes* directory. Our servlet is in the org.eclipsebook.ch09 package, and the directory structure must mirror the package structure, so put *Ch09_02.class* in *webapps\Ch09\WEB-INF\class\org\eclipsebook\ch09*:

```
webapps
|__ch09
    |__WEB-INF
        |__classes
        |   |__org
        |       |__eclipsebook
        |           |__ch09  Directory for the servlet code
        |__lib
```

To let Tomcat know that this new class is a servlet, you use a file named *web.xml* that holds configuration data for web applications. In this file, we use two XML elements, servlet and servlet-mapping, to connect the URL *Ch09_02* to the actual Java code for the servlet, org.eclipsebook.ch09.Ch09_02. You can see what *web.xml* looks like in Example 9-3.

Example 9-3. Updating web.xml

```xml
<?xml version="1.0" encoding="ISO-8859-1"?>
<!DOCTYPE web-app PUBLIC "-//Sun Microsystems, Inc.//DTD Web Application 2.3//EN"
"http://java.sun.com/dtd/web-app_2_3.dtd">
<web-app>
  <display-name>Example Applications</display-name>

  <servlet>
    <servlet-name>Ch09_02</servlet-name>
    <servlet-class>org.eclipsebook.ch09.Ch09_02</servlet-class>
  </servlet>

  <servlet-mapping>
    <servlet-name>Ch09_02</servlet-name>
    <url-pattern>/org.eclipsebook.ch09.Ch09_02</url-pattern>
  </servlet-mapping>

</web-app>
```

Create this new document, *web.xml*, in Eclipse now, by right-clicking the project and selecting New → File. To open *web.xml* in Eclipse, right-click it and select the Open With → Text Editor item (if you just double-click it, your default XML editor—for example, Internet Explorer in Windows—will open the file instead, unless you have an XML plug-in like XMLBuddy installed). Enter the XML in Example 9-3, store the file, and then copy it to the *Ch09* directory's *WEB-INF* directory:

```
webapps
|__ch09
    |__WEB-INF                  Information about Chapter 9's web applications
        |__classes
        |__lib
```

Finally, shut Tomcat down and restart it. We're ready to go; in the browser, navigate to the URL *http://localhost:8080/Ch09/org.eclipsebook.ch09.Ch09_02*, and you should see the results in Figure 9-4.

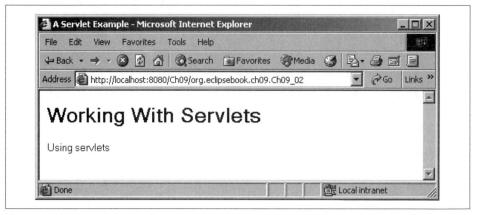

Figure 9-4. Viewing a new servlet

Not bad—we've used Eclipse to develop a new servlet. At this point, we've still been developing our code and then copying it to the Tomcat directories, but Eclipse can also handle the file handling for us.

Creating a Servlet in Place

The code we're developing needs to be in the Tomcat directories to run, and storing the compiled code we generate there is no problem with Eclipse. To see how this works, create a new project, Ch09_03. Enter the name of the project in the New Java Project dialog and click Next to bring up the second pane of this dialog. To set the default output folder for compiled code, click the Browse button next to the Default output folder box to open the Folder Selection dialog. Click the Create new folder button, and click the Advanced button in the New Folder dialog. Now select the Link to folder in the filesystem checkbox, and click the Browse button. Browse to the *jakarta-tomcat-4.1.29\webapps\Ch09\WEB-INF\classes* directory—the root directory for compiled servlet code—and click OK, bringing up the New Folder dialog again. In that folder, give this new folder the name output, as you see in Figure 9-5, and click OK.

Setting up the output folder this way means that the code we compile will automatically be placed in the *classes* folder (or, in our case, in the *classes\org\eclipsebook\ch09* folder, following the package name we're using). Now create a new class, Ch09_03, and enter the code for the servlet in Example 9-4 in it.

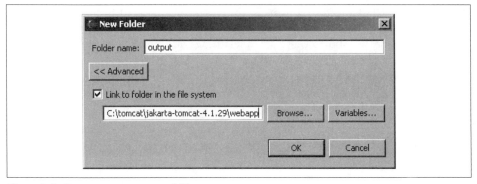

Figure 9-5. Creating a new output folder

Example 9-4. A new servlet

```java
import java.io.*;
import javax.servlet.*;
import javax.servlet.http.*;

public class ch09_03 extends HttpServlet
{
    public void doGet(HttpServletRequest request,
        HttpServletResponse response)
        throws IOException, ServletException
    {
        response.setContentType("text/html");
        PrintWriter out = response.getWriter();

        out.println("<HTML>");
        out.println("<HEAD>");
        out.println("<TITLE>");
        out.println("A Servlet Example");
        out.println("</TITLE>");
        out.println("</HEAD>");
        out.println("<BODY>");
        out.println("<H1>");
        out.println("Working With Servlets");
        out.println("</H1>");
        out.println("Developing servlets in place");
        out.println("</BODY>");
        out.println("</HTML>");
    }
}
```

Finally, add *servlet.jar* to the build path as before. When you build this project, *Ch09_03.class* will automatically be stored in the Tomcat *webapps\WEB-INF\classes\org\eclipsebook\ch09* directory, which is exactly where it should go.

We'll also need to edit *web.xml* to install this new servlet. This can be done in Eclipse using a *linked folder*. In this case, we're going to link to the *Ch09/WEB-INF* folder in the Tomcat installation, which holds *web.xml*. To create a linked folder, right-click the Ch09_03 project and select New → Folder. Click the Advanced button in the New Folder dialog, and select the Link to folder in the filesystem checkbox, then click the Browse button and browse to *jakarta-tomcat-4.1.29\webapps\Ch09\ WEB-INF*. Then click OK to bring up the New Folder dialog again, enter the name WEB-INF for this new folder in the Folder Name box, and click OK. This creates a new linked folder named *WEB-INF*, and you can access the contents of this folder, including *web.xml*, by opening it in the Package Explorer, as you see in Figure 9-6.

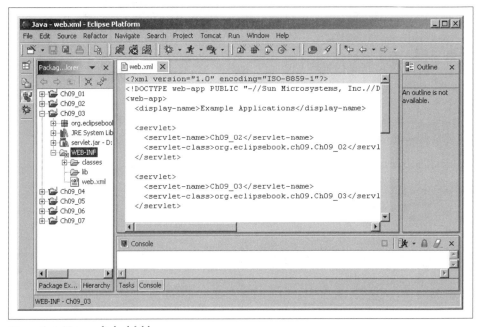

Figure 9-6. Using a linked folder

The *web.xml* to use in this project appears in Example 9-5 (note that servlet elements must be grouped together, followed by the grouped servlet-mapping elements—those elements should not be mixed, or Tomcat won't be able to parse the file, which means it won't start).

Example 9-5. The new version of web.xml

```
<?xml version="1.0" encoding="ISO-8859-1"?>
<!DOCTYPE web-app PUBLIC "-//Sun Microsystems, Inc.//DTD Web Application 2.3//EN"
"http://java.sun.com/dtd/web-app_2_3.dtd">
<web-app>
  <display-name>Example Applications</display-name>

  <servlet>
    <servlet-name>Ch09_02</servlet-name>
    <servlet-class>org.eclipsebook.ch09.Ch09_02</servlet-class>
  </servlet>
```

Example 9-5. The new version of web.xml (continued)

```
<servlet>
  <servlet-name>Ch09_03</servlet-name>
  <servlet-class>org.eclipsebook.ch09.Ch09_03</servlet-class>
</servlet>

<servlet-mapping>
  <servlet-name>Ch09_02</servlet-name>
  <url-pattern>/org.eclipsebook.ch09.Ch09_02</url-pattern>
</servlet-mapping>

<servlet-mapping>
  <servlet-name>Ch09_03</servlet-name>
  <url-pattern>/org.eclipsebook.ch09.Ch09_03</url-pattern>
</servlet-mapping>
```

```
</web-app>
```

Enter this new version of *web.xml* now, and restart Tomcat. Eclipse has taken care of all the file handling for us, so there's nothing to copy to the Tomcat directories—just navigate to the new servlet's URL, *http://localhost:8080/Ch09/org.eclipsebook.ch09. Ch09_03*, as you see in Figure 9-7.

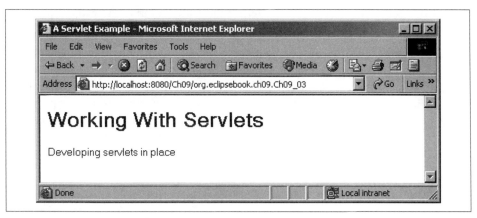

Figure 9-7. Developing a servlet in place

Getting better—now we've developed a servlet's code entirely in Eclipse. Eclipse has even done the file handling for us.

Connecting to a JavaBean

JSP files are able to connect to compiled Java code using JavaBeans, and developing those applications are no problem now that you know how to use linked folders. Here's an example, the Ch09_04 project. In this case, we'll use the bean in Example 9-6, which supports a property named msg that returns the message "No worries!"

Example 9-6. A JavaBean

```
package org.eclipsebook.ch09;

public class Ch09_04 {
    private String message = "No worries!";

    public void setMessage(String msg)
    {
        this.message = msg;
    }

    public String getMessage()
    {
        return this.message;
    }

    public Ch09_04()
    {
    }
}
```

This code's output, *Ch09_04.class* (note that you don't need *servlet.jar* in the build path here), goes into the *webapps\Ch09\WEB-INF\classes* directory, so use that directory as the output directory. After entering the code, compile the project to create *Ch09_04.class*.

In JSP, you can connect to the bean code in a variety of ways, including instantiating an object of the Ch09_04 class using Java in a JSP scriptlet. The recommended way of doing things, however, is to use the JSP jsp:useBean element to create a JavaBean object. Then use the jsp:getProperty element to get the value of a bean property, and use the jsp:setProperty element to set a bean property's value. You can see how this works in Example 9-7, where we're reading the current property of the bean's msg property, setting it to a new value, and reading that new value.

Example 9-7. Connecting to a JavaBean

```
<HTML>
    <HEAD>
        <TITLE>Setting a Property Value</TITLE>
    </HEAD>

    <BODY>
        <H1>Setting a Property Value</H1>

        <jsp:useBean id="bean1" class="org.eclipsebook.ch09.Ch09_04" />

        The message is: <jsp:getProperty name="bean1" property="message" />
        <BR>
        <jsp:setProperty name="bean1" property="message" value="Hello again!" />

        Now the message is: <jsp:getProperty name="bean1" property="message" />
    </BODY>
</HTML>
```

This JSP displays the original message in the msg property and the new value after it's been set. Using a linked folder, store this new JSP file in the *webapps\Ch09* directory, and navigate to *http://localhost:8080/Ch09/Ch09_04.jsp*, as you see in Figure 9-8.

Figure 9-8. Connecting to a JavaBean

At this point, then, we've been able to develop online Java code in Eclipse and write, compile, and install it in Tomcat. All that we've had to do outside Eclipse is start and stop Tomcat. And it turns out that you can do that from inside Eclipse, too.

Using the Sysdeo Tomcat Plug-in

The Sysdeo plug-in lets you start and stop Tomcat from inside Eclipse, and we'll take a look at using that plug-in here. You can download this plug-in for free from *http://www.sysdeo.com/eclipse/tomcatPlugin.html*. After expanding it in the *plugins* directory, activate it by selecting Window → Customize Perspective, opening the Other node, and selecting the Tomcat item, as you see in Figure 9-9.

This adds a Tomcat menu to Eclipse (shown in Figure 9-10) and adds three Tomcat buttons to the Eclipse toolbar that you can see under the Navigate menu; these buttons start, stop, and restart Tomcat.

To connect the Tomcat plug-in to the version of Tomcat you're using, select Window → Preferences and click the Tomcat node, as you see in Figure 9-11.

You use this dialog to connect the Tomcat plug-in to Tomcat itself. At this time, the Sysdeo plug-in for Eclipse 2.1.1 is in beta and does not yet work smoothly with the most recent version of Tomcat, Version 4.1.29, so for the next two examples, we'll use an earlier version of Tomcat (you can get earlier versions of Tomcat from the Apache archives at *http://archive.apache.org/dist/jakarta/*; the archives for all Tomcat 4+ versions are at *http://archive.apache.org/dist/jakarta/tomcat-4/archive/*). By the

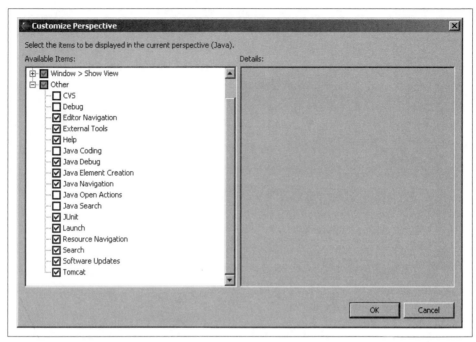

Figure 9-9. Activating the Tomcat plug-in

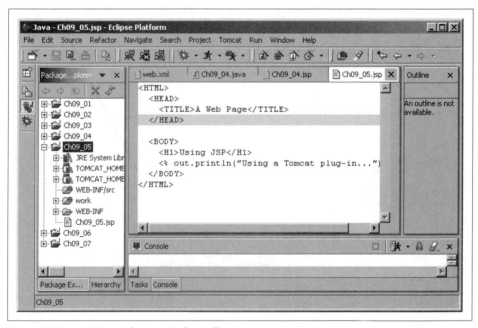

Figure 9-10. New Tomcat buttons in the toolbar

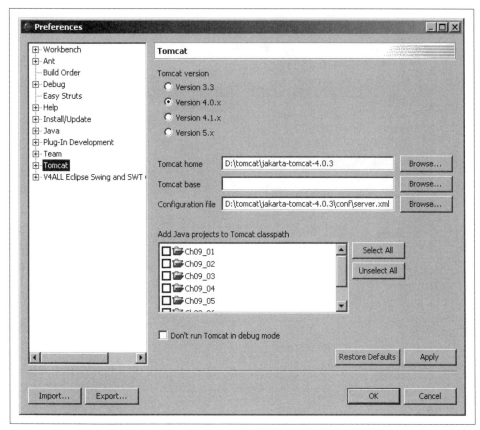

Figure 9-11. Connecting the Tomcat plug-in to Tomcat

time you read this, the Tomcat plug-in should be working with the current version of Tomcat; if not, download and use an earlier version of Tomcat from the Tomcat site if you want to use the plug-in.

In this dialog, you set the Tomcat home location, which is the parent directory of the Tomcat *bin* directory (equivalent to the CATALINA_HOME environment variable, detailed earlier). To set that location, click the Browse button next to the Tomcat home box, browse to the Tomcat installation directory, and click OK (this also fills in the Configuration file box automatically). Click OK to close the Preferences dialog.

Writing JSP with the Sysdeo Tomcat Plug-in

We'll start using the Tomcat plug-in with a JSP project. To create a new Tomcat project, select File → New → Project, select Java in the left box of the New Project dialog, select Tomcat Project in the right, and click Next. Give this new project the name Ch09_05 in the New Tomcat Project dialog and click OK. This creates a new Tomcat project with a number of folders already built-in, as you can see in the Package Explorer in Figure 9-12.

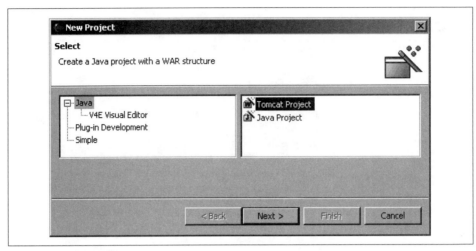

Figure 9-12. Creating a new Tomcat project

To create a new JSP project, right-click the project and select New → File, calling the new file *Ch09_05.jsp*. Enter the JSP you see in Example 9-8. Then simply save the file, and it's ready to run—no file copying needed.

Example 9-8. Creating a JSP with the Sysdeo plug-in

```
<HTML>
    <HEAD>
        <TITLE>A Web Page</TITLE>
    </HEAD>

    <BODY>
        <H1>Using JSP</H1>
        <% out.println("Using a Tomcat plug-in..."); %>
    </BODY>
</HTML>
```

The Tomcat plug-in lets you edit files locally and sets a Tomcat context for them by editing the Tomcat *server.xml* file in the Tomcat *conf* directory. In our example, here's what the plug-in adds to *server.xml* so Tomcat knows where to find our JSP file:

```
<Context path="/Ch09_05" reloadable="true"
docBase="D:\eclipse211\eclipse\workspace\Ch09_05"
workDir="D:\eclipse211\eclipse\workspace\Ch09_05\work\org\apache\jsp" />
```

This change to *server.xml* means that Tomcat can find our JSP, so start Tomcat by clicking the Start Tomcat button and navigate to *http://localhost:8080/Ch09_05/Ch09_05.jsp* in a browser (the URL here includes the project name, Ch09_05, not just the *Ch09* directory as the earlier non-plug-in examples did). You should see the results shown in Figure 9-13.

Figure 9-13. Creating a new JSP using the Sysdeo plug-in

 The Debug perspective will appear when you run Tomcat; when you're done with this example, terminate the Debug session and click the Remove All Terminated Launches button in the Debug view.

That's it—this JSP is running. As you can see, the Tomcat plug-in lets you develop code inside Eclipse, and it lets you start and stop Tomcat inside Eclipse as well.

Writing Servlets with the Sysdeo Tomcat Plug-in

The Sysdeo plug-in also helps write servlets, such as the one in Example 9-9. Up to this point, we've had to set the output directory to store servlets in the Tomcat directories, but the Tomcat plug-in can handle the details automatically.

Example 9-9. Creating a servlet with the Sysdeo plug-in

```
import java.io.*;
import javax.servlet.*;
import javax.servlet.http.*;

public class Ch09_06 extends HttpServlet {

        public void doGet(HttpServletRequest request,
            HttpServletResponse response)
            throws IOException, ServletException
    {
            response.setContentType("text/html");
            PrintWriter out = response.getWriter();

            out.println("<HTML>");
            out.println("<HEAD>");
            out.println("<TITLE>");
            out.println("A Web Page");
```

Example 9-9. Creating a servlet with the Sysdeo plug-in (continued)

```
            out.println("</TITLE>");
            out.println("</HEAD>");
            out.println("<BODY>");
            out.println("<H1>");
            out.println("Using Servlets");
            out.println("</H1>");
            out.println("Using a Tomcat plug-in...");
            out.println("</BODY>");
            out.println("</HTML>");
        }
}
```

To see this at work, create a new Tomcat project, Ch09_06. Add a new class, Ch09_06, to the project, putting that class in the org.eclipsebook.ch09 package. The new class is automatically stored in the *WEB-INF/src* directory, as you see in the Package Explorer in Figure 9-14.

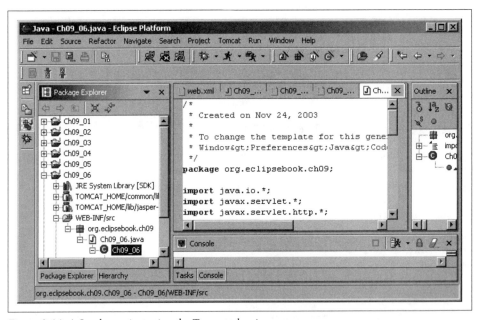

Figure 9-14. A Servlet project using the Tomcat plug-in

As before, the Tomcat plug-in edits the Tomcat *server.xml* document to let Tomcat know where to look for your files:

```
<Context path="/Ch09_06" reloadable="true"
docBase="D:\eclipse211\eclipse\workspace\Ch09_06"
workDir="D:\eclipse211\eclipse\workspace\Ch09_06\work\org\apache\jsp" />
```

There's one more thing to do before running this servlet. The Tomcat plug-in doesn't create a local *web.xml* file to tell Tomcat that *Ch09_06.class* is a servlet, as we have done in the earlier examples in this chapter. To let Tomcat run anonymous servlet classes that have not been defined in a *web.xml* file, you can enable the Tomcat "invoker" servlet by removing the comments around the `servlet-mapping` element in the *web.xml* file in the Tomcat *conf* directory:

```
<!-- The mapping for the invoker servlet -->
<!--
  <servlet-mapping>
    <servlet-name>invoker</servlet-name>
    <url-pattern>/servlet/*</url-pattern>
  </servlet-mapping>
-->
```

When you edit *web.xml* in the Tomcat *conf* directory, the servlet is ready to go; after saving *Ch09_06.java* and building the project, start Tomcat with the Tomcat plug-in's buttons and navigate to *http://localhost:8080/Ch09_06/servlet/org.eclipsebook. ch09.Ch09_06*. You should see the results that appear in Figure 9-15. Congratulations—now you're creating servlets with the Sysdeo Tomcat plug-in.

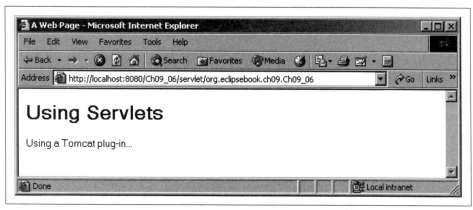

Figure 9-15. Running a servlet with the Tomcat plug-in

Alternatively, if you don't want to edit *web.xml* in the Tomcat *conf* directory to enable anonymous servlets, you can create a local *web.xml* for each project you create with the Tomcat plug-in. To do this, right-click the *WEB-INF* folder in the Package Explorer, select New → File, and enter the XML you see in Example 9-10.

Example 9-10. A web.xml file for use with the Sysdeo plug-in

```
<?xml version="1.0" encoding="ISO-8859-1"?>
<!DOCTYPE web-app PUBLIC "-//Sun Microsystems, Inc.//DTD Web Application 2.3//EN" "http://
java.sun.com/dtd/web-app_2_3.dtd">
<web-app>
  <display-name>Example Applications</display-name>
```

Example 9-10. A web.xml file for use with the Sysdeo plug-in (continued)

```
<servlet>
  <servlet-name>Ch09_06</servlet-name>
  <servlet-class>org.eclipsebook.ch09.Ch09_06</servlet-class>
</servlet>

<servlet-mapping>
  <servlet-name>Ch09_06</servlet-name>
  <url-pattern>/org.eclipsebook.ch09.Ch09_06</url-pattern>
</servlet-mapping>
```

```
</web-app>
```

If you create a local *web.xml* file like this on a project-by-project basis, you don't have to use the word "servlet" in the servlet's URL—in this case, you'll be able to navigate to the servlet with the URL *http://localhost:8080/Ch09_06/org.eclipsebook.ch09.Ch09_06*.

Debugging Web Projects

The Tomcat plug-in also lets you debug servlet code interactively. For example, say you put a breakpoint in the code for the Ch09_06 servlet we just developed at this line in the code:

```
out.println("<HTML>");
out.println("<HEAD>");
out.println("<TITLE>");
out.println("A Web Page");
out.println("</TITLE>");
out.println("</HEAD>");
out.println("<BODY>");
out.println("<H1>");
out.println("Using Servlets");
out.println("</H1>");
out.println("Using a Tomcat plug-in...");
out.println("</BODY>");
out.println("</HTML>");
```

When you start Tomcat and navigate to this servlet in a browser, execution will halt when the breakpoint is reached, and the Eclipse debugger will come up, as you see in Figure 9-16. You're free to single-step through the servlet's code at this point and debug what's going on.

You can also debug JSPs, but you have to work with the servlet code that the JSP is translated into. For example, your JSP *Ch09_04.jsp* in the *webapps/Ch09* directory is translated into the servlet code *Ch09_04_jsp.java* (this name can vary by Tomcat version) in the *work/localhost/ch09* directory before it's run (in the most recent versions of Tomcat, that's become the *work/Standalone/localhost/ch09* directory). The servlet file is the file that you actually debug.

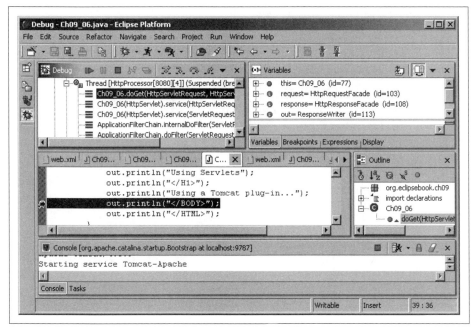

Figure 9-16. Debugging a servlet interactively

Deploying Web Applications

The last topic we'll take a look at in this chapter is all about deploying web applications. This process is easy enough—all you've got to do is create a compressed Web Archive (WAR) file of your application and drop it into the Tomcat *webapps* directory. The next time Tomcat is restarted, it'll expand that WAR file automatically, deploying the application.

As an example, we're going to deploy the servlet you see in Example 9-11. To make the WAR file creation easier, create this new project, Ch09_07, in its own folder, *Ch09_07*, in the *webapps* directory. Make this project a standard Java project (not a Tomcat project). Be sure you give the *Ch09_07* folder its own *WEB-INF* directory with the subdirectories *classes* and *lib*, and make the *classes* folder the output folder for the project. Now create *Ch09_07.java* as we have before, and, after entering the servlet's code into *Ch09_07.java*, build the project.

Example 9-11. A servlet to deploy

```
package org.eclipsebook.ch09;

import javax.servlet.http.HttpServlet;

import java.io.*;
import javax.servlet.*;
import javax.servlet.http.*;
```

Example 9-11. A servlet to deploy (continued)

```
public class Ch09_07 extends HttpServlet {
    public void doGet(HttpServletRequest request,
        HttpServletResponse response)
        throws IOException, ServletException
    {
        response.setContentType("text/html");
        PrintWriter out = response.getWriter();

        out.println("<HTML>");
        out.println("<HEAD>");
        out.println("<TITLE>");
        out.println("A Web Page");
        out.println("</TITLE>");
        out.println("</HEAD>");
        out.println("<BODY>");
        out.println("<H1>");
        out.println("Project Deployment!");
        out.println("</H1>");
        out.println("</BODY>");
        out.println("</HTML>");
    }
}
```

Also add the *web.xml* file you see in Example 9-12 to the project's *WEB-INF* folder to let Tomcat know about this servlet. That gets our servlet working, as you can check by navigating to *http://localhost:8080/Ch09_07/org.eclipsebook.ch09.Ch09_07*.

Example 9-12. web.xml for the servlet to deploy

```
<?xml version="1.0" encoding="ISO-8859-1"?>
<!DOCTYPE web-app PUBLIC "-//Sun Microsystems, Inc.//DTD Web Application 2.3//EN"
"http://java.sun.com/dtd/web-app_2_3.dtd">
<web-app>
  <display-name>Example Applications</display-name>

  <servlet>
    <servlet-name>Ch09_07</servlet-name>
    <servlet-class>org.eclipsebook.ch09.Ch09_07</servlet-class>
  </servlet>

  <servlet-mapping>
    <servlet-name>Ch09_07</servlet-name>
    <url-pattern>/org.eclipsebook.ch09.Ch09_07</url-pattern>
  </servlet-mapping>

</web-app>
```

The next step is to deploy this servlet by compressing it into a WAR file. An easy way to do that in Eclipse is to use Ant, and that can be done with the *build.xml* file you see in Example 9-13, which will compress all the files in the project into a WAR file named *Ch09_07war.war*.

Example 9-13. build.xml for the servlet to deploy

```xml
<?xml version="1.0" encoding = "UTF-8"?>
<project name="Ch09_07" default="Main Build" basedir=".">

    <property name="bin"
        location="d:/tomcat/jakarta-tomcat-4.1.29/webapps/ch09_07"/>
    <property name="wardir"
        location="d:/tomcat/jakarta-tomcat-4.1.29/webapps/ch09_07"/>
    <property name="warfile" location="${wardir}/Ch09_07war.war"/>
    <property name="build.compiler"
        value="org.eclipse.jdt.core.JDTCompilerAdapter"/>

    <target name="Main Build" depends="War">
        <echo message="Ant at work!"/>
    </target>

    <target name="War" >
        <jar destfile="${warfile}" basedir="${bin}"/>
    </target>

</project>
```

To create the WAR file, add *build.xml* to the project. Then right-click *build.xml*, select Run Ant, and click the Run button to create the WAR file *Ch09_07war.war*.

You can deploy the entire web application with this one file—just drop it into the Tomcat *webapps* directory on the user's machine and restart Tomcat. Taking its cue from the name of the WAR file, Tomcat will install the web application in a directory named *Ch09_07war* (note that we didn't name this WAR file *Ch09_07.war* because when Tomcat expanded that WAR file it would have overwritten the existing *Ch09_07* directory).

When the application has been deployed and installed by Tomcat this way, you can run it by navigating to *http://localhost:8080/Ch09_07war/org.eclipsebook.ch09.Ch09_07* in a browser, as you see in Figure 9-17. The servlet has been completely deployed.

Figure 9-17. Deploying a project

That completes this chapter on Eclipse and web development—as you can see, using Eclipse for web development is natural. Creating JSPs, creating servlets, installing files, starting and stopping Tomcat, creating web deployment packages—all of these tasks are no problem with Eclipse.

CHAPTER 10

Developing Struts Applications with Eclipse

In this chapter we're going to take a look at using Eclipse to write Struts-based web applications. This is going to give us experience not only using Struts, but also creating large-scale web applications, including handling build dependencies (where one file needs to be built before another), avoiding deleting files in the output folders when doing a full build (deleting all files in the output folder is called "scrubbing," which Eclipse does by default—and scrubbing a Struts application would delete needed files), organizing your source code files into a folder after the project has already been created, and other issues. We're also going to take a look at a popular Struts plug-in, Easy Struts, to help create Struts applications in Eclipse.

Although we're going to discuss Struts in overview here, we'll assume that if you want to follow the programming in detail, you already have some experience with Struts—in this book, our focus is on Eclipse, not Struts.

Struts is built on Model-View-Controller (MVC) architecture that has become popular in servlet/JSP programming. The original servlet/JSP programming architecture (sometimes called Model 1) was somewhat ad-hoc, using servlets, JSPs, and beans in a way that was completely up to the programmer. Since that time, web applications have become more large-scale, and the MVC architecture (sometimes called Model 2) has been adopted. In MVC programming, the view (often a JSP) handles the visual interface with the user, the model (often a JavaBean) handles the internal logic of the application, and the controller (often a servlet) handles the overall communication between the view and the model as well as forwarding user reqests as needed to other code.

In Struts terminology, the view is constructed using *forms* and the controller with *actions*. The model is often implemented with *form beans*.

Struts and Eclipse

We'll start by taking a look at the Struts example we're going to create using Eclipse, using the latest version of Tomcat available (Version 4.1.29 as of this writing), and the latest version of Struts (Version 1.1). When you navigate to the opening JSP, *http://localhost:8080/Ch10_01/Ch10_01.jsp*, you'll see a menu with a number of HTML controls, as appears in Figure 10-1.

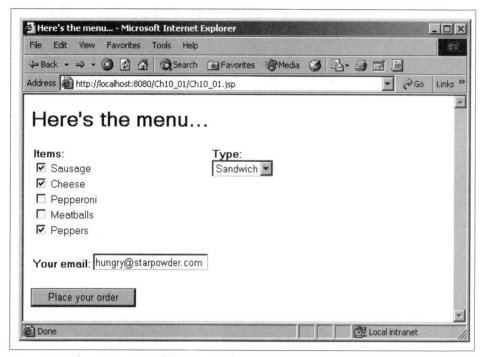

Figure 10-1. The opening view of the Struts application

The user can order a pizza or sandwich using the controls here and can also include his email address. Clicking the "Place your order" button sends the data in the form to an underlying bean and to the application's controller servlet, which displays a summary of the order, as you see in Figure 10-2.

Although these results look pretty simple, that's not to say that the implementation of this application is easy. Struts is not a lightweight framework; to create this example, you use these files, arranged in the Tomcat *webapps/Ch10_01* directory:

```
webapps
|
|__Ch10_01
    |   Ch10_01.jsp [View: Starting form]
    |   Ch10_05.jsp [View: Summary form]
    |
    |__WEB-INF
        |   struts-config.xml [Struts Configuration File]
        |   Ch10.tld  [Custom Tag Definitions]
        |   Struts TLD files [Struts Tag Definitions]
        |   web.xml [Application Descriptor File]
        |
```

```
|__lib
|       struts.jar  [Java Archive of Struts Classes]
|
|__classes
|   |   ApplicationResources.properties [Contains property data]
|   |
|   |__org
|      |
|      |__eclipsebook
|         |
|         |__ch10
|            |__Ch10_02.class  [Custom Tag 1 Implementation]
|               Ch10_03.class  [Custom Tag 2 Implementation]
|               Ch10_04.class  [Controller: Action servlet]
|               Ch10_06.class  [Model: Form bean]
```

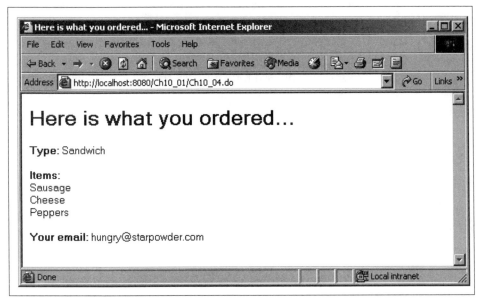

Figure 10-2. The Struts application's summary

The next step is to create this application using Eclipse. To follow along, create a simple Java project named Ch10_01, and create a new folder in the Tomcat *webapps* directory, *Ch10_01*. To get access to this folder in Eclipse, create a new folder by right-clicking the project and selecting New → Folder; name this folder *deployment*, and link it to the *webapps\Ch10_01* folder. Now, in Eclipse, create the folders you need for Java web applications—*WEB-INF*, *lib*, and *classes*—which will also create these folders in the Tomcat *webapps\Ch10_01* folder:

```
deployment
   |
   |__WEB-INF
      |
```

```
|__lib
|
|__classes
```

To handle the compiled output of this project, select the Project → Properties menu item, click the Browse button next to the Default output folder box, create a new folder named *output* linked to the *classes* directory, make sure that folder is selected in the Folder Selection dialog, and click OK. Doing so ensures that the compiled code will go into this directory (actually into *classes\org\eclipsebook\ch10*, following the name of the package we'll create here).

In this case, we purposely didn't create a *src* directory to hold the source code when creating this project as we have in the past, in order to demonstrate that it's easy enough to create a source code folder after a project has been created. To create a new source code folder, right-click the project and select New → Source Folder. Name the new source folder *src*.

Now add *servlet.jar* to the build path (it's in the Tomcat *common\lib* directory), as well as the Struts support JAR file, *struts.jar*. You can get *struts.jar* free at *http://jakarta.apache.org/struts/* in compressed format (the current version is 1.1). Unzip or untar the download to get *struts.jar*, and place that file in the application's *lib* directory. Besides *struts.jar*, we'll also need these JAR files from the download in this example, so place them in the *lib* directory as well:

- *commons-beanutils.jar*
- *commons-collections.jar*
- *commons-digester.jar*

You'll also need these Struts *.tld* (Tag Library Definition files) from the download in the application's *WEB-INF* directory; these files support the custom tags that Struts uses:

- *struts-bean.tld*
- *struts-html.tld*
- *struts-logic.tld*
- *struts-template.tld*

To get started with the code for this example, right-click the new folder and select New → Package to add a new package, *org.eclipsebook.ch10*, to the *src* folder. That sets up the build environment in Eclipse. Now it's time to write some code.

Creating the View

The first file that the user navigates to is the view file *Ch10_01.jsp*. In this file, we use various custom Struts tags to implement the display you see in Figure 10-1. For example, the `<html:form>` tag creates a Struts-enabled form that can display controls, as you see in Example 10-1; we're setting the form's action attribute to the name we'll give the controller, *Ch10_04.do*, so when the user clicks the Submit button (with the caption "Place your order"), the data in the form will be forwarded to the controller.

Example 10-1. A sample JSP

```
<%@ page contentType="text/html;charset=UTF-8" language="java" %>
<%@ taglib uri="/WEB-INF/struts-bean.tld" prefix="bean" %>
<%@ taglib uri="/WEB-INF/struts-html.tld" prefix="html" %>
<%@ taglib uri="/WEB-INF/struts-logic.tld" prefix="logic" %>
<%@ taglib uri="/Ch10" prefix="Ch10" %>

<HTML>
    <HEAD>
        <TITLE>Here's the menu...</TITLE>
    </HEAD>

    <BODY>
        <H1>Here's the menu...</H1>
        <html:errors/>
        <Ch10:type/>
        <Ch10:items/>

        <html:form action="Ch10_04.do">
            <TABLE>
                <TR>
                    <TD ALIGN="LEFT" VALIGN="TOP">
                        <bean:message key="items"/>
                        <BR>
                        <logic:iterate id="items1" name="items">
                            <html:multibox property="items">
                                <%= items1 %>
                            </html:multibox>
                            <%= items1 %>
                            <BR>
                        </logic:iterate>
                    </TD>
                    <TD ALIGN="LEFT" VALIGN="TOP">
                        <bean:message key="type"/>
                        <BR>
                        <html:select property="type">
                            <html:options name="type"/>
                        </html:select>
                    </TD>
                </TR>
                <TR>
                    <TD ALIGN="LEFT">
                        <BR>
                        <bean:message key="email"/>
                        <html:text property="email"/>
                    </TD>
                <TR>
            </TABLE>
```

Example 10-1. A sample JSP (continued)

```
                <BR>
            <html:submit value="Place your order"/>
        </html:form>
    </BODY>
</HTML>
```

Create this file by right-clicking the *deployment* folder in Eclipse and selecting New → File, which automatically stores *Ch10_01.jsp* in the *webapps/Ch10_01* folder.

As you see in Figure 10-1, the drop-down list we're presenting holds the items Pizza, Calzone, and Sandwich, and you can see the list of ingredients—Sausage, Cheese, Pepperoni, Meatballs, and Peppers—represented with a list of checkboxes. To make the items in these lists available to Struts HTML control in the view, we'll use two custom JSP tags, <Ch10:type> to return items like Pizza and Calzone, and <Ch10:items> to return items like Sausage, Cheese, and Pepperoni. As you can see in Example 10-1, we use the Struts <logic:iterate>, <html:multibox>, and <html:options> tags to create the needed HTML controls from those lists of items. You can see the implementation of these custom tags in Example 10-2 and Example 10-3. In Eclipse, create these files and store them in the *src* folder by right-clicking that folder and selecting New → Class, placing the new classes, Ch10_02 and Ch10_03, in the org.eclipsebook.ch10 package.

Example 10-2. A custom tag class for order types

```
package org.eclipsebook.ch10;

import javax.servlet.jsp.tagext.TagSupport;

public class Ch10_02 extends TagSupport
{
    public int doStartTag()
      {

        String[] typeArray = {"", "Pizza", "Calzone", "Sandwich"};

        pageContext.setAttribute("type", typeArray);

        return SKIP_BODY;
    }
}
```

Example 10-3. A custom tag class for pizza toppings

```
package org.eclipsebook.ch10;

import javax.servlet.jsp.tagext.TagSupport;

public class Ch10_03 extends TagSupport
{
```

Example 10-3. A custom tag class for pizza toppings (continued)

```
    public int doStartTag( )
      {
        String[] itemsArray = {"Sausage", "Cheese", "Pepperoni", "Meatballs", "Peppers"};

        pageContext.setAttribute("items", itemsArray);

        return SKIP_BODY;
      }
}
```

To make these custom tags work, we need a tag library descriptor file, which you can see in Example 10-4. This file, named *Ch10.tld*, goes into *deployment\WEB-INF*.

Example 10-4. The TLD for the custom tags

```
<?xml version="1.0"?>
<!DOCTYPE taglib PUBLIC "-//Sun Microsystems, Inc.//DTD JSP Tag Library 1.1//EN"
    "http://java.sun.com/j2ee/dtds/web-jsptaglibrary_1_1.dtd">

<taglib>
    <tlibversion>1.0</tlibversion>
    <jspversion>1.2</jspversion>
    <shortname>StrutsExample</shortname>
    <info>
        Supports the Struts Example
    </info>

    <tag>
        <name>type</name>
        <tagclass>org.eclipsebook.ch10.Ch10_02</tagclass>
        <bodycontent>empty</bodycontent>
    </tag>

    <tag>
        <name>items</name>
        <tagclass>org.eclipsebook.ch10.Ch10_03</tagclass>
        <bodycontent>JSP</bodycontent>
    </tag>
</taglib>
```

Creating the Controller

We've set things up in the view so the data in the HTML controls is sent to *Ch10_04.do*. That's the controller, or action servlet, in our application. We'll connect the extension *.do* to the action servlet for the application in *web.xml*. You can see how that's done in *web.xml* in Example 10-5, using the <servlet> and <servlet-mapping> elements, much as we did in the previous chapter.

Example 10-5. web.xml

```xml
<?xml version="1.0" encoding="ISO-8859-1"?>

<!DOCTYPE web-app
  PUBLIC "-//Sun Microsystems, Inc.//DTD Web Application 2.2//EN"
  "http://java.sun.com/j2ee/dtds/web-app_2_2.dtd">

<web-app>
    <display-name>Struts Example Application</display-name>

  <!-- Action Servlet Configuration -->
  <servlet>
    <servlet-name>action</servlet-name>
    <servlet-class>org.apache.struts.action.ActionServlet</servlet-class>
    <init-param>
      <param-name>application</param-name>
      <param-value>ApplicationResources</param-value>
    </init-param>
    <load-on-startup>2</load-on-startup>
  </servlet>

  <!-- Action Servlet Mapping -->
  <servlet-mapping>
    <servlet-name>action</servlet-name>
    <url-pattern>*.do</url-pattern>
  </servlet-mapping>

  <taglib>
    <taglib-uri>/Ch10</taglib-uri>
    <taglib-location>/WEB-INF/Ch10.tld</taglib-location>
  </taglib>

  <taglib>
    <taglib-uri>/WEB-INF/struts-bean.tld</taglib-uri>
    <taglib-location>/WEB-INF/struts-bean.tld</taglib-location>
  </taglib>

  <taglib>
    <taglib-uri>/WEB-INF/struts-html.tld</taglib-uri>
    <taglib-location>/WEB-INF/struts-html.tld</taglib-location>
  </taglib>

  <taglib>
    <taglib-uri>/WEB-INF/struts-logic.tld</taglib-uri>
    <taglib-location>/WEB-INF/struts-logic.tld</taglib-location>
  </taglib>

</web-app>
```

This file, *web.xml*, goes in the *deployment\WEB-INF* directory in the Eclipse project. That connects the extension *.do* to the action servlet in our application, but we haven't yet specified the actual code for that servlet. You do that in the *struts-config.xml* file, which also goes in the *deployment\WEB-INF* directory. For this example, the action servlet's code is to be *Ch10_04.class*, the summary page that should be displayed if there was no problem with the data entered by the user is *Ch10_05.jsp*, and the bean that will store the data from the user is *Ch10_06.class*. You can see how this works in Example 10-6.

Example 10-6. struts-config.xml

```xml
<?xml version="1.0" encoding="ISO-8859-1" ?>

<!DOCTYPE struts-config PUBLIC
          "-//Apache Software Foundation//DTD Struts Configuration 1.1//EN"
          "http://jakarta.apache.org/struts/dtds/struts-config_1_1.dtd">

<struts-config>

  <form-beans>
    <form-bean name="Ch10_06" type="org.eclipsebook.ch10.Ch10_06"/>
  </form-beans>

  <action-mappings>
    <action path="/Ch10_04"
      type="org.eclipsebook.ch10.Ch10_04"
      name="Ch10_06"
      scope="request"
      input="/Ch10_01.jsp">
      <forward name="OK" path="/Ch10_05.jsp"/>
    </action>

  </action-mappings>

</struts-config>
```

Now the data in the view will be sent to the Ch10_06 bean, and control will pass to the controller, Ch10_04. In the controller, we're passed an object of the bean class that holds the data the user entered into the view's HTML controls, and we'll check that data in the controller's code, as you see in Example 10-7. If the user hasn't entered some of the needed data, we'll display an error message; if the data is OK, we'll forward it on to the summary page, *Ch10_05.jsp*. This file, *Ch10_04.java*, goes into the *src* folder, as do all the other Java source files in the project.

Example 10-7. A forwarding class for Struts

```java
package org.eclipsebook.ch10;

import org.eclipsebook.ch10.Ch10_06;
import javax.servlet.http.HttpServletRequest;
import javax.servlet.http.HttpServletResponse;
import org.apache.struts.action.*;

public class Ch10_04 extends Action
{
```

Example 10-7. A forwarding class for Struts (continued)

```
    public ActionForward execute(ActionMapping mapping,
        ActionForm form,
        HttpServletRequest request,
        HttpServletResponse response)
    throws Exception {

        ActionErrors actionerrors = new ActionErrors( );

        Ch10_06 orderForm = (Ch10_06)form;

        String email = orderForm.getEmail( );
        if(email.trim( ).equals("")) {
            actionerrors.add(ActionErrors.GLOBAL_ERROR, new
                ActionError("error.noemail"));
        }

        String type = orderForm.getType( );
        if(type.trim( ).equals("")) {
            actionerrors.add("ActionErrors.GLOBAL_ERROR", new
                ActionError("error.notype"));
        }

        String[] items = orderForm.getItems( );
        if(items == null) {
            actionerrors.add("ActionErrors.GLOBAL_ERROR", new
                ActionError("error.noitems"));
        }

        if(actionerrors.size( ) != 0) {
            saveErrors(request, actionerrors);
            return new ActionForward(mapping.getInput( ));
        }

        return mapping.findForward("OK");
    }
}
```

The error messages referenced in the action servlet's code are stored in the file *ApplicationResources.properties*, which goes in the *deployment\WEB-INF\classes* directory in the Eclipse project. You can see this file in Example 10-8 (and it's connected to the action servlet in *web.xml*, Example 10-5).

Example 10-8. ApplicationResources.properties

```
email=<b>Your email:</b>
type=<b>Type:</b>
items=<b>Items:</b>

error.noemail=<li><font color="red">Please enter your email address.</font></li>
error.notype=<li><font color="red">Please select a type.</font></li>
error.noitems=<li><font color="red">Please select at least one item.</font></li>
```

Example 10-8. ApplicationResources.properties (continued)

```
errors.header=<font color="red">Please correct the following error(s):<ul>
errors.footer=</ul>
```

If the user omits some data in the view, he'll see one of the error messages in *ApplicationResources.properties*, as you see in Figure 10-3.

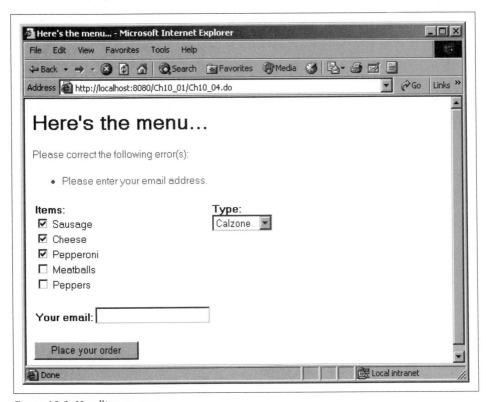

Figure 10-3. Handling an error

Creating the Model

We're almost done with the code for the project; the final two code files are the summary page that displays the data the user entered, *Ch10_05.jsp*, and the bean that acts as the model and stores the data the user entered, *Ch10_06.java*. In the summary page, *Ch10_05.jsp*, we use the data passed on to us in a bean object and various Struts tags to display that data, as you see in Example 10-9. This file goes into the *deployment* directory, the same as the original view, *Ch10_01.jsp*.

Example 10-9. The JSP to display order information

```
<%@ taglib uri="/WEB-INF/struts-bean.tld" prefix="bean" %>
<%@ taglib uri="/WEB-INF/struts-html.tld" prefix="html" %>
<%@ taglib uri="/WEB-INF/struts-logic.tld" prefix="logic" %>
```

Example 10-9. The JSP to display order information (continued)

```
<HTML>
    <HEAD>
        <TITLE>Here is what you ordered...</TITLE>
    </HEAD>

    <BODY>
        <H1>Here is what you ordered...</H1>
        <bean:message key="type"/>
        <bean:write name="Ch10_06" property="type"/>
        <BR>
        <BR>
        <bean:message key="items"/>
        <BR>
        <logic:iterate id="items1" name="Ch10_06" property="items">
            <%= items1 %>
            <BR>
        </logic:iterate>
        <BR>
        <bean:message key="email"/>
        <bean:write name="Ch10_06" property="email"/>
        <BR>
    </BODY>
</HTML>
```

Ch10_06.java, the bean that stores the data the user entered, supports properties corresponding to that data to make it accessible to the controller and the summary page. You can see how this works in Example 10-10. This file, like all the other *.java* files in the project, goes into the *src* folder.

Example 10-10. Form handler

```
package org.eclipsebook.ch10;
import org.apache.struts.action.ActionForm;

public class Ch10_06 extends ActionForm
{

    private String email = "";
    private String type = "";
    private String[] items;

    public String getEmail()
      {
        return email;
      }

    public void setEmail(String email)
      {
        this.email = email;
      }
```

Example 10-10. Form handler (continued)

```java
public String getType( )
  {
    return type;
}

public void setType(String type)
  {
    this.type= type;
}

public String[] getItems( ) {
    return items;
}

public void setItems(String[] items) {
    this.items = items;
}
}
```

That completes the entire application—our first large-scale Eclipse project—but it's still just about the minimum you need for a Struts application. Here's what the project looks like in overview in Eclipse:

```
Ch10_01
    |__src
    |  |__org.eclipsebook.ch10
    |       |__ Ch10_02.java
    |       |__ Ch10_03.java
    |       |__ Ch10_04.java
    |       |__ Ch10_06.java
    |
    |__JRE System Library
    |__servlet.jar
    |__struts.jar
    |
    |__deployment
        |
        |__WEB-INF
        |  |
        |  |__classes
        |  |  |__ApplicationResources.properties
        |  |
        |  |__lib
        |  |  |__commons-beanutils.jar
        |  |  |__commons-collections.jar
        |  |  |__commons-digester.jar
        |  |  |__struts.jar
        |  |
        |  |__Ch10.tld
        |  |__struts-bean.tld
        |  |__struts-config.xml
        |  |__struts-html.tld
```

```
|  |__struts-logic.tld
|  |__struts-template.tld
|  |__web.xml
|
|__Ch10_01.jsp
|__Ch10_05.jsp
```

Before building, there's one thing to note: the code for the action servlet, *Ch10_04.java*, uses objects of the `Ch10_06` class to hold the data the user passed to us:

```
public class Ch10_04 extends Action
{
    public ActionForward execute(ActionMapping mapping,
        ActionForm form,
        HttpServletRequest request,
        HttpServletResponse response)
    throws Exception {

        ActionErrors actionerrors = new ActionErrors();

        Ch10_06 orderForm = (Ch10_06)form;

        String email = orderForm.getEmail();
        .
        .
        .
```

That dependency could be a problem if *Ch10_04.java* were built before *Ch10_06.java*. Although this would be an issue using a build tool like Ant, it's not a problem here. It turns out that Eclipse checks build dependencies like this automatically and resolves them by compiling files in the correct order.

On the other hand, if you have circular dependencies, where file A depends on file B, which in turn depends on file A, you'll get an error. You can enable or disable circular dependencies for a project (the default is disabled) with the Window → Preferences → Java → Compiler → Build Path page, as you see in Figure 10-4. In that dialog, select the Use project settings radio button; then you can set the Circular dependencies item to Error or Warning.

Note also that we've deselected the "Scrub output folders on full build" checkbox in Figure 10-4. To see why that's important, build the project now using either the Project → Build Project or Project → Rebuild Project menu items. When you select the Project → Rebuild Project menu item, which builds everything from scratch, you'll get the expected result, which means all our *.class* files will appear in the *org\eclipsebook\ch10* folder under the *classes* folder, which is what we want:

```
deployment
|
|__WEB-INF
    |
    |__classes
```

```
|__org
   |__eclipsebook
      |__ch10
         |__Ch10_02.class
         |__Ch10_03.class
         |__Ch10_04.class
         |__Ch10_06.class
```

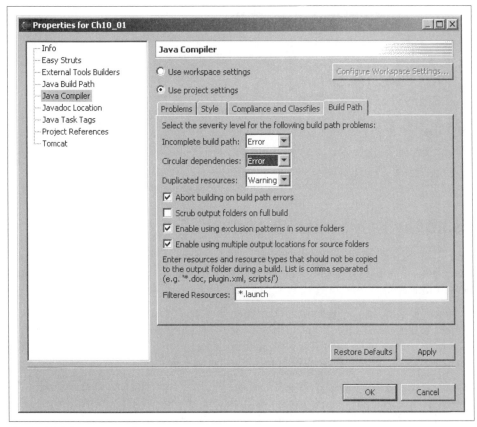

Figure 10-4. Setting compiler options

However, there's a problem: by default, Eclipse *scrubs*—deletes the contents of—the output folder, which we've linked to the *classes* folder. And that folder held the file *ApplicationResources.properties*, which has now been deleted (scrubbing happens by default if you select the Project → Rebuild Project menu item but not if you select the Project → Build Project item).

Accidental scrubbing is the kind of issue we haven't had to deal with when creating smaller projects, but in a larger project with many files, it can be a problem. To solve it, deselect the "Scrub output folders on full build" checkbox, as you see in

Figure 10-4. Now if you rebuild the project, *ApplicationResources.properties* will be preserved and the *.class* files will be built:

```
deployment
  |
  |__WEB-INF
      |
      |__classes
          |__ApplicationResources.properties
          |__org
              |__eclipsebook
                  |__ch10
                      |__Ch10_02.class
                      |__Ch10_03.class
                      |__Ch10_04.class
                      |__Ch10_06.class
```

Now that the project is built, you can run it as you saw in Figures 10-1 and 10-2.

As you can see, there was a lot of code and folder-juggling here, as there usually is when creating Struts applications. There's an Eclipse plug-in that can make life somewhat easier, the Easy Struts plug-in, and we'll take a look at using it next.

Using the Easy Struts Plug-in

The Easy Struts plug-in is available for free from *http://sourceforge.net/projects/easystruts*. This plug-in adds Struts support to a project and has a number of code-generation wizards that let you create actions, forms, and so on.

To use this plug-in, Easy Struts recommends that you start by creating a Tomcat project using the Sysdeo Tomcat plug-in we looked at in Chapter 9 (which means that we'll use an older version of Tomcat in this example, as we did when using the Tomcat plug-in in the previous chapter). Call this Tomcat project Ch10_02.

To work with Easy Struts, you start by configuring the plug-in. Select Window → Preferences, then select the Easy Struts item and the Struts 1.1 tab. Add the Struts JAR files and TLD files so the plug-in knows where to find them, as you see in Figure 10-5. Accept the other defaults by clicking OK.

To add Struts support to the Ch10_02 project, right-click that project and select New → Other, then select the Easy Struts item in the left list and Add Easy Struts support in the right list, as shown in Figure 10-6.

Clicking Next brings up the next pane in the dialog, shown in Figure 10-7, where you can select Struts options; set the package to org.eclipsebook.ch10 and click Finish.

With the current version of the plug-in, you must also select Project → Properties, click the Java Build Path item, followed by the Order and Export tab, then select the TOMCAT_HOME item, and move it, using the Up button, above the TOMCAT_HOME/common/lib/servlet.jar and TOMCAT_HOME/lib/jasper-runtime.jar items so that TOMCAT_HOME

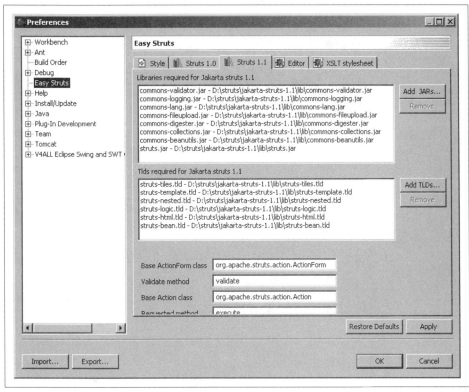

Figure 10-5. Configuring the Easy Struts plug-in

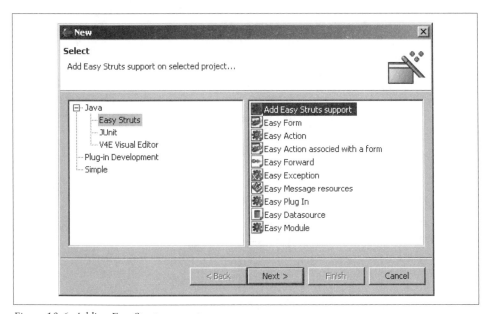

Figure 10-6. Adding EasyStruts support

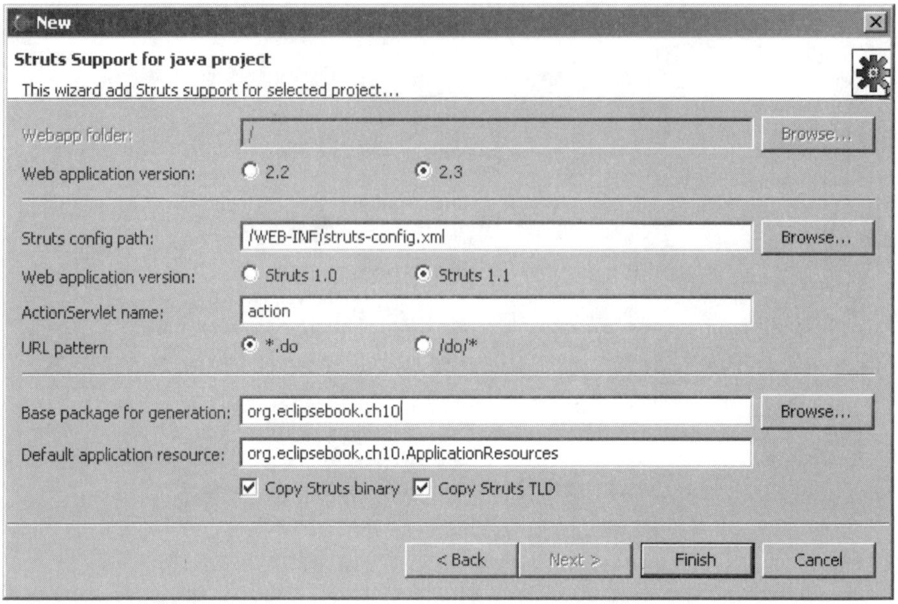

Figure 10-7. Configuring Struts support

will be defined before being used. Making this change removes the warning sign Eclipse displays in the project's icon in the Package Explorer.

Adding Easy Struts support adds the Struts JAR files to the project automatically. To create an input form and a corresponding bean to hold the input form's data, right-click the project and select New → Other, select the Easy Struts item in the left list and the Easy Form item in the right list (you can see this item in Figure 10-6), and click Next to open the dialog you see in Figure 10-8.

Give this new form bean the name Ch10_06 to match the name of our bean in the project we just developed, select the (Create JSP) input checkbox so that Easy Struts will create a JSP form connected to this form bean, and name the JSP form Ch10_01. jsp, as in our earlier project.

Easy Struts gives you some rudimentary support for creating properties in the form bean, along with associated HTML controls in the JSP page. To do that, you click the Add button next to the Form properties box. The only one of our controls that is simple, however, is the text box where the user can enter his email address (the other controls are a more advanced checkbox list and a select control, which Easy Struts can't help us with), so click the Add button, enter the name of the property to add, email, leave its type as java.lang.String, and select the HTML text control as the associated control to create in the JSP form. When done, click Finish to add the new property to the form and click Finish to create *Ch10_01.jsp* and *Ch10_06.java*. You can see the resulting *Ch10_01.jsp* in Example 10-11 and *Ch10_06.java* in Example 10-12. They're good starts, but a lot of programming is required to make them match our earlier code.

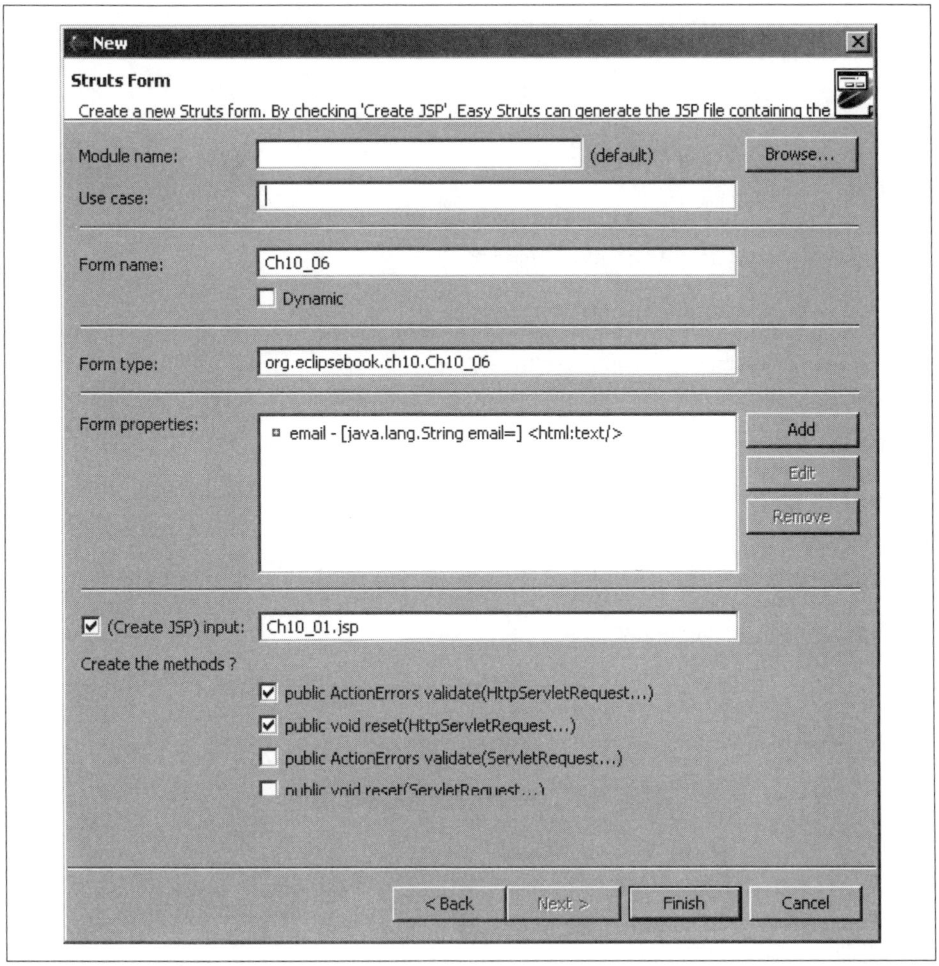

Figure 10-8. Creating a form

Example 10-11. Generated JSP file

```jsp
<%@ taglib uri="/WEB-INF/struts-bean.tld" prefix="bean"%>
<%@ taglib uri="/WEB-INF/struts-html.tld" prefix="html"%>
<html>
    <head>
        <meta name = "Generator" content = "Easy Struts Xslt generator for Eclipse
        (http://easystruts.sf.net).">

        <title>Struts Form for Ch10_06</title>
    </head>
    <body>
        <html:form action="/[ACTION_PATH]">
            email : <html:text property="email"/><html:errors
                property="email"/></br>
            <html:submit/><html:cancel/>
```

Example 10-11. Generated JSP file (continued)

```
        </html:form>
    <body>
</html>
```

Example 10-12. Generated Java file

```java
package org.eclipsebook.ch10;

import javax.servlet.http.HttpServletRequest;

import org.apache.struts.action.ActionErrors;
import org.apache.struts.action.ActionForm;
import org.apache.struts.action.ActionMapping;

/**
 * Ch10_06.java created by EasyStruts - XsltGen.
 * http://easystruts.sf.net
 * created on 12-02-2003
 *
 * XDoclet definition:
 * @struts:form name="Ch10_06"
 */
public class Ch10_06 extends ActionForm {

    // --------------------------------------------------------- Instance Variables

    /** email property */
    private String email;

    // --------------------------------------------------------- Methods

    /**
     * Method validate
     * @param ActionMapping mapping
     * @param HttpServletRequest request
     * @return ActionErrors
     */
    public ActionErrors validate(
        ActionMapping mapping,
        HttpServletRequest request) {

        throw new UnsupportedOperationException(
            "Generated method 'validate(...)' not implemented.");
    }

    /**
     * Returns the email.
     * @return String
     */
    public String getEmail() {
        return email;
    }
```

Example 10-12. Generated Java file (continued)

```
    /**
     * Set the email.
     * @param email The email to set
     */
    public void setEmail(String email) {
        this.email = email;
    }

}
```

To create an action servlet, right-click the project, select New → Other, select Easy
Struts in the list on the right as before, select Easy Action in the list on the right, and
click Next. This opens the dialog you see in Figure 10-9.

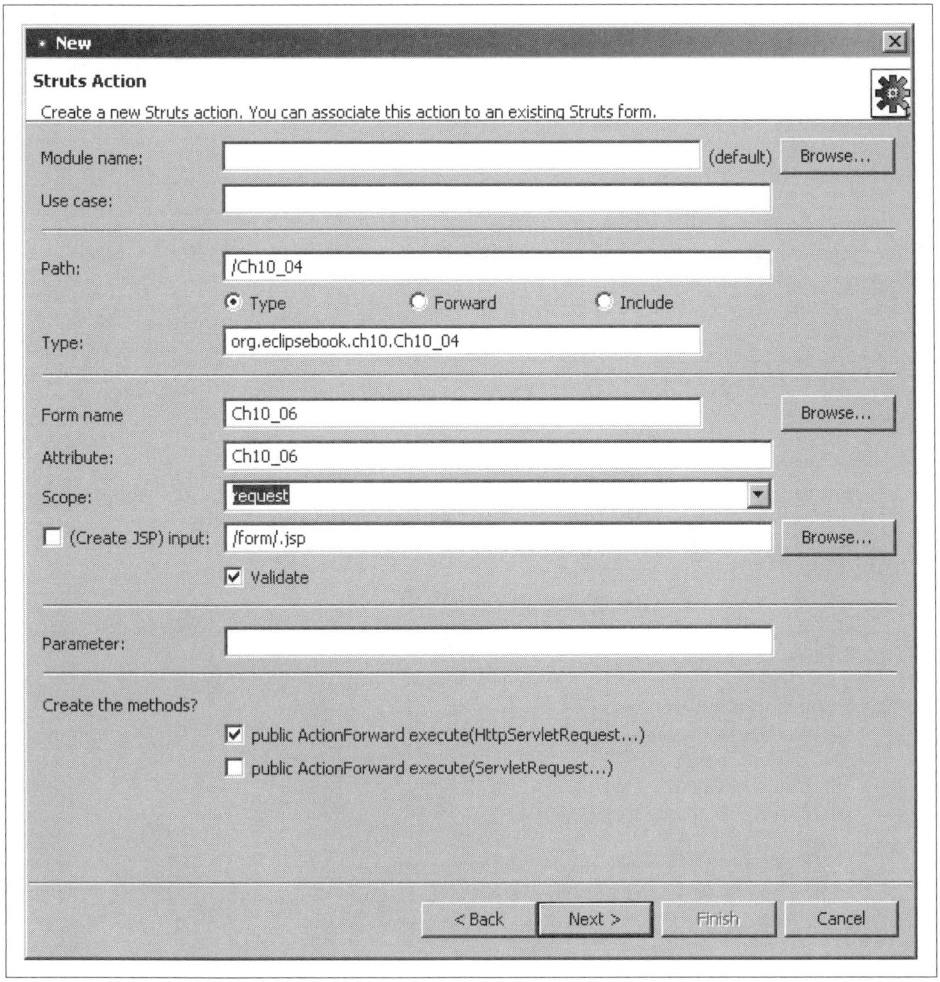

Figure 10-9. Creating an action

Clicking the Next button takes you to the next pane, where you can create forwards to other servlets and JSPs; in this case, just click Finish to generate the action servlet skeleton for *Ch10_04.java* you see in Example 10-13. As you can see, the backbone of an action servlet is there, but it will take a lot of work to add all the code we had in our earlier version of this file.

Example 10-13. Generated servlet code

```java
package org.eclipsebook.ch10;

import javax.servlet.http.HttpServletRequest;
import javax.servlet.http.HttpServletResponse;

import org.apache.struts.action.Action;
import org.apache.struts.action.ActionForm;
import org.apache.struts.action.ActionForward;
import org.apache.struts.action.ActionMapping;

/**
 * Ch10_04.java created by EasyStruts - XsltGen.
 * http://easystruts.sf.net
 * created on 12-02-2003
 *
 * XDoclet definition:
 * @struts:action path="/Ch10_04" name="Ch10_06" input="/form/.jsp" validate="true"
 */
public class Ch10_04 extends Action {

    // -------------------------------------------------------- Instance Variables

    // -------------------------------------------------------- Methods

    /**
     * Method execute
     * @param ActionMapping mapping
     * @param ActionForm form
     * @param HttpServletRequest request
     * @param HttpServletResponse response
     * @return ActionForward
     * @throws Exception
     */
    public ActionForward execute(
        ActionMapping mapping,
        ActionForm form,
        HttpServletRequest request,
        HttpServletResponse response)
        throws Exception {
        Ch10_06 Ch10_06 = (Ch10_06) form;
        throw new UnsupportedOperationException(
            "Generated method 'execute(...)' not implemented.");
    }

}
```

As you can see, Easy Struts provides skeletal code for the various parts of a Struts program, and it's up to you to fill in the details. We're not going to go through the whole process here, but if you're interested, the Ch10_02 file in the download for this book is the resulting application—the same as the one we created earlier in this chapter—but it's based on Easy Struts.

That completes our look at Eclipse and building Struts projects manually and with a plug-in. Struts applications need a lot of code and multiple files, but that's been useful to us since it gave us a look at developing larger scale applications with Eclipse. In the next two chapters, we're going to take a look at developing our own plug-ins.

CHAPTER 11

Developing a Plug-in: The Plug-in Development Environment, Manifests, and Extension Points

In this chapter and the next, we're going to start modifying Eclipse itself. So far, we've been using it as we've downloaded it, adding a few prebuilt plug-ins as needed. Now we're going to start creating our own plug-ins. Eclipse was built as an extensible IDE, and we're going to extend it.

As you know, plug-ins are stored in folders in the *plugins* directory, and that's where the ones we create will go. These folders typically have names like *org.eclipse.swt. win32_2.1.1* or *org.junit_3.8.1*, where the folder name is the plug-in name, followed with an underscore and a version number. When Eclipse loads a plug-in that has several folders in the *plugins* directory, it checks the version number in order to load only the most recent version.

You'll typically find the following files in every plug-in's folder:

*.jar
    Java code for the plug-in

about.html
    Displayed when the user asks for info about the plug-in

plugin.properties
    Holds string data used by *plugin.xml*

plugin.xml
    Plug-in manifest that describes the plug-in to Eclipse

lib
    Holds additional JAR files

icons
    Directory for icons (GIF format is standard)

We'll see these various files as we develop plug-ins, but we'll start with the minimum needed. The *plugin.xml* file is the plug-in manifest, which tells Eclipse about the plug-in. In fact, that's the only file you really need to create a plug-in as far as Eclipse is concerned.

All You Really Need Is plugin.xml

Creating a very simple plug-in is easy enough—all you need is a working *plugin.xml*. To show how this works, you can use a text editor to create a new plug-in manifest, *plugin.xml*, for a fictional plug-in named org.eclipsebook.first. In this case, we'll set the plug-in's name, ID, version number, and the name of its provider like this:

```
<?xml version="1.0" encoding="UTF-8"?>
<plugin
    id="org.eclipsebook.first"
    name="First Plug-in"
    version="1.0.0"
    provider-name="Steve">
</plugin>
```

Just store *plugin.xml* in *plugins\org.eclipsebook.first_1.0.0* and restart Eclipse. You can find the new plug-in in the plug-in registry, which is where Eclipse holds data about all current plug-ins. To see that data, select Help → About Eclipse Platform and click the Plug-in Details button, opening the About Eclipse Platform Plug-ins dialog you see in Figure 11-1.

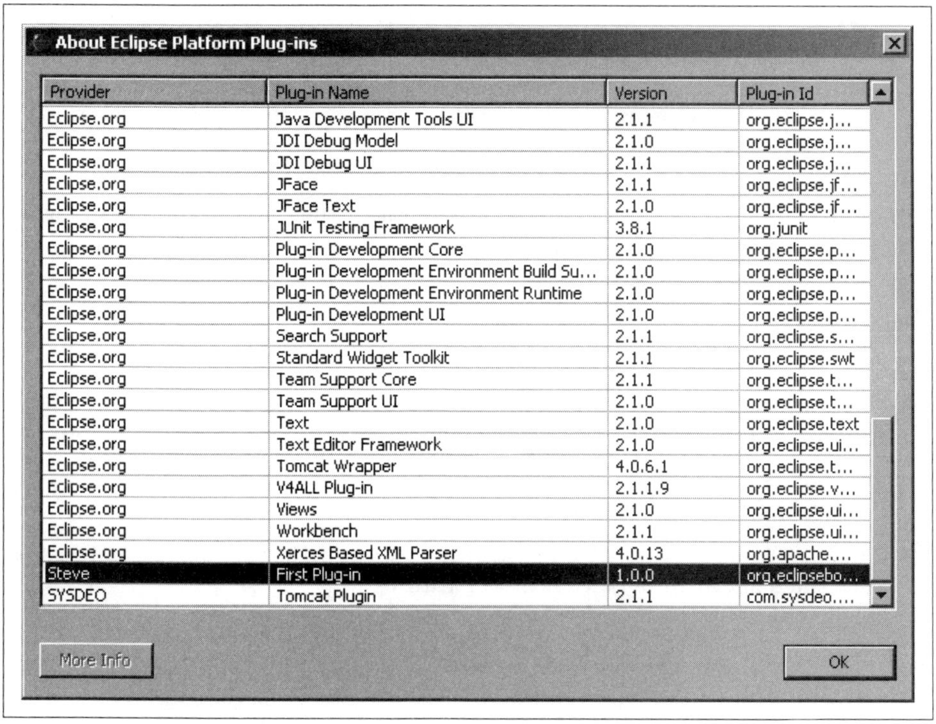

Provider	Plug-in Name	Version	Plug-in Id
Eclipse.org	Java Development Tools UI	2.1.1	org.eclipse.j…
Eclipse.org	JDI Debug Model	2.1.0	org.eclipse.j…
Eclipse.org	JDI Debug UI	2.1.1	org.eclipse.j…
Eclipse.org	JFace	2.1.1	org.eclipse.jf…
Eclipse.org	JFace Text	2.1.0	org.eclipse.jf…
Eclipse.org	JUnit Testing Framework	3.8.1	org.junit
Eclipse.org	Plug-in Development Core	2.1.0	org.eclipse.p…
Eclipse.org	Plug-in Development Environment Build Su…	2.1.0	org.eclipse.p…
Eclipse.org	Plug-in Development Environment Runtime	2.1.0	org.eclipse.p…
Eclipse.org	Plug-in Development UI	2.1.0	org.eclipse.p…
Eclipse.org	Search Support	2.1.1	org.eclipse.s…
Eclipse.org	Standard Widget Toolkit	2.1.1	org.eclipse.swt
Eclipse.org	Team Support Core	2.1.1	org.eclipse.t…
Eclipse.org	Team Support UI	2.1.0	org.eclipse.t…
Eclipse.org	Text	2.1.0	org.eclipse.text
Eclipse.org	Text Editor Framework	2.1.0	org.eclipse.ui…
Eclipse.org	Tomcat Wrapper	4.0.6.1	org.eclipse.t…
Eclipse.org	V4ALL Plug-in	2.1.1.9	org.eclipse.v…
Eclipse.org	Views	2.1.0	org.eclipse.ui…
Eclipse.org	Workbench	2.1.1	org.eclipse.ui…
Eclipse.org	Xerces Based XML Parser	4.0.13	org.apache.…
Steve	First Plug-in	1.0.0	org.eclipsebo…
SYSDEO	Tomcat Plugin	2.1.1	com.sysdeo.…

Figure 11-1. The plug-in registry

You can see the new, fictional plug-in in the registry, near the bottom.

If an Eclipse project has a plug-in manifest, it's considered a plug-in project.

That's a nice exercise but it doesn't go very far in extending Eclipse. Developing a real plug-in involves creating multiple files, including multiple code files. The good news is that Eclipse has built-in wizards to help you out.

Using the Plug-in Development Environment

The Eclipse platform is already a conglomeration of over a hundred plug-ins, and they build on each other using *extension points*. An extension point lets one plug-in build on what another plug-in exports. In this chapter, we're going to use extension points to add new menus, buttons, and so on to Eclipse in a plug-in.

Plug-ins can only make use of classes exported by other plug-ins, which makes extension points especially important. For example, to let a plug-in make use of prebuilt Java code, you can wrap JAR files inside plug-ins and let other plug-ins depend on it. Much support for custom plug-ins is already built into several standard plug-ins that come with Eclipse.

Using the Eclipse Plug-in Development Environment (PDE), you can build plug-ins that will build on the standard extension points available. Here are the types of plug-in projects that the PDE will create for you:

Plug-in projects
> A standard plug-in

Fragment projects
> An add-on or addition to a plug-in (sometimes used for internationalization)

Feature projects
> Projects that contain one or more plug-ins

Update site projects
> Web site that can automatically install features

The PDE has a number of built-in Wizards, and we're going to make use of that support in our next example. This example will create a simple plug-in that supports both a menu item and a button in the toolbar. To create the plug-in project, select File → New → Project. Select Plug-in Development in the left box of the New Project dialog and Plug-in Project in the right box, as shown in Figure 11-2. Then click Next.

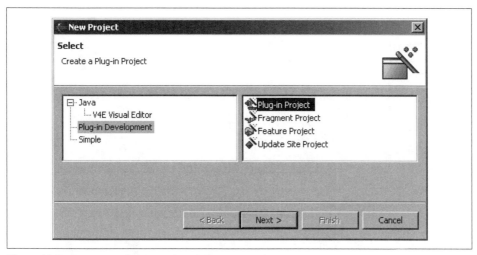

Figure 11-2. Creating a plug-in project

In the next pane, name the project org.eclipsebook.ch11.Ch11_01, as you see in Figure 11-3, and click Next. This project name will also be the ID of the plug-in when it comes time to use it in Eclipse.

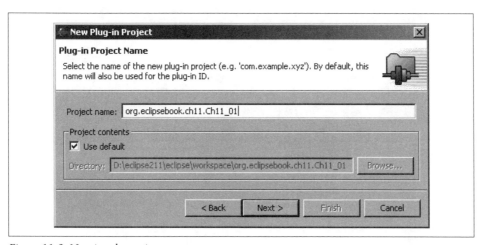

Figure 11-3. Naming the project

In the next pane, make sure the "Create a Java project" radio button is selected, as you see in Figure 11-4, and click Next.

The next pane is the Plug-in Code Generators pane, shown in Figure 11-5. We're going to select the built-in "Hello, World" example here, so select the "Hello, World" item in the left box and click Next. (This pane also allows you to create other types of plug-in projects, such as plug-ins with editors, views, and so on.)

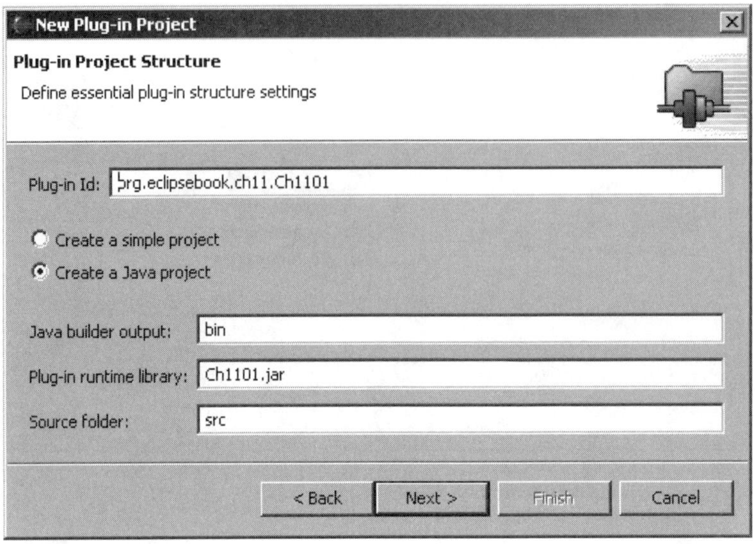

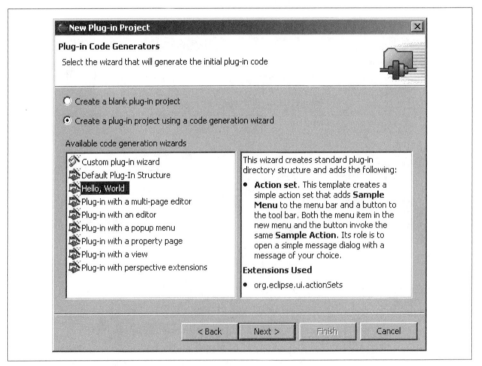

Figure 11-4. Setting the project type

Figure 11-5. Creating a Hello, World example

In the following pane you can configure the plug-in. Enter a provider name—we'll use Eclipse Book—and accept the other defaults, which appear in Figure 11-6. Click Finish to create the code for this plug-in (clicking Next here would let you set the text the plug-in displays in its message box, but the default text is fine).

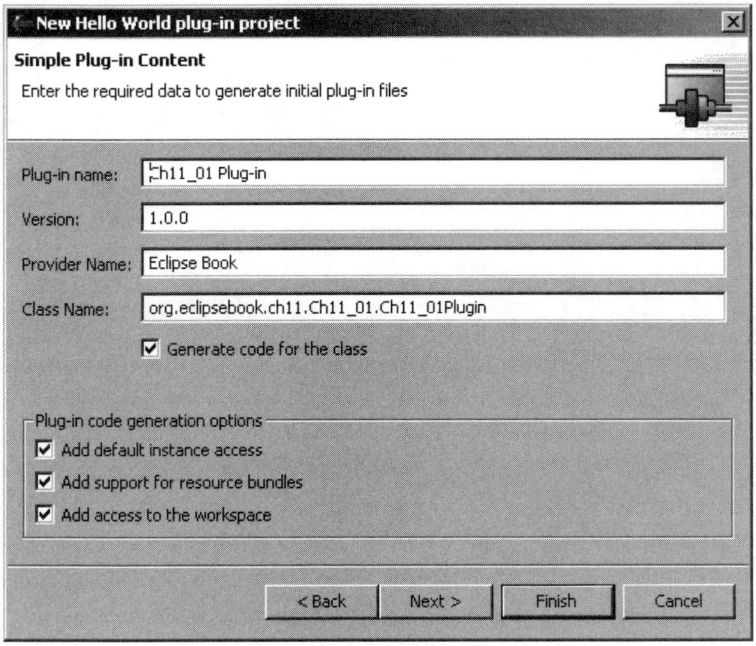

Figure 11-6. Configuring the plug-in

Clicking Finish opens the plug-in manifest editor, as you see in Figure 11-7, where it's displaying a Welcome page. You can open the editor later yourself by double-clicking *plugin.xml* in the Package Explorer.

The plug-in manifest editor looks simple, but there's a lot going on here. Note, in particular, the tabs at the bottom of the editor:

Welcome
> The Welcome page you see in Figure 11-7, describing the plug-in

Overview
> Holds summary information for the plug-in, such as name, version, provider name, and so on

Dependencies
> Indicates the plug-ins required for this plug-in

Runtime
> Indicates the libraries needed to run this plug-in

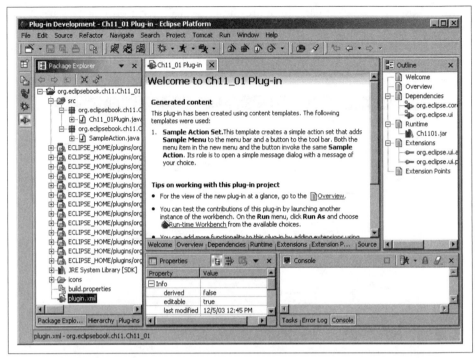

Figure 11-7. The plug-in manifest editor

Extensions
> Indicates the extensions points used by the plug-in

Extension Points
> Indicates the extension points defined by the plug-in

Source
> An XML editor that lets you edit the source code for *plugin.xml*

The manifest editor lets you edit *plugin.xml*, either directly by clicking the Source button, or by using the various tabs in the editor. For example, to build on the standard extension points, you can click the Extensions tab and use the Add button to add functionality to your plug-in, as we'll do later in this chapter. When you make changes this way, the PDE edits *plugin.xml* for you automatically, saving you the trouble of editing raw XML.

Using the Run-time Workbench

At this point, you could create *Ch11_01.jar*, and install that JAR file, *plugin.xml*, and so on in the *plugins* directory and you'd be ready to go—the new plug-in would support a menu item and a toolbar button. But for testing purposes, Eclipse offers a shortcut: the Run-time Workbench. This is a workbench that you can launch from Eclipse and use to test plug-ins.

To run the Run-time Workbench, select the plug-in project in the Package Explorer, select Run → Run, open the Run-time Workbench node in the left box, and select the Run-time Workbench item under that node, as you can see in Figure 11-8. Then select the JRE you want to use when working with the Run-time Workbench (you don't need to do this step if you have an installed JRE you've named JRE2, which is what the Run-time Workbench seaches for by default). Then click Run. (The next time, you can simply select Run → Run As → Run-time Workbench.)

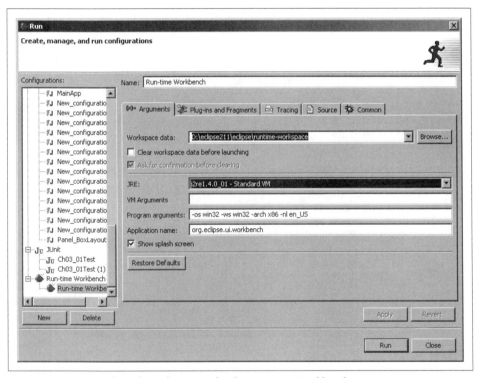

Figure 11-8. Setting a launch configuration for the Run-time Workbench

This starts the Run-time Workbench, but we're not done yet. To see the results of this plug-in, select Window → Customize Perspective → Other and select the checkbox for the Sample Action Set item, which is defined by our plug-in, and click OK. This adds the menu defined by the new plug-in, Sample Menu, to the menu bar and a button with the Eclipse icon to the toolbar just under that menu, as you can see in the Run-time Workbench in Figure 11-9.

When you select the Sample Menu → Sample Action item or click the New button, the plug-in displays a message box with the message "Hello, Eclipse World", as you see in Figure 11-10.

Congratulations—you've created a working Eclipse plug-in that's running. To end the example, close the Run-time Workbench.

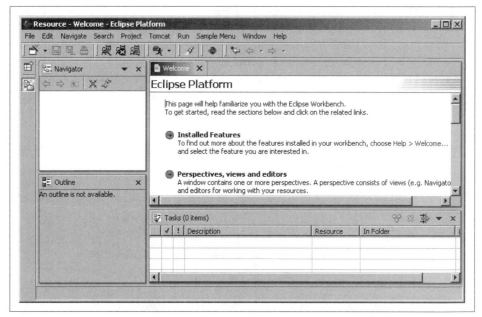

Figure 11-9. The Run-time Workbench

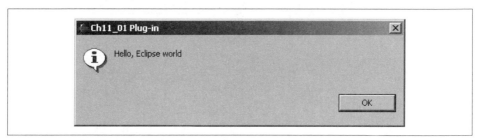

Figure 11-10. The plug-in's message box

 You can debug your code as you would any other. Just select Run → Debug As → Run-time Workbench.

In this case, the PDE wizards created the needed code for this sample plug-in. In the next example, we're going to build the code ourselves.

Creating a Standard Plug-in

In this example, we're going to be responsible for creating our own plug-in. Like the previous example, this plug-in is going to have its own menu item and toolbar button, but this time, we're going to do the legwork ourselves.

Start by selecting File → New → Project. In the New Project dialog, select Plug-in Development and Plug-in Project, and click Next. In the next pane, enter the new project's name, `org.eclipsebook.ch11.Ch11_02`, and click Next to open the Plug-in Project Structure pane. Click Next again to accept the defaults.

In the Plug-in Code Generators pane, select the Default Plug-In Structure item as shown in Figure 11-11, and click Next.

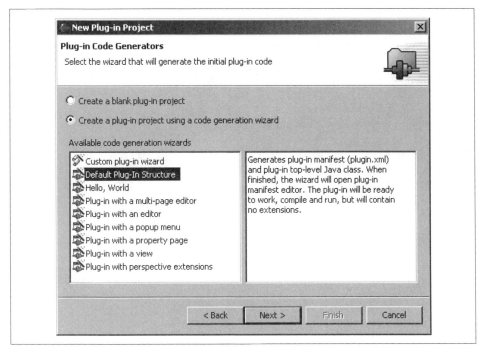

Figure 11-11. Setting the plug-in's code wizard

In the following pane, the Simple Plug-in Content pane shown in Figure 11-12, set the provider name—we'll use `Eclipse Book` in this example. We won't need the convenience methods the wizard can generate for us, so deselect the checkboxes in the "Plug-in code generation options" box. Then click Finish.

This should generate the `Ch11_02` plug-in, and open the manifest editor in Eclipse. Click the Source page, which displays the XML in *plugin.xml*:

```
<?xml version="1.0" encoding="UTF-8"?>
<plugin
    id="org.eclipsebook.ch11.Ch1102"
    name="Ch11_02 Plug-in"
    version="1.0.0"
    provider-name="Eclipse Book"
    class="org.eclipsebook.ch11.Ch11_02.Ch11_02Plugin">
```

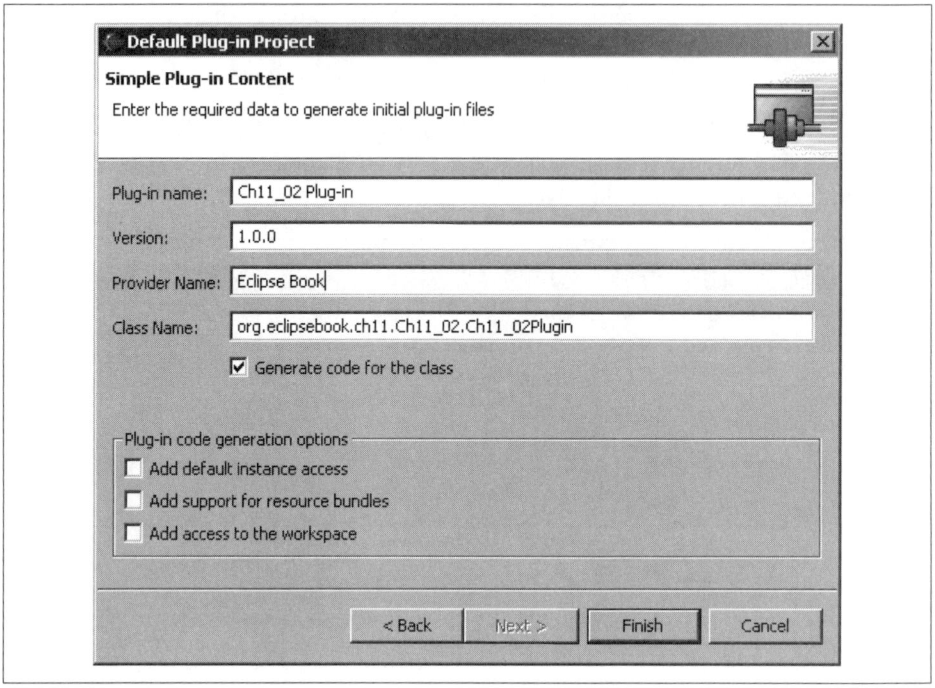

Figure 11-12. Setting code options

```
<runtime>
    <library name="Ch1102.jar"/>
</runtime>
<requires>
    <import plugin="org.eclipse.core.resources"/>
    <import plugin="org.eclipse.ui"/>
</requires>
```

```
</plugin>
```

That's our new plug-in's manifest. Our goal in this plug-in is to add a new menu item and a button in the toolbar. To make things happen in a plug-in, you define *actions* and *action sets*.

An action represents a command that the user can trigger. To implement what goes on in an action, you extend the Action class. You can work with the same Action object in a variety of situations, as when the user selects a menu item or clicks a toolbar button—the action object will make the same thing happen in either case. In this way, the same action can be initiated by different user-interface elements.

As you can guess from the name, an action set is a set of actions. You tie actions to user-interface elements like menus and toolbars with an action set (the <actionSet> element in *plugin.xml* typically contains both <menu> elements and <action> elements). An action is a Java object defining what you want to have happen when the user issues a specific command, and an action set ties actions to user-interface elements.

You create action sets as extensions of the `org.eclipse.ui.actionSets` extension point, which is how you implement menu items or buttons in a plug-in. You could implement this extension in the XML in *plugin.xml* directly, but it's much easier to use the manifest editor.

Creating an Action Set

To see how to create an action set to tie a menu and toolbar button to an action, click the Extension tab in the manifest editor and click Add to open the New Extension wizard you see in Figure 11-13. Select the Generic Wizards item in the left box, the Schema-based Extension in the right box, and click Next.

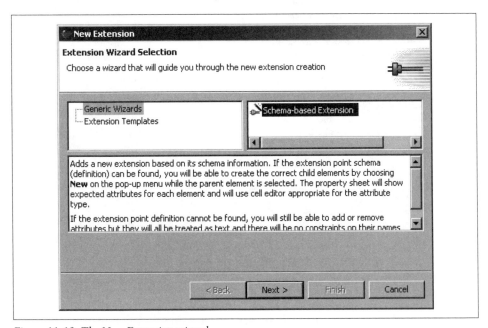

Figure 11-13. The New Extension wizard

The next pane is the Extension Point Selection pane, which you can see in Figure 11-14. In this case, we want to add support for a menu item and a toolbar button, which is all handled together in our action set, so select the `org.eclipse.ui.actionSets` extension point, and click Finish.

This adds the base extension we'll need for toolbar and menu support. To create the action set that we'll use, right-click the `org.eclipse.ui.actionSets` item in the All Extensions box and select the New → actionSet item, creating a new action set as you see in Figure 11-15.

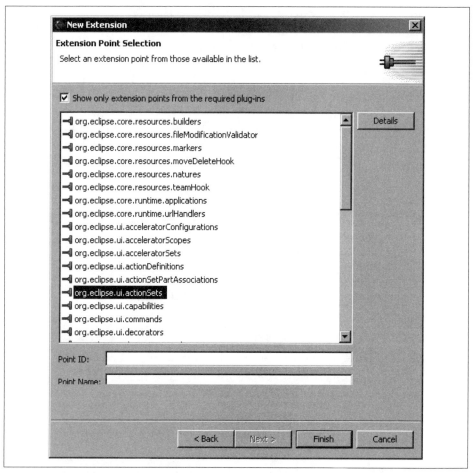

Figure 11-14. Selecting an extension point

To set the properties of this new action set, select it and, in the Properties view, set the `label` property to New Action Set and the `visible` property to true. Using the manifest editor in this way lets you edit the XML in *plugin.xml* automatically; here's the new XML we've created, indicating that this extension contains an action set:

```
<extension
    point="org.eclipse.ui.actionSets">
  <actionSet
      label="New Action Set"
      visible="true"
      id="org.eclipsebook.ch11.Ch11_02.actionSet1">
  </actionSet>
</extension>
```

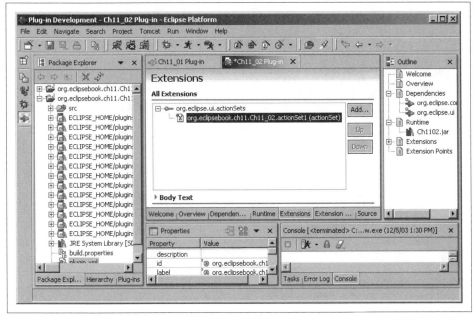

Figure 11-15. Creating an action set

Creating a Menu

To create a new menu, right-click New Action Set in the Extensions tab and select New → menu. In the Properties view, set the `id` property of the new menu to new-Menu, and the `label` property to New Menu, as you see in Figure 11-16.

To add a menu item here, we'll create a menu separator, which acts as a placeholder and will allow us to add items to this menu at runtime. To add the menu separator, right-click New Menu and select New → separator. In the Properties view, set the separator's name property to newGroup, as you see in Figure 11-17.

Our action set has a new menu at this point, and the next step is to tie an action to that menu. If you have multiple menus and multiple toolbar buttons, they could all go into the same action set (which would group your toolbar buttons next to each other in the toolbar).

Creating an Action

Now we'll add a new action to connect Java code to the menu and toolbar handling supported by the action set. To create a new action, right-click the New Action Set item in the All Extensions box and select New → action.

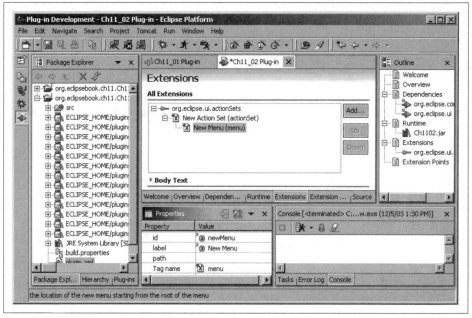

Figure 11-16. Creating a new menu

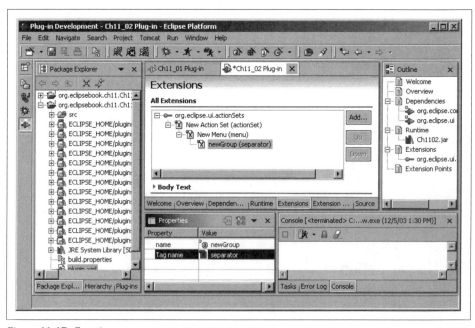

Figure 11-17. Creating a menu separator

To customize this action, we'll create a menu item and toolbar item that will display the message "No worries." To do that, select the new action in the Extensions box. In the Properties view, set the label property to New Action and the toolTip property to No worries. Next, set the menubarPath property to newMenu/newGroup and the toolbarPath property to newGroup.

Now we need to connect this action to Java code. To do that, select the action, New Action, in the All Extensions box, and click the ellipsis ("...") button that appears when you select the class property in the Properties view. This opens the Java Attribute Editor you see in Figure 11-18. Click the Generate a new Java class radio button, enter org.eclipsebook.ch11.Ch11_02 in the Package name box (or click the Browse button and select that package), and name the class NewAction, as you see in the figure. Then click Finish.

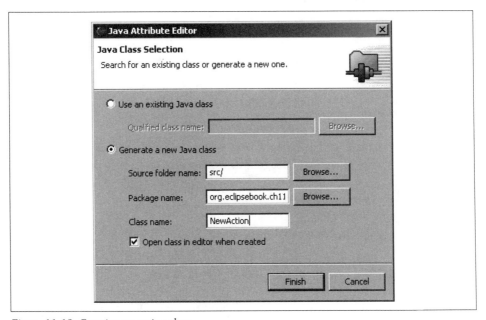

Figure 11-18. Creating an action class

This will create a new <action> element in *plugin.xml*:

```
<action
      label="New Action"
      tooltip="No worries."
      class="org.eclipsebook.ch11.Ch11_02.NewAction"
      menubarPath="newMenu/newGroup"
      toolbarPath="newGroup"
      id="org.eclipsebook.ch11.Ch11_02.action1">
</action>
```

In addition, a new Java file, *NewAction.java*, has been created and added to the project. The framework of the plug-in is in place; all that's left is to write the code that will actually display a message box when the toolbar button or menu item is selected.

Writing the Code

Open *NewAction.java* now. To display a message box, we'll need an object implementing the Workbench window interface, `IWorkbenchWindow`. The object we need is passed to the init method in *NewAction.java*, so begin by creating a private class variable, `workbenchWindow`, to hold it:

```
public class NewAction implements IWorkbenchWindowActionDelegate {
    private IWorkbenchWindow workbenchWindow;
       .
       .
       .
```

We'll store the workbench window passed to us in the `init` method in this variable this way:

```
public void init(IWorkbenchWindow window)  {
    workbenchWindow = window;
}
```

Now use this variable and the `openInformation` method of the `MessageDialog` class to display a message box with the message "No worries." in the `run` method:

```
public void run(IAction action)  {
    MessageDialog.openInformation(
    workbenchWindow.getShell( ),
    "New Plug-in",
    "No worries.");
}
```

Then save all files. That completes the plug-in development; to test this new plug-in, launch the Run-time Workbench. Select Window → Customize Perspective as before, and select the box next to the New Action Set item. Doing so should give you the result you see in Figure 11-19, where you can see the default square button icon Eclipse uses for toolbar buttons and the new menu, New Menu.

When you select the New Menu → New Action menu item or click the new button, you should see the New Plug-In message box, shown in Figure 11-20. Congratulations—the new plug-in is doing exactly what it should.

Automatically Customizing a Perspective

The business of having to customize the perpective every time you launch a new plug-in using Window → Customize Perspective is a little cumbersome. There's a way around it if you use the extension point `org.eclipse.ui.perspectiveExtensions` in *plugin.xml*, which can add the plug-in to a perspective automatically. It's easy

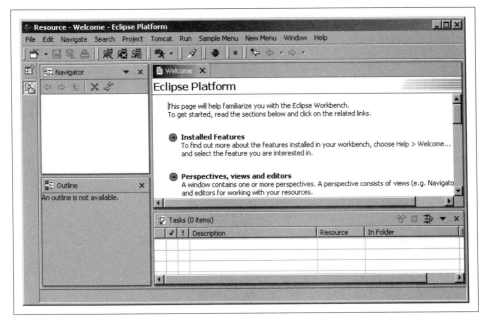

Figure 11-19. Using the new plug-in

Figure 11-20. The message from the new plug-in

enough to make this change simply by editing the XML in *plugin.xml* to use the extension point org.eclipse.ui.perspectiveExtensions. For example, to automatically add our plug-in to the Java perspective, you can use the org.eclipse.ui. javaPerspective class like this in *plugin.xml*:

```
<?xml version="1.0" encoding="UTF-8"?>
<plugin
    id="org.eclipsebook.ch11.Ch1102"
    name="Ch11_02 Plug-in"
    version="1.0.0"
    provider-name="Eclipse Book"
    class="org.eclipsebook.ch11.Ch11_02.Ch11_02Plugin">

    <runtime>
        <library name="Ch1102.jar"/>
    </runtime>
```

```
<requires>
   <import plugin="org.eclipse.core.resources"/>
   <import plugin="org.eclipse.ui"/>
</requires>

<extension
      point="org.eclipse.ui.actionSets">
   <actionSet
         label="New Action Set"
         visible="true"
         id="org.eclipsebook.ch11.Ch11_02.actionSet1">
      <menu
            label="New Menu"
            id="newMenu">
         <separator
               name="newGroup">
         </separator>
      </menu>
      <action
            label="New Action"
            tooltip="No worries."
            class="org.eclipsebook.ch11.Ch11_02.NewAction"
            menubarPath="newMenu/newGroup"
            toolbarPath="newGroup"
            id="org.eclipsebook.ch11.Ch11_02.action1">
      </action>
   </actionSet>
</extension>
<extension
   point = "org.eclipse.ui.perspectiveExtensions">
   <perspectiveExtension
      targetID="org.eclipse.ui.javaPerspective">
      <actionSet
         id="org.eclipsebook.ch11.Ch11_02.actionSet1">
      </actionSet>
   </perspectiveExtension>
</extension>
</plugin>
```

To automatically add the plug-in to the Resource perspective, use the class org.eclipse.ui.resourcePerspective instead. Save *plugin.xml* after you make these changes and restart the Run-time Workbench. The plug-in should be installed on startup.

CHAPTER 12

Developing a Plug-in: Creating Editors and Views

In this chapter, we're going to create custom editors and views in plug-ins. Plug-in development is a huge topic by itself, and it can take dozens of files to create a commercial plug-in. Fortunately, the Eclipse PDE comes with a number of wizards that will write up the plug-in's code framework for you, saving significant time. We'll see how to use those wizards in this chapter, rewriting the code they generate to make the plug-in do what we want.

Creating a Multi-Page Editor

The first example in this chapter is going to create a multi-page editor associated with the file extension we're going to specify: *.xyz*. When the user double-clicks a file with that extension in the Package Explorer, Eclipse will use our editor to open and edit it. That editor will have two tabs corresponding to its two pages—the default tab will display the text contents of the file, and the Sorted tab will display those contents sorted in alphabetical order. You can create files with the *.xyz* extension using the New → File menu item, but this plug-in example is also going to have a built-in wizard that will create *.xyz* files for the user and place default text in them.

Creating the Code

To create the code skeleton for this example, select New → Project, and in the New project dialog, select Plug-in Development in the left box, Plug-in Project in the right box, and click Next. Give the name of the project as `org.eclipsebook.ch12.Ch12_01` in the following pane, and click Next. Leave the defaults selected in the Plug-in Project Structure pane to make this a Java project, and click Next again to bring up the Plug-in Code Generators pane shown in Figure 12-1.

Select the Plug-in with a multi-page editor item, as you see in the figure, and click Next. In the following pane, set the Provider name to `Eclipse Book` and click Next again. In the next pane that appears, set the File Extensions item to xyz to associate the plug-in with that extension, as you see in Figure 12-2, and click Next again.

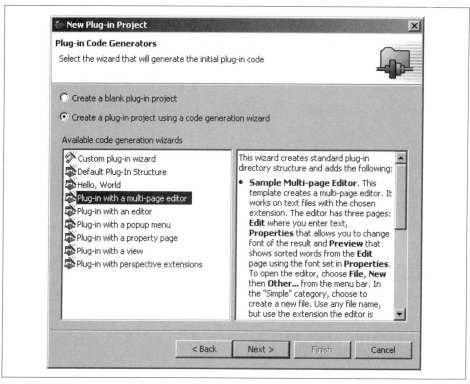

Figure 12-1. Creating a plug-in with a multi-page editor

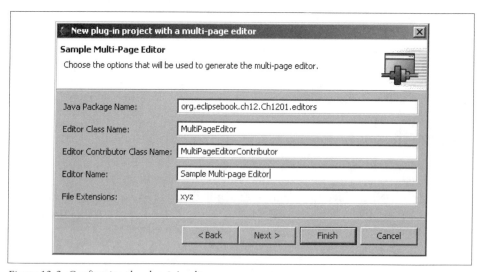

Figure 12-2. Configuring the plug-in's editor

In the next pane, set the file extension to xyz, and give file.xyz as the initial file name, as shown in Figure 12-3. Then click Finish to create the code skeleton for this plug-in.

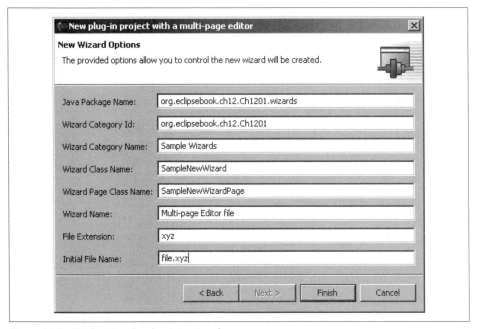

Figure 12-3. Configuring the plug-in's wizard

Here are the files the PDE wizard creates and adds to the *src* folder in the org. eclipsebook.ch12.Ch12_01 project:

```
src
|__org.eclipsebook.ch12.Ch12_01
|    |__Ch12_01Plugin.java              The standard plug-in file
|
|__org.eclipsebook.ch12.Ch1201.editors
|    |__MultiPageEditor.java             The editor's code
|    |__MultiPageEditorContributor.java  The editor actions (menus/toolbar items)
|
|__org.eclipsebook.ch12.Ch1201.wizards
|    |__SampleNewWizard.java             The wizard's code
|    |__SampleNewWizardPage.java         The code for the wizard's page
|
|__plugin.xml
```

Dissecting the Wizard

This plug-in supports both a wizard and a multi-page editor. We're going to focus on the editor, but it's instructive to take a brief look at the wizard as well. The job of the wizard is to create a new file, *file.xyz*, and to add it to the project. The Java code that does this is the SampleNewWizard class, which extends the Eclipse Wizard class. The visual page that the wizard displays to the user is supported in the SampleNewWizardPage class; that class constructs a composite SWT object that displays the controls the user will interact with. Here's how code in SampleNewWizard creates the page the wizard will display:

```
public class SampleNewWizard extends Wizard implements INewWizard {
    private SampleNewWizardPage page;
    private ISelection selection;

    public SampleNewWizard( ) {
        super( );
        setNeedsProgressMonitor(true);
    }

    public void addPages( ) {
        page = new SampleNewWizardPage(selection);
        addPage(page);
    }
        .
        .
        .
```

After the user has filled in the data the wizard asks for (which is the project to add the new file to and the name of the file) and clicked Finish, the SampleNewWizard class's doFinish method is called. This method is passed both the name of the project to add the new file to and the name of the file. Take a look at this method's code, which shows how to create a new file, add it to an Eclipse project, and open that file in Eclipse—some of the most impressive things you can do in a plug-in:

```
private void doFinish(
    String containerName,
    String fileName,
    IProgressMonitor monitor)
    throws CoreException {
    // create a sample file
    monitor.beginTask("Creating " + fileName, 2);
    IWorkspaceRoot root = ResourcesPlugin.getWorkspace().getRoot( );
    IResource resource = root.findMember(new Path(containerName));
    if (!resource.exists( ) || !(resource instanceof IContainer)) {
        throwCoreException("Container \"" + containerName +
          "\" does not exist.");
    }
    IContainer container = (IContainer) resource;
    final IFile file = container.getFile(new Path(fileName));
    try {
        InputStream stream = openContentStream( );
        if (file.exists( )) {
            file.setContents(stream, true, true, monitor);
        } else {
            file.create(stream, true, monitor);
        }
```

```
            stream.close( );
        } catch (IOException e) {
        }
        monitor.worked(1);
        monitor.setTaskName("Opening file for editing...");
        getShell().getDisplay().asyncExec(new Runnable( ) {
            public void run( ) {
                IWorkbenchPage page =
                    PlatformUI.getWorkbench( )
                        .getActiveWorkbenchWindow().getActivePage( );
                try {
                    page.openEditor(file);
                } catch (PartInitException e) {
                }
            }
        });
        monitor.worked(1);
    }
```

The default text in the new file is set when doFinish opens a new input stream to read the contents it should place in the file. That's done in the openContentStream method, which we're going to modify in order to place our own text, "Here is the sample text.", into the new file by default. Here's the new code to add to this method:

```
    private InputStream openContentStream( ) {
        String contents =
        "Here is the sample text.";
        return new ByteArrayInputStream(contents.getBytes( ));
    }
```

That modifies the wizard to fill the new file with the default text we've specified.

Coding a Multi-Page Editor

The real action in this example takes place in *MultiPageEditor.java*, the Java support for the editor that edits *.xyz* files. (*MultiPageEditorContributor.java* is also part of the editor, but it is peripheral to this discussion since it provides the support for menu and toolbar actions, which we discussed in Chapter 11.) The goal here is to add two pages to this editor: a simple text-editing page that displays the text in an *.xyz* file and a second page that displays the text sorted in alphabetical order. To set up those two pages, we're going to adapt the code written for us by the PDE wizard.

In *MultiPageEditor.java*, the MultiPageEditor class supports the editor we're creating (this class extends the MultiPageEditorPart class, which is an Eclipse class that uses an SWT tab folder control to display editor pages). To display the text in the first page of the editor, this example uses an org.eclipse.editors.ui.text.TextEditor object named editor; to display the sorted text in the second page, it uses an org.eclipse.editors.custom.StyledText object named text. After creating those objects, you can use the MultiPageEditorPart class's addPage method to add the two new pages to the editor. To do that, you override the `MultiPageEditor` class's `createPages` method, which is responsible for creating the pages in the editor and is called automatically when the editor starts. Here's how that looks in our modified code:

```java
public class MultiPageEditor extends MultiPageEditorPart {

    private TextEditor editor;

    private StyledText text;

    public MultiPageEditor() {
        super();
    }

    void createPage0() {
        try {
            editor = new TextEditor();
            int index = addPage(editor, getEditorInput());
            setPageText(index, editor.getTitle());
        } catch (PartInitException e) {
            ErrorDialog.openError(
                getSite().getShell(),
                "Error creating nested text editor",
                null, e.getStatus());
        }
    }

    void createPage1() {
        Composite composite = new Composite(getContainer(), SWT.NONE);
        FillLayout layout = new FillLayout();
        composite.setLayout(layout);
        text = new StyledText(composite, SWT.H_SCROLL | SWT.V_SCROLL);
        text.setEditable(false);

        int index = addPage(composite);
        setPageText(index, "Sorted");
    }

    protected void createPages() {
        createPage0();
        createPage1();
    }
```

That creates and adds the two pages we're going to use in this editor. The next step is to enable actions like File → Save or File → Save As when the user selects them in the standard Eclipse menu system or toolbar. To do that, you override the doSave and doSaveAs methods, using the getEditor method to get the IEditorPart object that does the actual work, and calling that object's methods of the same names. This code has been provided for us by the PDE wizard already:

```java
public void doSave(IProgressMonitor monitor) {
    getEditor(0).doSave(monitor);
}
```

```
public void doSaveAs( ) {
    IEditorPart editor = getEditor(0);
    editor.doSaveAs( );
    setPageText(0, editor.getTitle( ));
    setInput(editor.getEditorInput( ));
}

public boolean isSaveAsAllowed( ) {
    return true;
}
```

We still need to sort the words to be displayed in the sorted editor. You can catch page changes by overriding the pageChange method, and if the new page holds the sorted editor (the standard text editor is page 0, the sorted text editor is page 1), we'll sort the words before displaying them with a custom method named sort:

```
protected void pageChange(int newPageIndex) {
    super.pageChange(newPageIndex);
    if (newPageIndex == 1) {
        sort( );
    }
}
```

In the sort method, we get access to the unsorted text in the plain text editor (the editor object) like this: String unsortedText = editor.getDocumentProvider( ). getDocument(editor.getEditorInput()).get( ). The next step is to sort that text by breaking it up into an ArrayList of words using the StringTokenizer class, breaking on spaces, tabs, new lines, and carriage returns. Here's what that looks like:

```
void sort( ) {
    String unsortedText = editor.getDocumentProvider( )
        .getDocument(editor.getEditorInput()).get( );

    StringTokenizer stringTokenizer =
        new StringTokenizer(unsortedText, " \t\n\r");
    ArrayList wordArrayList = new ArrayList( );
    while (stringTokenizer.hasMoreTokens( )) {
        wordArrayList.add(stringTokenizer.nextToken( ));
    }
    .
    .
    .
```

After breaking the words up into an ArrayList, the next step is to sort those words and reassemble them. The final step is to put the result into the StyleText control, text, which displays the sorted text in the editor's second page. Here's the code:

```
void sort( ) {
    String unsortedText = editor.getDocumentProvider( )
        .getDocument(editor.getEditorInput()).get( );

    StringTokenizer stringTokenizer =
        new StringTokenizer(unsortedText, " \t\n\r");
```

```
    ArrayList wordArrayList = new ArrayList();
    while (stringTokenizer.hasMoreTokens()) {
        wordArrayList.add(stringTokenizer.nextToken());
    }

    Collections.sort(wordArrayList, Collator.getInstance());
    StringWriter sortedText = new StringWriter();
    for (int loopIndex = 0; loopIndex < wordArrayList.size(); loopIndex++) {
        sortedText.write(((String) wordArrayList.get(loopIndex)));
        sortedText.write(System.getProperty("line.separator"));
    }

    text.setText(sortedText.toString());
}
```

That sorts and displays the text in *file.xyz* in the Sorted tab's editor, which completes our custom version of *MultiPageEditor.java*. We've set up our new editor and handled its text in code. To see this editor at work, start the Run-time Workbench and create a new Java project, testProject. Now right-click on testProject and select New → Other to open the New dialog you see in Figure 12-4. Select the Sample Wizards item in the left box and the Multi-page Editor file item on the right and click Next to open the new wizard.

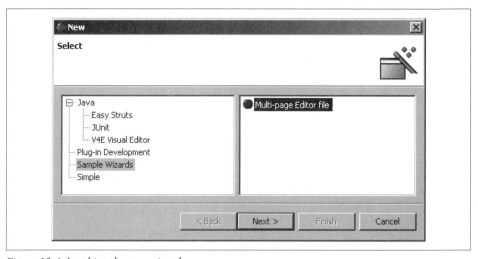

Figure 12-4. Invoking the new wizard

Your new wizard indicates the name of the new file, *file.xyz* by default, and asks you to specify a container for the file, as shown in Figure 12-5. Browse to testProject with the Browse button and click Finish to create the file.

That creates *file.xyz* and opens it for editing with the sample text we specified, as shown in Figure 12-6. Note that you can also see *file.xyz* in the Package Explorer.

Our multi-page editor has two tabs: file.xyz and Sorted. Clicking the Sorted tab displays the second editor, containing the sorted text as you see in Figure 12-7.

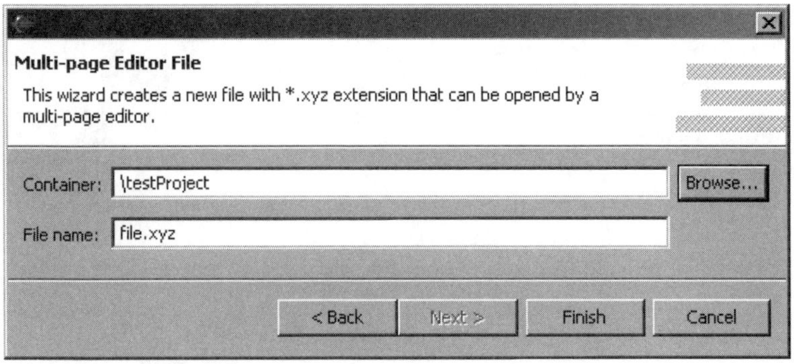

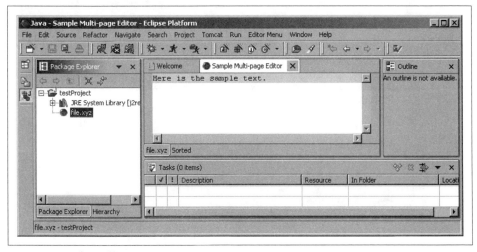

Figure 12-5. Using the new wizard

Figure 12-6. Editing file.xyz

Our customized editor is working as it should—it'll open any *.xyz* file you double-click in the Package Explorer. You can make changes to the text in that file in the editor's first page, and save the new text with Eclipse's File → Save or File → Save As menu items or the corresponding toolbar buttons. We've added our own editor to Eclipse—not bad!

Creating a View

In the next example, we're going to use a plug-in to create a new view. Start by creating a new plug-in project named `org.eclipsebook.ch12.Ch12_02`. In the Plug-in Code Generators pane, which you see in Figure 12-8, select the "Plug-in with a view" wizard and click Next.

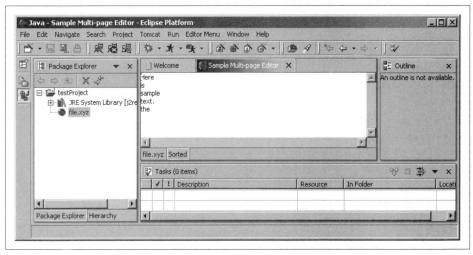

Figure 12-7. Viewing the sorted text

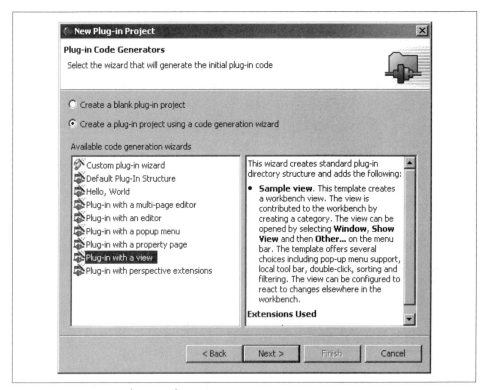

Figure 12-8. Creating a plug-in with a view

In the following pane, give Eclipse Book as the provider's name and click Next again to bring up the Main View Settings dialog you see in Figure 12-9. In this pane, you set the name of the view and its category—we'll stick with the defaults, which will make this a table-based view (i.e., the items in the view will be displayed in a table control) named Sample View in the category Sample Category. Click Next again to bring up the final pane of this wizard.

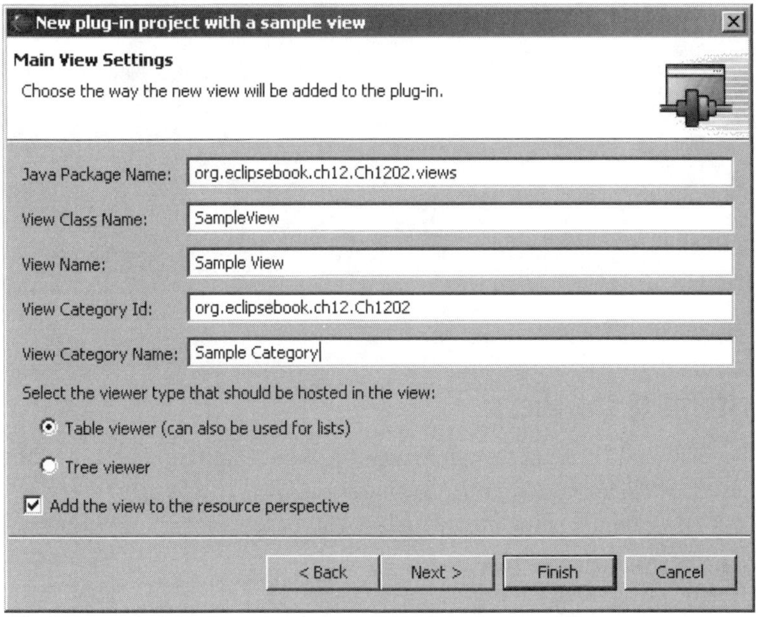

Figure 12-9. Configuring the view

The last pane, shown in Figure 12-10, lets you configure the view's actions, such as responding when the user double-clicks an item in the view. Leave the defaults selected and click Finish to create the framework for this plug-in.

Here are the files created and added to the project's *src* folder:

```
src
|__org.eclipsebook.ch12.Ch12_02
|    |__Ch12_02Plugin.java            The standard plug-in file
|
|__org.eclipsebook.ch12.Ch1202.views
|    |__SampleView.java                The view file
|
|__plugin.xml
```

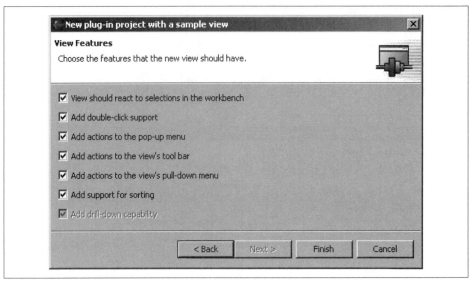

Figure 12-10. Configuring the view's actions

Adding Items to the View

The new view is supported in *SampleView.java*, which we're going to adapt so that it will display four clickable items. In *SampleView.java*, the SampleView class extends the ViewPart class, which is the abstract class you base views on in plug-ins:

```
public class SampleView extends ViewPart {
    private TableViewer viewer;
    private Action action1;
    private Action action2;
    private Action doubleClickAction;
        .
        .
        .
```

Eclipse gets the content displayed in the view by calling methods in an object that implements the IStructuredContentProvider interface. We're going to adapt the code in the class used to create that object, the ViewContentProvider class, to make the view display a set of four items, "Item 1" to "Item 4" in this example. Here's the code:

```
class ViewContentProvider implements IStructuredContentProvider {
    public void inputChanged(Viewer v, Object oldInput, Object newInput) {
    }
    public void dispose() {
    }
    public Object[] getElements(Object parent) {
        return new String[] { "Item 1", "Item 2", "Item 3", "Item 4" };
    }
}
```

The view is created when Eclipse calls the createPartControl method. Here's how the code uses our ViewContentProvider class to get the content for the view:

```
public void createPartControl(Composite parent) {
    viewer = new TableViewer(parent, SWT.MULTI | SWT.H_SCROLL | SWT.V_SCROLL);
    viewer.setContentProvider(new ViewContentProvider());
    viewer.setLabelProvider(new ViewLabelProvider());
    viewer.setSorter(new NameSorter());
    viewer.setInput(ResourcesPlugin.getWorkspace());
    makeActions();
    hookContextMenu();
    hookDoubleClickAction();
    contributeToActionBars();
}
```

That sets up our four new items, "Item 1" to "Item 4", in the view. These items will appear in a table, one on top of the other. The next step is to actually do something when the user wants to work with one of these items.

Configuring View Actions

The rest of the code in *SampleView.java* supports the view's actions when you click, double-click, or right-click items in the view. We'll change the code in the makeActions method to customize the view's actions to display an appropriate message when an item is selected or double-clicked; you get access to the object corresponding to the item that was selected or double-clicked this way: Object obj = ((IStructuredSelection)selection).getFirstElement(). Here's the modified code that will determine which item the user wants to work with and display a message that indicates the item by name:

```
private void makeActions() {
    action1 = new Action() {
        public void run() {
            ISelection selection = viewer.getSelection();
            Object obj =
                ((IStructuredSelection)selection).getFirstElement();
            showMessage("You selected " + obj.toString());
        }
    };
    action1.setText("Action 1");
    action1.setToolTipText("Action 1 tooltip");
    action1.setImageDescriptor(PlatformUI.getWorkbench().getSharedImages().
        getImageDescriptor(ISharedImages.IMG_OBJS_INFO_TSK));

    action2 = new Action() {
        public void run() {
            showMessage("Action 2 executed");
        }
    };
    action2.setText("Action 2");
    action2.setToolTipText("Action 2 tooltip");
    action2.setImageDescriptor(PlatformUI.getWorkbench().getSharedImages().
```

```
        getImageDescriptor(ISharedImages.IMG_OBJS_TASK_TSK));
    doubleClickAction = new Action( ) {
        public void run( ) {
            ISelection selection = viewer.getSelection( );
            Object obj =
                ((IStructuredSelection)selection).getFirstElement( );
            showMessage("You double-clicked " + obj.toString( ));
        }
    };
}
```

As you can see, the code that the PDE wizard creates is designed to be relatively easily modified. To see this new view at work, start the Run-time Workbench and select Window → Show View → Other. Select the Sample View item in the Sample Category folder, as you see in Figure 12-11, and click OK to display the new view.

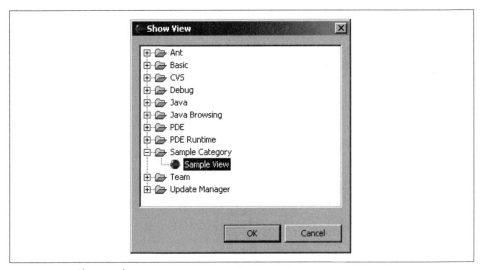

Figure 12-11. Showing the new view

The new view appears in Figure 12-12, where you can see the four sample items we created at the bottom of Eclipse. Very cool—we've added a new, functional view to Eclipse.

Right-clicking an item and selecting the Action Item 1 executes the code we've added to display the message box you see in Figure 12-13, where the selected item is identified.

Similarly, double-clicking an item displays the message box you see in Figure 12-14, where the double-clicked item is identified in a message box.

That's what we wanted to do—create a new view and handle user actions with the items in the view. We've been able to create plug-ins with views, editors, and even wizards. Now that you've gotten the basics of plug-in creation under your belt, our last topic in this chapter will be about how to deploy your plug-ins.

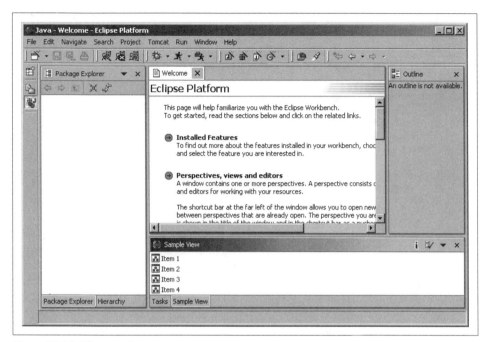

Figure 12-12. *The new view*

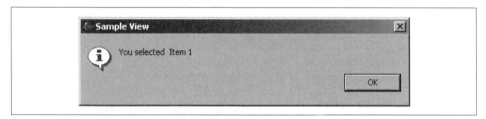

Figure 12-13. *Selecting an item*

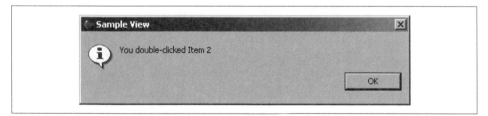

Figure 12-14. *Double-clicking an item*

Deploying a Plug-in

Eclipse makes it relatively simple to create deployment packages for plug-ins. To deploy a plug-in, select File → Export, selecting the "Deployable plug-ins and fragments" item in the Export dialog, as you see in Figure 12-15.

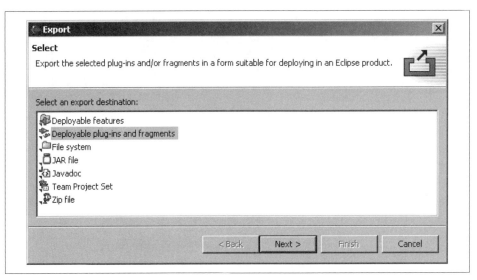

Figure 12-15. Deploying plug-ins

Click Next to open the "Deployable plug-ins and fragments" pane you see in Figure 12-16. You can deploy plug-ins as either *.jar* or *.zip* files; here, we'll deploy both plug-ins in a *.zip* file. Enter the fully qualified name of the *.zip* file to create—*plugins.zip*—in the File name box and select both plug-in projects from this chapter.

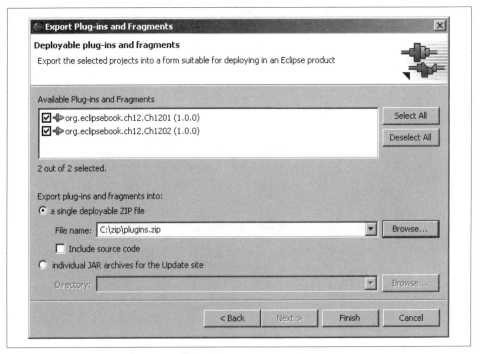

Figure 12-16. Creating a plug-in .zip file

This packages both plug-ins (including a *plugin.xml* and a *.jar* file for each) in the *plugins.zip* file. Unzipping that file in the Eclipse distribution directory installs the plug-ins—the two files for the first plug-in will be installed in *eclipse\plugins\ org.eclipsebook.ch12.Ch1201_1.0.0*, and the files for the second plug-in will be installed in *eclipse\plugins\org.eclipsebook.ch12.Ch1202_1.0.0*.

CHAPTER 13

Eclipse 3.0

Eclipse 3.0 is on the way, and we'll get a look at what's coming in this chapter. As of this writing, 3.0 is still in beta version.

This chapter is going to use the most recent beta of Eclipse 3.0, milestone build 6. Eclipse 3.0 is being designed to be as compatible as possible with Versions 2.0 and 2.1, and the update team says, "We will provide a comprehensive Eclipse 3.0 Porting Guide that covers all areas of breaking API changes, and describes how to port existing 2.1 plug-ins to 3.0." You'll also be able to import 2.0 and 2.1 projects into 3.0, but you'll get a dialog saying that the project needs to be modified and probably won't work with earlier versions after that, so make sure you copy your projects first.

A Look at Eclipse 3.0

At this point, Eclipse 3.0 looks a lot like Eclipse 2.1, as you can see in Figure 13-1.

As we're going to see, some new buttons, menu choices, and views have appeared, but fundamentally, Eclipse 2.0 users will have no difficulty slipping right into this new version of Eclipse.

On the other hand, the Eclipse team has been experimenting with the look of views, editors, and perspectives in Eclipse 3.0, and there's no guarantee that Eclipse 3.0 will keep looking like Figure 13-1.

Some of the changes the Eclipse team is contemplating include rounding view tabs instead of the square ones currently in use, only presenting a single editor tab at once instead of stacking them (you can reach other editor tabs with arrow buttons), and displaying icons for perspectives at top right, not at left.

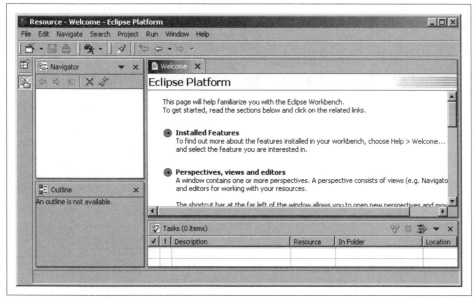

Figure 13-1. The current build of Eclipse 3.0

Creating a Java Project

For Java programmers, the fundamental Eclipse task is creating a Java project. As you're going to see, the process is (so far) virtually identical to working in Eclipse 2.1.

To create a new project, right-click the Navigator view and select New → Project, opening the New Project dialog. Select the Java item in the pane on the left and Java Project in the pane on the right and click Next. These dialogs you see in Figure 13-2 are just as we've seen before. Name this new project Ch13_01 and click Next.

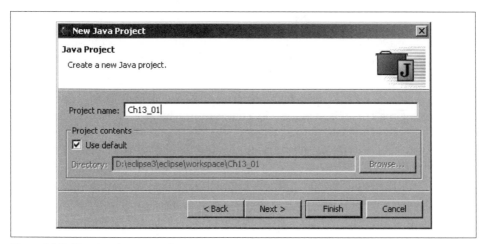

Figure 13-2. Naming the new project

This brings up the familiar dialog you see in Figure 13-3, where you can set project settings, such as the source folder and the import and export order—all items we're already familiar with. Click Finish to create the project.

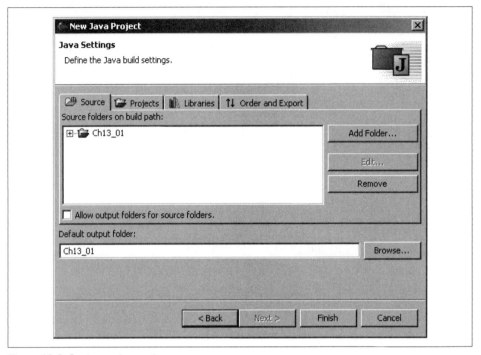

Figure 13-3. Setting project options

Eclipse 3.0 will ask if you want to switch to the Java perspective; click OK. The new Java perspective looks much like what we've seen before, except that the Tasks view has now been renamed the Problems view, as you see in Figure 13-4.

To create a new class, right-click the project and select New → Class, opening the New Java Class dialog you see in Figure 13-5. This is the same dialog we've worked with throughout this book, so just enter the new class's name, Ch13_01, and package, org.eclipsebook.ch13, and click Finish.

Opening the new Java file in the Java editor reveals some changes—for example, the new shape of the cursor, as you see in Figure 13-6. That's the *smart insert* cursor, which is covered a little later in this chapter—see the upcoming section "Smart Insert Mode." Note also the two new buttons in the Outline view—Hide Local Types and Link With Editor.

At left in the new JDT editor is the Quick Diff bar, which lets you track differences to particular lines as compared to what's been saved on disk (or, if you configure it, to what's in a CVS repository).

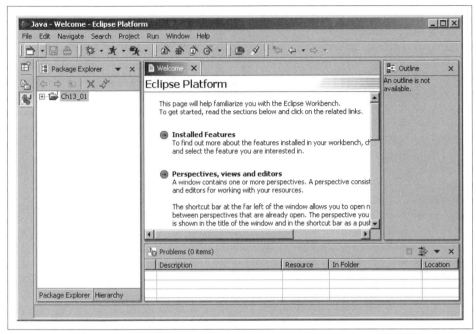

Figure 13-4. The Eclipse 3.0 Java perspective

To see how Quick Diff works, enter `System.out.println("Hello");` in the main method, and save the file (only the Save diskette icon appears in the toolbar now, not the Save All diskette icon). Next, change the line to `System.out.println("Hello from Eclipse 3.0");` and let the mouse hover over the Quick Diff bar as you see in Figure 13-7. The original version of the code will appear, and you can restore it by clicking it.

Quick Diff is also being made available to plug-ins.

To run this code, select Run → Run As → Java Application (note the new Run → Run As → JUnit Plug-in Test menu item as well), giving the results you see in the Console view in Figure 13-8. That's it; you've created and run a Java application in Eclipse 3.0. As you can see, the procss is very similar to what you would see in Eclipse 2.1.

Note the new buttons in the Console view: Pin Console, Display Selected Console, and Remove All Terminated Launches.

That recreates a familiar task for us in Eclipse 3.0, and, as you can see, it works much as we've seen before.

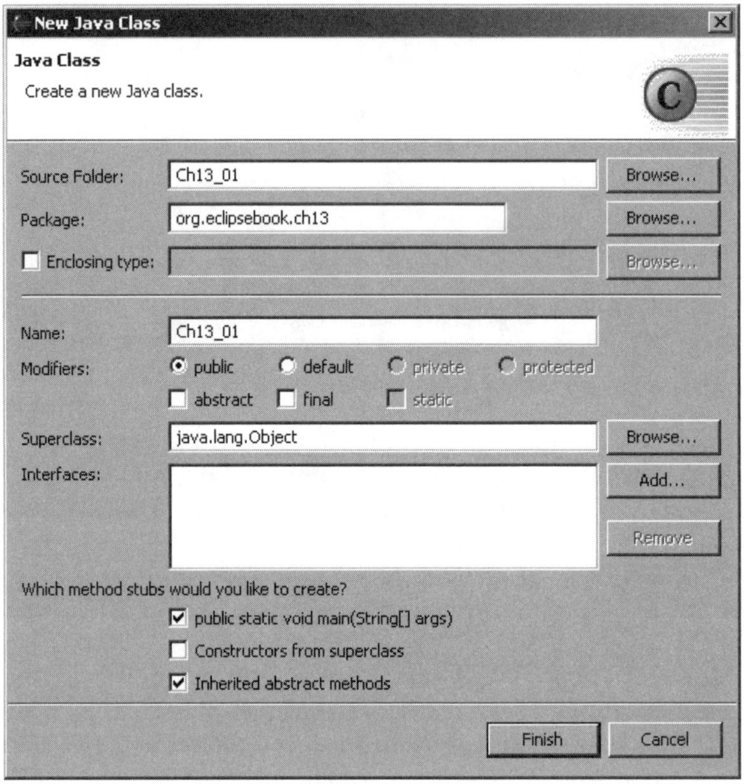

Figure 13-5. Creating a new class

Perhaps the biggest change in Version 3.0 is that the Eclipse platform has been broadened for use as a general hosting tool, designed to work with general applications, not just IDEs. Now general applications will be able to populate the menu bar and toolbars, and the assumed data model will no longer be necessarily centered on the workspace. We'll be seeing more on that as Eclipse 3.0 nears launch.

There are also specific changes to the various parts of Eclipse—the Eclipse platform itself, the JDT, SWT, and so on—and we'll examine them on a case-by-case basis.

Changes to the Eclipse Platform

There are a number of changes to the Eclipse platform in Eclipse 3.0. Many of the changes take place behind the scenes—for example, when resources are changed, auto-builds now occur in the background so you don't have to wait, and there's a new Progress view that lets you keep track of those changes. Disabled features can now be uninstalled to free disk space (select Help → Software Updates → Manage Configuration, turn off the disabled feature filter, and select Uninstall from the context menu of the disabled feature to uninstall it).

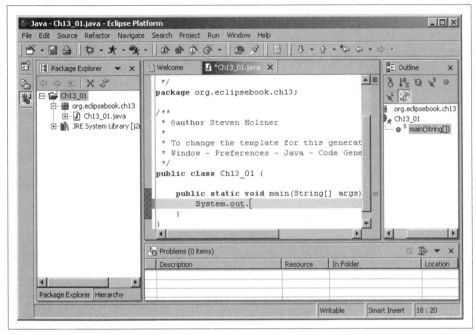

Figure 13-6. Using the Java editor

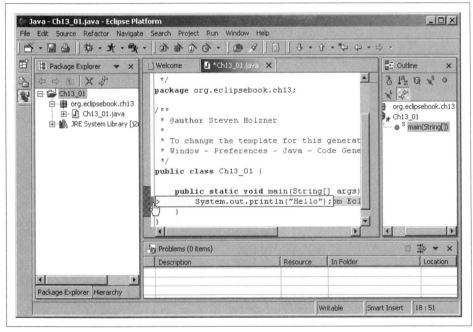

Figure 13-7. Using Quick Diff

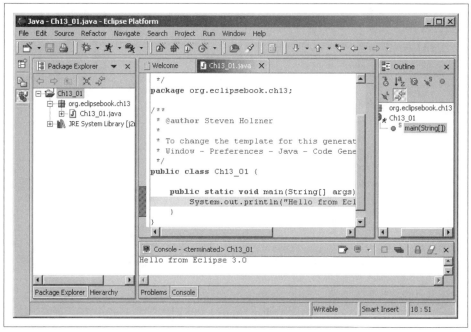

Figure 13-8. Running the code

Now you can have Eclipse automatically check for updates—check out the Window → Preferences → Install/Update → Automatic Updates preference page.

Some of the changes are more evident, however. One of the most handy changes is that you can now use regular expressions in the File search page. Select Search → File to open the dialog you see in Figure 13-9—note the new "Regular expression" checkbox.

Not familiar with regular expressions? Click the "Regular expression" checkbox and press F1 for an overview of how to use regular expressions to match text.

You can also edit files outside the workspace now, using the new File → Open External File menu item, which opens the dialog you see in Figure 13-10. Select a file and click Open to open it in an external editor.

The annotations that appear in various editors are also being elaborated in Eclipse 3.0. In Eclipse 2.1, there are 6 such annotation types that can be customized (such as problems and warnings), but in the Eclipse 3.0 Window → Preferences → Editors → Text Editor preference page, there are now 12, as you can see in Figure 13-11.

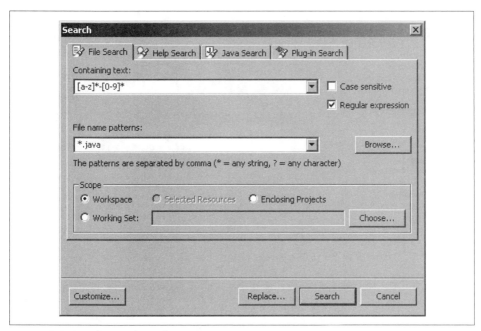

Figure 13-9. Searching with regular expressions

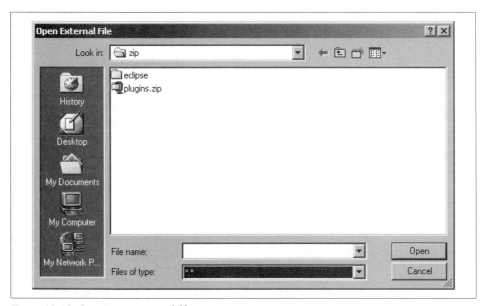

Figure 13-10. Opening an external file

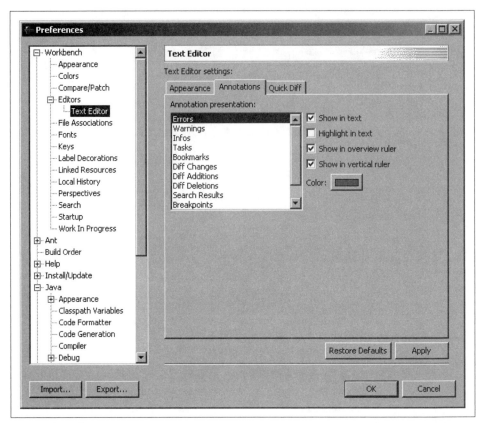

Figure 13-11. Customizing annotations

Besides using underlining and squiggly underlining for annotations, you can also now display annotations using background highlighting.

There are new editing functions built into all text editors as well. You can now move lines up and down with Alt+Arrow Up and Alt+Arrow Down, you can insert a new line above or below the current line with Ctrl+Shift+Enter and Shift+Enter. You can convert selected text to lowercase or uppercase with Ctrl+Shift+Y or Ctrl+Shift+X. And you can toggle the Quick Diff bar with Ctrl+Shift+Q (as well as the Window → Preferences → Workbench → Editors → Text Editor → Quick Diff preference page).

A major focus in Eclipse 3.0 is greater usability. A number of dialogs are being redesigned to make them easier to use; for example, the new Customize Perspective dialog (Window → Customize Perspective) appears in Figure 13-12. The checkboxes and display in this dialog make working with it far simpler than before.

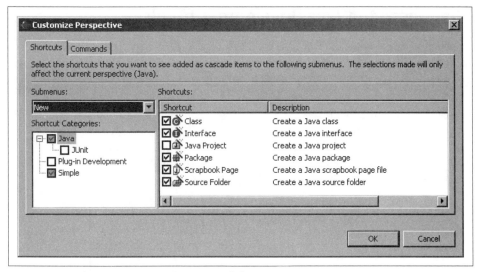

Figure 13-12. The new Customize Perspective dialog

The Eclipse team is also tackling the Eclipse learning curve. It's not clear how this will shake out, but here's what they're saying now:

> Users who are new to an Eclipse-based product can find their first experiences with it overwhelming, even daunting. The initial experience would be improved if a product could preconfigure the workbench to show only the subset of function that a new user really needs; welcome pages could be personalized for particular users roles or levels of experience.

 The Eclipse team is definitely recognizing that the Eclipse learning curve is steep. In Version 3.0, there's a new emphasis on having Eclipse train new users with active help links and F1 help.

There are many other proposed changes to the Eclipse platform as well—here's a sampling:

- Support splitting in text editors to let users view two sections of text at once.
- Store user settings and preferences independently of workspaces so they can be used across many workspaces.
- Allow plug-ins to be added and removed dynamically, without having to restart Eclipse.
- Allow plug-in deactivation to lessen the load on system resources.
- Add a security model that can be used by all plug-ins, including user authentication.
- Use the XML support in J2SE 1.4 instead of the Xerces plug-in.
- Port SWT to 64-bit operating environments.

Changes to the Java Development Tools

The major enhancements in Eclipse 3.0 are to the JDT, as you might expect. The changes so far are mostly for usability and convenience, and they're designed to help you program Java better. It's not clear which ones will be around in the final release of Eclipse 3.0, but we'll take a look at what's available now.

Quick Hierarchy Views

You can now select a type, method, or package reference in the JDT editor and press Ctrl+T to see a quick type hierarchy view, as appears in Figure 13-13.

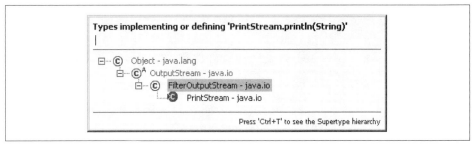

Figure 13-13. Showing a quick hierarchy

You can also now open a view that shows a method call hierarchy by selecting Navigate → Open Call Hierarchy (or by pressing Ctrl+Alt+H) in the JDT editor (or, for that matter, any of the Java views that show methods).

Creating Constructors from Fields

You can also create a constructor that fills various fields easily in Eclipse 3.0. For example, say you added a String field to a class this way:

```
public class Ch13_01 {

    private String text;

    public static void main(String[] args) {
        System.out.println("Hello from Eclipse 3.0");
    }

}
```

To create a constructor that fills this field in Eclipse 3.0, select Source → Generate Constructor Using Fields, opening the dialog you see in Figure 13-14.

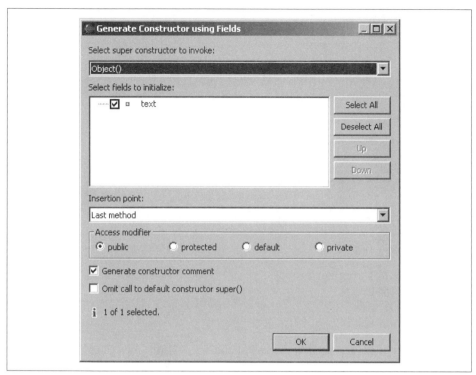

Figure 13-14. Creating a constructor using a field

You select fields you want to fill in the constructor and click OK; in this case, here's the constructor created:

```java
public class Ch13_01 {

    private String text;

    public static void main(String[] args) {
        System.out.println("Hello from Eclipse 3.0");
    }

    /**
     * @param text
     */
    public Ch13_01(String text) {
        super();
        this.text = text;
    }
}
```

Creating Factory Methods

You can go further as well—you can convert your constructor into a factory method with the new Refactoring → Introduce Factory item. Just select a constructor declaration or a call to the constructor in the JDT editor and select that menu item. For example, say you added this call to the Ch13_01 constructor in your code:

```java
public class Ch13_01 {

    private String text;

    public static void main(String[] args) {
        Ch13_01 ch13_01 = new Ch13_01("Hello");
        System.out.println("Hello from Eclipse 3.0");
    }

    /**
     * @param text
     */
    public Ch13_01(String text) {
        super();
        this.text = text;
    }
}
```

Selecting the constructor call and the Refactoring → Introduce Factory item opens the dialog you see in Figure 13-15.

Figure 13-15. Creating a factory method

Clicking OK creates a new factory method, createCh13_01, replaces the call to the constructor with a call to that method, and makes the original constructor private:

```java
public class Ch13_01 {

    private String text;

    public static void main(String[] args) {
        Ch13_01 ch13_01 = createCh13_01("Hello");
        System.out.println("Hello from Eclipse 3.0");
    }
```

```
public static Ch13_01 createCh13_01(java.lang.String text) {
    return new Ch13_01(text);
}

/**
 * @param text
 */
private Ch13_01(String text) {
    super( );
    this.text = text;
}
}
```

More on refactoring: now you can also move public static final fields between classes and interfaces, as well as static inner types between classes. The Refactoring → Change Method Signature now lets you rename parameters in overridden methods as well.

This is the general trend in Eclipse 3.0—giving you more control over tasks you already perform. For example, the dialog for the JDT editor's Source → Add Constructors from Superclass command now displays a dialog that lets you select which of the superclass's constructors should be added to the current class. Other commands now give you considerably more control, such as the code generation dialogs for the Source → Generate Getter and Setter, Source → Override/Implement Methods, and Source → Generate Delegate Methods. You can indicate where the generated method will be inserted and—for getters and setters—the sort order.

While discussing getter/setter generation, it's worth noting that you can find new templates for getters and setters in the Window → Preferences → Java → Code Generation → Code and Comments preference page.

Smart Insert Mode

There's a new typing mode in the JDT editor—*smart insert mode*—in addition to the standard overwrite and insert mode. Smart insert mode adds functionality for Java programmers, such as automatically wrapping Java strings to code lines as you type them. You can toggle between these three modes by repeatedly clicking the Insert key and watching the status bar indicator (set to Smart Insert in Figure 13-8).

To configure smart insert mode, select Window → Preferences → Java → Editor → Typing, opening the dialog you see in Figure 13-16. Besides the options you see in that dialog, there are others being considered for smart insert, such as automatically inserting semicolons at the end of lines.

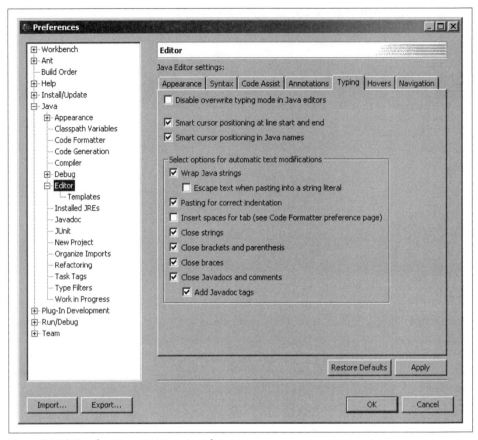

Figure 13-16. Configuring smart insert mode

Creating Block Comments

Besides commenting out blocks of code using single-line comments, you can also comment out code using Java block comments. For example, if you select this code:

```java
public class Ch13_01 {

    private String text;

    public static void main(String[] args) {
        System.out.println("Hello from Eclipse 3.0");
    }
}
```

and then select the Source → Add Block Comment (note that the Source → Comment item is still available for commenting out blocks with single-line comments), you'll get this result:

```
public class Ch13_01 {

    private String text;

/*  public static void main(String[] args) {
        System.out.println("Hello from Eclipse 3.0");
    }
*/}
```

To uncomment a block, select it and then select Source → Remove Block Comment.

New Views

Eclipse 3.0 also comes with some new views: Javadoc, Error log, and Declaration. You can show these as you would any view, using Window → Show View. For example, the Error log view, which holds errors in the Eclipse *.log* file, appears in Figure 13-17.

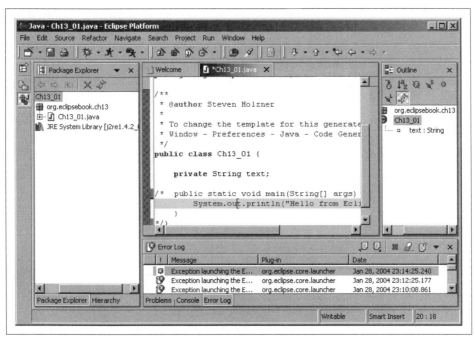

Figure 13-17. The Error log view

Additional Changes

Besides the changes to the JDT already discussed, there are plenty of other smaller changes. Here's an overview of the most significant of these:

- When you select a local variable in the JDT editor and press F3 (or select Navigate → Open Declaration), the JDT editor displays the variable's declaration.

- The JDT compiler now adds more checks to find and mark styling issues. To turn them on, see Window → Preferences → Java → Compiler → Style.

- Instead of adding a closing brace as soon as an opening brace has been entered, the JDT editor now waits until a new line is added after the opening brace.

- There are some new Quick Assists in the JDT editor—Split and join variable declaration, and Create field from parameter.

- The launch configuration page now lets you set environment variables.

- The JDT compiler can now indicate when projects are compiled against a binary library whose version is incompatible with what is being generated. For example, you might be trying to generate 1.1-compatible class files while compiling using a Java 1.3 library. See Window → Preferences → Java → Compiler → Build Path.

- You can now implement searches to include projects that enclose the current project.

- The JDT editor's Go To Next/Previous Error toolbar buttons were replaced by Go To Next/Previous Annotation drop-down style buttons, which allow you to choose which annotations you want to move to.

- The JDT compiler can find and mark unused exceptions that are declared but not thrown. Enable this with Window → Preferences → Java → Compiler → Unused Code.

There are plenty of plans for new improvements to Eclipse 3.0 in upcoming releases. Here's a sampling:

- Generalize the JDT editor to handle other Java-like source files, such as SQLj and JSP.

- Mark overridden methods with override indicators.

- Handle new J2SE 1.5 functionality and extensions to Java, such as generic types, autoboxing, static imports, and so on. The final version of Eclipse 3.0 will probably ship before J2SE 1.5 does, but the Eclipse team is working on including support for it already.

Other Changes

There are some other changes to various other subprojects in Eclipse 3.0, including CVS and Ant control as well as the PDE and SWT.

Eclipse now ships with the latest version of Ant, which is Version 1.5.4. The Ant launch configuration is all new, letting you work with Ant in a separate Java VM (you can set the options for choosing the Ant JRE on the JRE tab of the Ant launch configuration).

As far as CVS goes, you can now use the Team → Show Annotation item to open the CVS Annotation view. If you select a line in the JDT editor, the CVS Annotation view will indicate who released the change—which means you can track who released a bug.

There have been a couple of improvements to SWT as well. SWT now lets you embed Swing and AWT widgets inside SWT on other platforms besides Windows. As of this writing, however, this only works in Windows with JDK 1.4 and above, and on GTK and Motif with early versions of Sun JDK 1.5.

SWT shells can now have irregular shapes as well. You can define these shapes with combinations of rectangles and polygons. And SWT has a new browser widget that can display HTML documents. As of this writing, however, this widget is only supported in Windows (and uses Internet Explorer 5.0 or above) and Linux GTK (where it uses Mozilla 1.4 GTK2).

There aren't many changes to the PDE in the current milestone build of Eclipse 3.0. Two significant ones are that the PDE now supports JUnit testing for plug-in development, and that there is also a special build configuration editor that lets you edit a plug-in's *build.properties* file.

Other changes that are being contemplated include improvements to the PDE editors and debuggers, as well as supporting context-sensitive help for plug-ins.

That's it for our look at Eclipse 3.0. There's little question that there will be other changes before the final version is released, so keep your eyes peeled.

Index

We'd like to hear your suggestions for improving our indexes. Send email to *index@oreilly.com*.

G

Generate Getter and Setter dialog box, 36
Generate Javadoc dialog box, 47
get method
    depicted, 70
    purpose, 65, 66, 71
GET requests (HTTP), 200
getChecked method, 186
getDefault method (Display), 162
getEditor method, 266
getFirstElement method, 273
getIDsOfNames method, 192
getMessage method, 36
getProperty element (JSP), 206
getSelection method, 181
getSelectionIndices method, 165
getter methods, 35, 36, 291
getText method, 177
getWriter method, 200
GIF format, 242
graphical user interface (see GUI)
GridLayout class (SWT), 163
Group (SWT control), 152
GUI (graphical user interface)
    AWT and, 133–135, 149
    drag-and-drop, 141
    Eclipse workbench and, 7
    Java applets and, 130–133
    plug-ins and, 142
    Swing applications, 135–141
    SWT window and, 191
    V4ALL plug-in, 142–148
    views and, 9

H

handleEvent method (Listener), 177
HEAD tag, 95
Help → About Eclipse Platform menu
    item, 243
Help → About item, 175
Help → Software Updates → Manage
    Configuration menu item, 282
help component (Eclipse), 8
Hewlett-Packard, 2
Hierarchy view
    depicted, 12, 54
    Eclipse 3.0 and, 288
    finding class members, 19
history
    comparing code with, 104
    resource changes and, 8

hit counts, 82–84, 86
Hitachi, 2
hot code replacement, 91–92
HPUX Motif
    launch configuration, 157
    SWT and, 150, 151
HP-UX operating system, 7
HTML
    AWT and, 133
    browser widgets and, 295
    help component and, 8
    Java and, 199
    JSP pages and, 236
    METHOD attribute, 200
<html:form> tag (Struts), 222
<html:multibox> tag (Struts), 224
<html:options> tag (Struts), 224
HTTP GET requests, 200
HTTP POST requests, 200
HttpServlet class, 41, 200

I

IBM
    Eclipse and, 2
    OTI and, 3
    Standard Widget Toolkit, 138, 149
icons directory, 242
id property (menus), 255
IDE (integrated development
    environment), 1, 242
IEditorPart objects, 266
images, toolbars and, 176
Import dialog box, 26
Import menu item, 26
importing
    AWT support, 133
    classes, 37
    projects, 26
    scrapbook pages, 22
    sorting items, 42
infinite loops, 78
inheritance trees, 13
init method, 258
Inspect menu item, 89
installing
    Eclipse, 4, 5
    JUnit, 66, 67
    plug-ins, 6
    problems, 5
    Tomcat web server, 195–197
instantiating objects, 206

Wizard class, 263
wizards
    creating multi-page editors, 261–269
    creating plug-ins, 244
    creating views, 269–274
    New Extension wizard, 253
    PDE and, 244
workbenches
    Eclipse 3.0 and, 287
    editor window, 9
    overview, 7
    views and, 9
    (see also Run-time Workbench)
working sets, 56, 61
workspace
    Eclipse 3.0, 287
    editing files outside, 284
    overview, 8
    patch files and, 109
    projects as folders in, 14
workspace directory, 142

X

Xerces plug-in, 287
XML
    Ant build file, 116, 117
    Eclipse 3.0 and, 287
    help component and, 8
    plug-in xml code, 251
    servlet elements, 201, 204, 213
    syntax errors and, 129
    well-formed, 127
XML Buddy, 198, 201
XML editors, 125, 198
XML files, 124

Z

ZIP files, 276

About the Author

Steve Holzner is an award-winning author who has been writing about Java topics since Java first appeared. He's a former *PC Magazine* contributing editor whose many books have been translated into 18 languages around the world. His books have sold more than 1.5 million copies, and many of his bestsellers have been on Java.

Steve graduated from MIT and got his Ph.D. from Cornell; he's been a very popular member of the faculty at both MIT and Cornell, teaching thousands of students over the years and earning an average student evaluation over 4.9 out of 5.0. He also runs his own software company and teaches week-long classes on Java to corporate programmers around the country.

Colophon

Our look is the result of reader comments, our own experimentation, and feedback from distribution channels. Distinctive covers complement our distinctive approach to technical topics, breathing personality and life into potentially dry subjects.

The animals on the cover of *Eclipse* are ornate butterflyfish (*Chaetodon ornatissimus*). Ornate butterflyfish are easily recognized by their white skin marked with orange diagonal, parallel stripes. A black eye-band runs vertically down the head to conceal the eye—an adaptation that confuses predators as to the direction the fish will flee when attacked. Butterflyfish have laterally compressed bodies that enable them to swim stealthily through coral crevices. These reef-dwelling fish are native to the tropical marine waters of the Indo-Pacific, inhabiting both shallow lagoons and seaward reefs.

Mature butterflyfish are characteristically monogamous and travel in mated pairs. During the day, the home-ranging pairs search for food; at night, they sleep hidden in reef recesses. Adults usually spawn at dusk, rising 30 to 50 feet above their habitats into the water column, where they release a white cloud of gametes before quickly returning to the bottom. The abandoned, tiny, buoyant, fertilized eggs are dispersed by the currents. Once hatched, usually within 30 hours of fertilization, the larvae are protected by bony armor, which is shed during the juvenile stage. Juveniles are solitary until they reach sexual maturity, about a year after birth.

Ornate butterflyfish have short jaws and brush-like teeth for nipping off the coral polyps that sustain their diets. Because they are corallivorous, ornate butterflyfish do not survive well away from the reef. These highly sensitive fish are more susceptible to diseases, bacterial infections, and starvation when kept in a home aquarium.

Marlowe Shaeffer was the production editor and proofreader for *Eclipse*. Jane Ellin was the copyeditor. Reg Aubry and Mary Anne Weeks Mayo provided quality control. Lucie Haskins wrote the index.

Ellie Volckhausen designed the cover of this book, based on a series design by Edie Freedman. The cover image is a 19th-century engraving from the Dover Pictorial Archive. Emma Colby produced the cover layout with QuarkXPress 4.1 using Adobe's ITC Garamond font.

David Futato designed the interior layout. This book was converted by Julie Hawks to FrameMaker 5.5.6 with a format conversion tool created by Erik Ray, Jason McIntosh, Neil Walls, and Mike Sierra that uses Perl and XML technologies. The text font is Linotype Birka; the heading font is Adobe Myriad Condensed; and the code font is LucasFont's TheSans Mono Condensed. The illustrations that appear in the book were produced by Robert Romano and Jessamyn Read using Macromedia FreeHand 9 and Adobe Photoshop 6. The tip and warning icons were drawn by Christopher Bing. This colophon was written by Marlowe Shaeffer.

Related Titles Available from O'Reilly

Java

Ant: The Definitive Guide

Enterprise JavaBeans, *3rd Edition*

Hardcore Java

Head First Java

Head First Servlets & JSP

Head First EJB

J2EE Design Patterns

Java and SOAP

Java & XML Data Binding

Java & XML

Java Cookbook

Java Data Objects

Java Database Best Practices

Java Enterprise Best Practices

Java Enterprise in a Nutshell, *2nd Edition*

Java Examples in a Nutshell, *3rd Edition*

Java Extreme Programming Cookbook

Java in a Nutshell, *4th Edition*

Java Management Extensions

Java Message Service

Java Network Programming, *2nd Edition*

Java NIO

Java Performance Tuning, *2nd Edition*

Java RMI

Java Security, *2nd Edition*

Java ServerPages, *2nd Edition*

Java Serlet & JSP Cookbook

Java Servlet Programming, *2nd Edition*

Java Swing, *2nd Edition*

Java Web Services in a Nutshell

Learning Java, *2nd Edition*

Mac OS X for Java Geeks

NetBeans: The Definitive Guide

Programming Jakarta Struts

Tomcat: The Definitive Guide

WebLogic: The Definitive Guide

O'REILLY®

Keep in touch with O'Reilly

1. Download examples from our books

To find example files for a book, go to:

www.oreilly.com/catalog

select the book, and follow the "Examples" link.

2. Register your O'Reilly books

Register your book at *register.oreilly.com*

Why register your books?
Once you've registered your O'Reilly books you can:

- Win O'Reilly books, T-shirts or discount coupons in our monthly drawing.
- Get special offers available only to registered O'Reilly customers.
- Get catalogs announcing new books (US and UK only).
- Get email notification of new editions of the O'Reilly books you own.

3. Join our email lists

Sign up to get topic-specific email announcements of new books and conferences, special offers, and O'Reilly Network technology newsletters at:

elists.oreilly.com

It's easy to customize your free elists subscription so you'll get exactly the O'Reilly news you want.

4. Get the latest news, tips, and tools

www.oreilly.com

- "Top 100 Sites on the Web"—PC Magazine
- CIO Magazine's Web Business 50 Awards

Our web site contains a library of comprehensive product information (including book excerpts and tables of contents), downloadable software, background articles, interviews with technology leaders, links to relevant sites, book cover art, and more.

5. Work for O'Reilly

Check out our web site for current employment opportunities:

jobs.oreilly.com

6. Contact us

O'Reilly & Associates
1005 Gravenstein Hwy North
Sebastopol, CA 95472 USA

TEL: 707-827-7000 or 800-998-9938
(6am to 5pm PST)

FAX: 707-829-0104

order@oreilly.com
For answers to problems regarding your order or our products. To place a book order online, visit:

www.oreilly.com/order_new

catalog@oreilly.com
To request a copy of our latest catalog.

booktech@oreilly.com
For book content technical questions or corrections.

corporate@oreilly.com
For educational, library, government, and corporate sales.

proposals@oreilly.com
To submit new book proposals to our editors and product managers.

international@oreilly.com
For information about our international distributors or translation queries. For a list of our distributors outside of North America check out:

international.oreilly.com/distributors.html

adoption@oreilly.com
For information about academic use of O'Reilly books, visit:

academic.oreilly.com